WASTING YOUR WILDCARD

WASTING YOUR WILDCARD

The Method and Madness of Fantasy Football

DAVID WARDALE

YELLOW JERSEY PRESS
LONDON

7 9 10 8 6

Yellow Jersey Press
20 Vauxhall Bridge Road,
London SW1V 2SA

Yellow Jersey Press is part of the Penguin Random House group of companies
whose addresses can be found at global.penguinrandomhouse.com

Penguin
Random House
UK

First published in Yellow Jersey in 2018

penguin.co.uk/vintage

A CIP catalogue record for this book is available from the British Library

ISBN 9781787290167

Typeset in 11/16 pt Baskerville MT Pro by
Integra Software Services Pvt. Ltd, Pondicherry

Printed and bound in Great Britain by Clays Ltd, Elcograf S.p.A.

Penguin Random House is committed to a sustainable future for our
business, our readers and our planet. This book is made from
Forest Stewardship Council® certified paper

To my wife and three sons — all the reality I've ever needed.

CONTENTS

PREFACE

On May 30, 2015, at well past seven in the evening, Arsenal striker Olivier Giroud scored deep into stoppage time at the end of that season's FA Cup final.

The Daily Telegraph's Jason Burt was glowing in his praise of the match, even employing an Oxford comma with a flourish to suit the occasion: 'After the grubbiness and depression of the Fifa Congress and the septic re-election of Sepp Blatter, here was a raucous, cleansing occasion. An FA Cup final rich in tradition, with two grand old clubs, two vociferous tribes of support, and an atmosphere that built rapidly.'

Giroud's goal, on the face of it, meant little to many beyond his tall and knowingly good-looking self, his (presumably) equally attractive family and those Gunners' fans who had a particular thing for seeing opponents ground into the dirt. It was, after all, the fourth Arsenal goal in a 4–0 rout of Aston Villa; the proverbial icing on the metaphorical cake baked in the sportswriters' cliche kitchen, because they wanted it more at the end of the day.

But try telling that to George Watley.

That goal, that 90+3-minute goal at the very end of a match Arsenal had already won, meant a lot to George. His Fantasy team, Build Your Skills, gained an extra five points from Giroud's last-gasp strike, taking him three clear of one Victor Vassallo's Rabatmalta 1 side.

Three points clear. Top of the league. Winner of the season's The Sun Dream Team competition. Bragging rights. Glory.

And £260,000.

Unless you're a failed banker, a hedge fund manager or Olivier Giroud, that's a life-changing sum of money – enough for a couple of rooms in London or most of the houses in Waterloo Walk, Sunderland (Google it, you'll see). And all because George happened to nail a game of Fantasy Football.

It's a game often derided as 'the acceptable face of Dungeons & Dragons', but show me anyone who's won a quarter of a million quid from an expertly woven soul trap spell in the very bowels of Castle Dwe'eb and I'll change my name to Nigel, Comte de Farage, Quaffer of Ales, Slayer of Dragons, Man of the People.

Fantasy Football is big. Huge. Global. It can make some very rich, others modestly better off and the rest of us happy, delirious, deranged, despairing, frustrated and obsessed – occasionally all at the same time.

The big question, as ever, is why.

The answer, perhaps surprisingly for a game mainly centred around the obscenely wealthy English Premier League, has very little to do with money, despite George's Fantasy payday.

The winner of the world's biggest Fantasy Football competition, the Fantasy Premier League (FPL), has to see off more than five million competitors to claim their prize. But they don't win money, just a couple of all-expenses-paid trips to a football match of their choice, a video game console and a few other bits and baubles from the Premier League's main sponsors.

Should you score the most points from one set of fixtures, you're crowned the Manager of the Week. Your prize? A FIFA video game, a ball, a rucksack and … a mug. Be still, your Fantasy heart.

No, it's all about the glory with the FPL. Thirty-eight Gameweeks, months of planning, weeks of agonising, days of double-checking, hours of second-guessing and then a final fateful moment before you press 'Submit' on your transfers, your captain and your team and let real football players dictate your Fantasy life. All that for a weekend away or, more likely, an FPL-branded stress ball.

Whatever players' FPL motivations, money clearly isn't the defining one. So what exactly does make a Fantasy Football manager tick? Like anything else, different people have different motivations.

But the unifying reason is surely to win. Not the overall game – that is the preserve of experts with an unholy mix of skill, hard graft and luck. No, winning mini-leagues against colleagues, friends or family – sometimes for a bit of cash, always for a season's worth of unbearable smugness – drives most people on.

And the desire to improve, to rise higher and out-smug rivals in ever more unbearable ways, is constant. To do so requires a shedload of work – spreadsheets, form guides, tips and tricks from all and sundry. Some of that can be found in the pages that follow.

But Fantasy Football, like any other game, is as much about the players as what they play. Without them, there would be no game. Without them, nobody would care. And the thing is, when you begin scratching beneath the neat and well-maintained surface of Fantasy Football, you realise that players do care. They care a lot. Far too much, in many cases.

Some are best avoided, unless you need the money or their organs. Others demand our attention, be it for their expertise, their obsession or their cheerful lack of scruples. The rest are just along for the absurd and (mostly) harmless ride.

Talking to them has made me realise how important and far-reaching this frippery of a game is becoming. It's introduced me to a whole new community of people happy to help and to share their love, knowledge and experience. And it's also helped me to become a better Fantasy Football manager.

I can't guarantee that this book will do the same for you – you've probably been a lot better than me all along – but you never know . . .

CHAPTER ONE

FANTASY FOOTBALL – WHY AND WHO

Rather than asking 'why play Fantasy Football?', the more pertinent question might be 'why not?'.

The obvious first answer to that is 'I don't know anything about football'. But that doesn't matter. No, really. It doesn't matter.

I asked an old colleague of mine whether he plays Fantasy. His answer: 'I did it once. I was put off for life when my wife beat me choosing players like Scott Minto … because she liked his name.'

Fantasy Football is a game of sweet science and skill wrapped in a sickly coating of luck. Ask anyone with a half-decent track record and an ounce of self-awareness and they'll agree. You can plot and plan your way through season after season, shave the odds, maybe even cut dirty great lumps off them, but you're still, occasionally, beholden to slices of good or bad fortune as you go.

Okay, so losing to a team of Mintos sits at the more extreme end of the bad luck spectrum; bad enough that 1990s Glenn Hoddle might have suggested my colleague was Vlad the Impaler in a previous life. But even one seemingly innocuous action can have disastrous consequences in Fantasy, a sort of reverse butterfly effect that comes at the end of a chain of events while wearing shorts and a bad haircut.

Twitter user Bhavik (@bkbaz2011) would agree. His 2011–12 season came down to the actions of Sergio Aguero following the

Argentinian striker's famous last-minute goal to win the league title for Manchester City.

'Aguero scored versus QPR in that dramatic game. Four points for me and I thought I'd just won my mini-league by one point. But then he removes his shirt, gets a yellow card and that's minus one point. So I end up drawing with my rival.' Nine months of effort ruined in a nanosecond of celebratory South American nippleage. I bet Scott Minto never got booked for that.

The saying that 'football is all about opinions' is true enough. What remains only implied, however, is that nearly all of them are wrong. Or perhaps more accurately, not entirely right. Just because people know what they're looking at doesn't mean they know what they see.

There's a common argument that people play Fantasy to demonstrate that they 'know football' and yet large chunks of the game's players know nothing of the sort. They're not scouts with the expert eye to recognise talent, nor coaches with the level of tactical awareness to turn a match with their decisions. They don't know football, they know *about* it.

'About' is an apt word – their knowledge revolves around football, involves what surrounds it. They know the history and the lore, the clubs, the grounds, the managers and the players. They know the strong and the weak, the injured, the out of form, the best and the rest. They know what we could all know if we had the time or inclination. It's not secret knowledge, after all. Television, radio, websites, message boards, social media and newspapers – it's all there, if you want it.

Fantasy Football doesn't require knowledge *of* the game and *how* it's played and plays out. It requires knowledge *about* the game – who plays it, when and where.

To use another sport for an analogy, there are racing tipsters out there, very successful ones who are in profit over the years for the horses they've backed and the odds they've scanned. Have any of these people been a successful trainer or a champion jockey? Have any of them even got on a horse? If you met any of them, I'd wager that you'd know the answer to that last question immediately.

There are Fantasy players who know nothing about football. They're rare, thankfully, because to lose to them is infuriating. Humiliating, if you're that way inclined. They know enough about the rules of the game (the Fantasy one) to pick their team based on prices, to bring in new players based on what they can afford to spend and, well, that's it. That is their strategy. And occasionally, very occasionally, it works.

Helen Bonynge, retired, living in Sydney, Australia, is a classic example. 'If you can't beat them you have to join them. My husband and friends play so I joined in too, so I knew what it was all about ... great fun.'

And her tactics? 'It's funny to hear people talking like they really own those players!! Me, I hardly know the players and when I want to buy one I just go down the list to the first one I can afford ... no spreadsheets for me.'

That sort of comment will send a sickened shudder through many reading it, an inglorious mix of contempt and despair welling inside them. In a game where so many overthink, such a prime example of underthink, or hardlythink, is anathema. And some of that contempt will be laced with fear.

Helen's highest moments are 'when I beat my husband and friends'. Oh, how they must love that. All that thought and agonising and doubt laid to waste by a rival who knows only that the price is right.

Helen is not alone but she remains an exception, not the rule. If it were any other way, nobody would play the game. It would be too random, annoying ... pointless – and it's already enough of those three anyway.

But nobody should fool themselves that their Fantasy achievements are any indicator of their footballing expertise. Most are not experts; they merely have knowledge of the knowledge of the experts. They are experts in expertise. They know what is there for all to know, and then they apply it.

So if Hardlythink Helen is an exception, what does the average Fantasy player have that she does not? One word: love.

The vast majority of Fantasy Football players love football. That's not a surprise, of course. The way that love has been reshaped by Fantasy Football might be, however.

I'll use myself as an example. I love football. I am old enough to know better, and also not to care. It has run through my life, a constant seam mined for delight, despair, disgust and distraction. And fellowship, to a degree, although my circle of friends has included few fellow addicts of either the game or, since the 1990s, the game about the game. Football has, over time, kept me in work and defined much of my play.

I was born in the 1960s and came to football in the early 70s. Genealogy made me an Arsenal fan, although by the time I actually turned up my immediate family had moved from north London to the Midlands, so father-son bonding at Highbury was not on the agenda, most notably because my father was often not at home of a weekend anyway. On the rare occasions, usually during the packed Christmas schedule, that he did take me to see Arsenal, it would be an away game.

My first Arsenal game was at the City Ground in Nottingham. I think we won 1–0, but I was young and more taken with the specimen sitting next to me in the main stand than anything happening on the pitch. Not my father, I hasten to add, but a blotchy-moist shambles of a man who exuded a uniquely sharp but fuggy aroma of cigarettes, beer and sweat ('Bin Dipper Pour Homme') and who spent almost the entire match head down and swaying in his seat, only occasionally looking up at the game to utter the same two words, like a mantra: 'Fucking shithouse.'

I was entranced, frightened and perplexed in equal measure, and it taught me a valuable life lesson right there – if in doubt, don't look 'em in the eye. And maybe another – there's nothing good coming from a smell that bad.

An equally visceral experience occurred at Filbert Street, Leicester, in the Spion Kop end reserved for away supporters. I have no recollection of the score there at all – I was too busy staying on my feet in the swirling, angry sea of footballing humanity that trapped me and pulled me back and forth across the concrete terracing in surges both random and merciless.

I loved it.

Football on the telly was a rare commodity back then, little more than FA Cup finals and the major international tournaments that England, as I progressed from single digits to my teens, completely failed to qualify for.

By then I'd been injected with two powerful doses of FA Cup final heartbreak watching Arsenal lose, and one of almost unbearably painful joy when my brave boys had beaten Man United 3–2 with a last-gasp goal – but only after blowing a 2–0 lead.

Bitter defeats and bittersweet wins were, I now realise, the perfect introduction to a life-long investment in the fortunes of your club and country. But if I'm being honest, it was an investment I never truly made.

Sure, I wept when I finally got to see England at the World Cup in 1982, only for them to ghost out of the tournament in Spain. Two goalless draws and a horrible miss from the obviously unfit Kevin Keegan – our only truly world-class player who had been sidelined for almost the entire tournament with a back injury – left me in tears as a teenager. And then I moved on to watch one of the greatest matches I'll ever see, Italy beating Brazil 3–2 in an encounter of fluidity and drama. Paolo Rossi's hat-trick, the impossibly cool Socrates, Brazil's carefree attacks versus Italy's calculated counters, all of it combined to wash away those tears in a deluge of excitement.

Because it was football, not Arsenal or England, that was the main attraction. Following club or country could be a thing of both beauty and angst, but nothing was bigger than the game. Not Alan

Sunderland's regrettable moustache/perm combo, not Pat Jennings and his shovel hands, not even my boyhood hero Liam 'Chippy' Brady.

Football, be it good, bad or indifferent, was everything. And by the 1980s, it was incredibly bad. Shamefully so.

Did any other country's fans have to watch their team with one eye on the pitch and the other on the crowd? English fans did, the tear gas floating like the first signs of fire into camera shot to announce that it was on again; that the shame was out to play.

Fans trashing, charging and fighting, always fighting. And fans dying, chased or burned or crushed. English football in the 1980s was a basket case; a toxic mess of underfunding, overcrowding, establishment contempt and death.

Yet still I loved it. In hindsight, I was in an abusive relationship. The Hand of God slapped me down and I got up, hoping it would be the last of the cheap shots. Heysel, Bradford and Hillsborough – lives lost so cheaply to tribalism, underinvestment and incompetence – but I still convinced myself it would change.

Incredibly, I was right.

Italia 90 – English football's redemption. It started, typically ugly, with scenes of sunburnt fans battered by Italian police and extended to a storm-soaked Sardinian pitch on which England and the Republic of Ireland lumped their way to an unedifying 1–1 draw that many, both at home and abroad, considered so wonderfully apt for the knuckle-dragging Little Englanders who followed the sport.

But the apes evolved, and when England were finally gone from that World Cup, they went with pride. Yes, pride – an emotion I had all but given up on feeling about the national team. The goals of Gary Lineker, *that* goal from David Platt and the man-child Paul Gascoigne reduced to semi-final tears shared by a nation seemingly cured of the 'English Disease' ... all of that combined to provide football with a perfect platform to change, to grow and move on.

And, for once, it actually did. The 1990s ushered in what we have today, for better or for worse. But, despite the obscene wealth, and the strutting egos and oligarch playthings that that has enabled, it is almost entirely for the better. Football in the 90s became rich and safe and ... attractive.

No coincidence, then, that Fantasy Football took off at the very same time. And it provided another level of interest and investment in a sport that had begun to wear me down. I had spent so much of my early life caring about football, and that care had not been returned. I had learned to care less about the game just, ironically, at a time when I started getting paid to write about it. Football was earning me a living, but where was the love, the joy and the wonder? Why should I care beyond the next pay cheque?

Fantasy Football taught me to care again. It returned some of the joy and threw in a whole new heap of interest. It made football matter once more, albeit for the most trivial of reasons – the state of my Fantasy team.

And I'm not alone in this view. Peter Kouwenberg is one of the best FPL managers around. When I spoke to him, he was number one in the Fantasy Football Scout website's all-time Career Hall of Fame thanks to his consistently high finishes over the years.

He, too, believes that Fantasy Football brings the love back to an increasingly unlovable game. 'For someone who grew up on Championship Manager and Sensible World of Soccer, FPL is a great managerial-type game, but rooted in the real world.

'It's clever because I actually dislike the way the real game has gone, with diving called "being clever" and the obscene money being chucked around in a country whose public sector is on its knees, but I follow the Premiership avidly and hypocritically due to FPL. As a Forest fan, that's the closest interest I'll have in the Prem.'

Fantasy Football has also gone a small way towards repairing one of the greatest disconnects in the game – the gap between player and fan.

Even without the rose-tinted spectacles of nostalgia, there is no doubt that football has been reshaped – some would say irrevocably deformed – by money. Players now earn vast sums of it, while the fans themselves are also wealthier. They have to be or they're not getting in to watch the game, what with the cost of a ticket these days.

Gone are the days of football as the working-class game, played and watched by people separated only by ability and a few extra quid a week in wages. Players don't travel to the game with the fans on the bus any more, they don't get fish and chips on their way back and they don't retire to run a pub or a bookies or sell insurance.

The link between purveyor and consumer is broken – except, rather strangely, in Fantasy Football. Whether they know it or not, every week people play Fantasy Football on equal terms with many professional footballers. Stoke City striker and ex-England international Peter Crouch is rather good at it. Bournemouth and Bosnia goalkeeper Asmir Begovic is in twelve mini-leagues, one of which involves another seventeen of his Premier League club's squad.

Premier League footballers earn ridiculous amounts of money. That's not their fault. If someone decided to hand you a huge wage increase, would you turn it down? What you then did with your new-found wealth is a different question, but deriding footballers for being paid too much money is like criticising a waiter for the cost of your dinner – the blame for that lies almost entirely elsewhere.

All that money brings with it all manner of complications for a pro footballer – envy, desire, the threat of blackmail and robbery – which in turn makes going for a 'normal' night out almost impossible. Bubbles form as the player becomes ever more isolated from his fans.

Fantasy Football is, in however trivial a way, perhaps the only unplanned and unscripted forum in which pro footballers can now interact with us civilians, on equal terms and using the same tools. No agents, publicists or media advisers; just the player and the fan.

Ed Shardlow, a financial planner from London, experienced this phenomenon directly during the 2006–07 season. 'I was trying to impress my new girlfriend by taking her to the new Dans Le Noir restaurant in London, where you eat in the pitch-black with blind waiters. It must have worked as we've been together for over ten years and she's now my wife and mother to our baby boy.

'We were sat opposite each other in the darkness, at one end of a table of six, with two other couples. We introduced ourselves to the couple next to us, and then I overheard them talking to the couple at the other end and worked out that the guy was a professional footballer called Jay and was talking with an American accent.'

At the time, there was only one American called Jay playing Premier League football – a Watford defender called Jay DeMerit. In Ed's words, Jay was 'a decent pick when Watford were in the Premier League. Good attacking player who got a couple of goals and seven clean sheets from twenty-nine starts'. Yep, Ed is most definitely a Fantasy Football manager.

The conversation then went as follows:

Ed: 'Jay, what's your surname?'

Jay: 'DeMerit.'

Ed: 'You're actually in my Fantasy Football team!'

Jay: 'Oh, cool!'

The evening progressed in pleasant, if pitch-black, fashion until it was time to go. 'We all said what a pleasure it had been and Jay said to me: "I'll try to play well for your Fantasy team this weekend." To which I replied: "Don't worry. You're only in there because you're cheap."'

There are silences, there are awkward silences and then there are awkward silences horrifically accentuated by the fact that you can't see the face of the person you've just jokingly insulted.

'I tried to gauge his reaction and reassure him that I was kidding. I couldn't see his face, and he couldn't see my expression. It felt really awkward for a second or so before he laughed and the tension dissolved. Fortunately, we were able to look each other in the eye outside in the light and make sure there was no ill feeling.'

Without Fantasy Football, that whole experience would never have happened. Instead, it would have been a fan/player interaction in which the player held all the power, who was an object of awe, adulation or envy. Fantasy Football turned all that on its head, giving Ed, the humble civilian, the power to bring the hero down, however gently, from his pedestal.

For the record, in Asmir Begovic's Bournemouth mini-league, Nathan Ake, Charlie Daniels, Steve Cook and Brad Smith all picked themselves for their opening-day squads in 2017–18. Self-confidence or rampant vanity? You decide. Asmir, meanwhile, left all his Chelsea players on his Fantasy bench when Bournemouth played the Blues in real life. Superstition, or a smart move not to open himself up to accusations of throwing the match for his own Fantasy gain? Again, that's your call.

There's a saying that football is the most important unimportant thing in the world. If true, what the hell does that make its Fantasy spin-off? Who cares, because it is a beautifully harmless outlet for the love of football its players share. Okay, so love is both the sweetest thing and something that you give a bad name.

Fantasy Football is all that – and we all know players in both of those camps. But it is also the most exciting, maddening and all-consuming of fripperies that is played in all four corners (in-swinging and out, left or right) of the world, and everywhere else in between.

Football is the global game and Fantasy Football its precocious little brother. The latter cannot survive without the former but, increasingly, the relationship is truly symbiotic. When the players paid to play a game also play – entirely willingly and for no money – a game about the game they play, you're either on to a good thing or about to implode in a bizarre feedback loop. At the time of writing, it was still very much the former.

So who is the typical Fantasy Football manager? Worst case scenario, as dreamt up by someone with no time for, interest in or love towards Fantasy Football, would be something along the lines of:

Male. Middle-aged. Needs to lose weight and gain friends. Straight. Possible virgin, although might have paid to address that issue somewhere down the line. Ideal woman: Xena, Warrior Princess, or Harley Quinn. Occupation: something in computers. Likes: the Microsoft Office suite, sci-fi and the impersonal nature of the internet. Dislikes: eye contact and reality TV. Hobbies if Fantasy Football not available: Doctor Who figurines and serial murder.

Best case scenario: Male. Middle-aged. Needs to lose weight and gain friends. Straight. Married, two children, one of whom has an unusual middle name (e.g., Wembley, Radamel or Clattenburg). Long-suffering wife. Ideal woman: Countdown numbers genius Rachel Riley. Occupation: something in computers. Likes: the Microsoft Office suite, sci-fi and the impersonal nature of the internet. Dislikes: waiting for children to grow up enough (a bright seven-year-old or an average teen) so that beating them at Fantasy Football is a satisfying experience. Hobbies if Fantasy Football not available: Peppa Pig figurines and alcohol.

Typical Fantasy Football player stories include Arsenal fan WA from America: 'I happened to strike up a conversation at a wine tasting with a Spurs fan and avid FPLer from the UK, which led to some obvious banter. He asked how my team was doing. I told him it was my first season but I thought I was doing okay, to which he asked about my overall ranking. I couldn't remember exactly what it was but told him I thought it was somewhere around 5k.

'His stunned reaction caused me to question my recollection so while we sat there tasting wine (and boring everyone else around us) I pulled up my team on my phone and verified that I was in fact at 5k.'

SB, another Arsenal fan, from Manchester, England: 'Fantasy Football got me in trouble as well in actual, real football. My partner is a Bolton fan and we went to a game against Everton back when Bolton were in the Premier League.

'I had Joleon Lescott and Mikel Arteta in my FPL team. It was 1–1 when Everton got a corner. Arteta took it and Lescott scored and I jumped up and cheered. This went down like a lead balloon as I tried to explain I was, of course, not happy that Everton had scored, but they were both in my Fantasy Football team and I would get mega points. My other half was not happy at all and still tells this story to people when we speak about FF.'

Or maybe JB, a Brighton fan, also from England: 'I dreamt that I had the most insanely brilliant instinct that Wayne Rooney was going to have a ridiculously strong weekend (at the time he wasn't even starting for United) and so I went to transfer him into my team and it wouldn't let me. I started panicking and getting in a right sweat about it and then realised (as it happens in dreams, things are never quite right) that I was six hours late to make the transfer.

'Rooney went on to score seven goals that Gameweek (only in my dream obvs). Hahaha, so unrealistic but a genuine dream/nightmare.'

Typical – and true – stories from Fantasy Football addicts who, to give them their full names are:

Wendy Adams, forty-eight, an insurance agent from Fullerton, California. Pay-off line from story: 'I pulled up my team on my phone and verified that I was in fact at 5k, not really having a clue at this point that it was actually a fairly impressive rank for an American chick playing her first season.'

Sal Browning, thirty-seven, a senior exhibitions co-ordinator at the Museum of Science and Industry in Manchester.

Jules Breach, thirty, sports journalist and presenter of the Fantasy Premier League's television show.

Typical Fantasy Football players they most assuredly are, the point being that the only thing truly typical about an FF player is a love of football and its Fantasy offshoot. Yes, Fantasy Football is still a male-dominated pursuit. But it isn't an exclusively male one, and the number of women playing the game grows every year.

Not that sexism doesn't occur. It does in real life, so it would be astonishing if it didn't in Fantasy Land as well. When I asked Jules Breach whether she'd encountered much in her career, she said the following: 'I get asked this question a lot and I think the fact the question is still being asked says it all.

'Hopefully one day soon us girls won't have to address these issues any longer. Generally, I don't get many comments along those lines, but there's always going to be a few narrow-minded people who spoil the party.

'Some people think they're being funny, others probably don't like the fact that there are females that know more than them about a sport they feel should be male-dominated.'

Professional sport in general, and football in particular, is an incredibly exclusive bubble in which many ex-pros seem to think that only their opinion is valid because, like a Vietnam veteran, 'you weren't there, man'. It's a 'show us your medals' mentality beloved of the deeply unimaginative, someone who cannot begin to comprehend that empathy, intelligence and a deep knowledge of a sport can lead to a complete appreciation of what it takes to play it at any level, be it high or low.

We can't all be Adele, after all, but we still know when someone's singing out of tune. 'I've been asked silly questions like "do you actually like football?",' Jules goes on, 'and "do you actually play FPL?" I have to laugh at these questions; it's crazy to think that some people think it can all be an act. I live, breathe and *love* football, and I'm pretty certain my passion shows through my work.

'Sometimes I wonder if there's an element of having to prove yourself slightly more as a girl, but maybe that's just me personally being a perfectionist and nothing to do with my sex.

'The Fantasy community are very accepting and I've met loads of lovely players through social media, both girls and guys. It's like a little family online and we all share one thing in common – our desperation to *win!*'

That's the beauty of Fantasy Football. There's a bottom line to it – the entirely objective matter of your overall ranking or your mini-league position. If you, like 'American chick' Wendy, finish in the top

5,000 of a game played by millions worldwide, you clearly know your stuff. The fact that you're one sausage short of a picnic, so to speak, or that some of your fellow managers struggle to make eye contact because they're staring at the milk delivery system attached to your chest, is neither here nor there. Forget 'show us your medals'. How about 'check out my overall ranking'?

'There's always work that can be done to tackle issues of sexism, though,' Jules adds. 'Maybe I'm one of the lucky ones who hasn't had to deal with it much, but I know some of my female colleagues have done. There are lots of positive steps happening now though; more women working in sport, more being done to make pay equal and more women playing sport across the globe.

'I know I personally am very proud to be one of the many women working in sport.'

There's no doubt that some women have suffered unhealthily large doses of sexism in the world of football. Just ask David Moyes, if you need a man to confirm it. But is Fantasy Football sexist? Only in so far as there are sexists playing it. There are also racists, homophobes and people who love Piers Morgan because 'he's only saying what we're all thinking'. I tweeted Piers, by the way, to ask him whether he played Fantasy Football. I received no reply, so I'm fervently hoping that means he doesn't.

And does Fantasy Football have a typical player? Again, only in so far as we all share a love for an entirely inconsequential game that has a nasty habit of taking over too much of our waking (and occasionally dreaming) thoughts, be we male or female, young or old, working as a shelf stacker or as the senior exhibitions co-ordinator at the Museum of Science and Industry in Manchester.

But is there a typical Fantasy Football demographic? David Pugh, The Daily Telegraph's marketing director when the newspaper launched its ground-breaking Fantasy Football game in the mid-1990s, told industry magazine Campaign in 1997: 'The typical Telegraph Fantasy Football player is thirty-five, male and professional, which is the type of reader the paper was trying to attract. So the data was good to use to try to get these people to read the Telegraph on other days besides Wednesday [when its weekly FF game was featured in the paper].'

North America, which cottoned on to Fantasy sports as a mass-market pursuit three decades before the UK, has also produced huge amounts of research on the subject. According to a 2015 round-up of that research put out by the Sports Management Degree Hub website, Fantasy sports players as a percentage of the US population were 20 per cent male, 5 per cent female. The average age of a player was thirty-four, a chunky 78 per cent had a college degree and 66 per cent were in full-time employment, earning on average close to $100,000 a year.

Those are American figures, so not directly applicable to us Fantasy Football managers across the globe. But they do at least stick another knife into the lazy assumption that we are all sweaty old male keyboard warriors with nothing better to do in our tragic little lives than play Tunnels and Trolls and Football.

If you're reading this and now realise that you're a highly desirable demographic for advertisers to prey on, well done. But feel free to spend your hard-earned money how the hell you want to.

And if you don't fit the bill because you're either above or below some consumerist benchmark dreamt up by voracious capitalists seeking to exploit you for all you're worth (or not worth, as the case may be), congratulations – you've just stuck it to The Man.

CHAPTER TWO

THE HISTORY OF THE GAME(S)

Much like space exploration, fake breasts and gun crime, Fantasy sports had its trail blazed in America. The first Fantasy Football league, the snappily titled Greater Oakland Professional Pigskin Prognosticators League, was set up in 1963. That was an American football league, with a golfing equivalent reportedly up and running even earlier than that.

American sports – and specifically gridiron and baseball – have had a long and very happy relationship with stats, so it is not surprising that Fantasy games, which tend to rely on any number of performance indicators that then translate into points, evolved Stateside.

Even so, that first league was decidedly old school. The managers used a draft system to pick their players and the only scoring metric was a touchdown.

Speaking to the Chicago Tribune in 2015, one of the Pigskin Prognosticators' founder members, a then ninety-year-old Andy Mousalimas, described the appeal of the new game. 'We knew it was something special. We couldn't wait for the games. We'd go and root for the opposition, and fans would look at us and say "what the hell are you doing rooting for that guy?".'

That remains, for some, one of the key problems with all Fantasy sports – the reshaping of allegiances based on who you have in your particular side, be they the good, the bad or Troy Deeney.

The big question is why did it take real football – I refuse to ever call it soccer – and, in particular, the Brits, so long to embrace the concept of Fantasy sports?

The reasons I offer are in no way definitive, more a tentative crumb or two added to a debate that hasn't exactly raged over the years – if it has even raged at all.

The UK has a long and proud tradition of discovery and invention. Sod Thomas Edison, for instance, because it was Joseph Swan who, in 1880, first patented the light bulb, while Brits also gave the world its first taste of a chocolate bar, the cash machine (complete with a four-digit password), the worldwide web and the spill-free dog bowl.

How such a small island could churn out all this stuff probably comes down to climate, a deeply misplaced sense of superiority, a taste for pissing about in sheds and a centuries-old attitude to sex – the ultimate occupation for a restless mind – that ran along the lines of 'well, the French take that sort of thing rather too seriously, so we'd jolly well better not then'.

The result was repressed homosexuality and sado-masochism for the ruling classes, Carry On films for the rest of us and a slew of inventions from people with nothing saucier on their hands than a bit of time.

As for sport, the British were masters at inventing it, exporting it and then getting progressively worse at it for pretty much all of the reasons above, plus an outdated notion that we really shouldn't be trying too hard to be good at anything that doesn't involve annoying the rest of Europe or taking over vast swathes of the world for commercial gain – frequently at the same time.

Such ridiculous generalisations and stereotypes no longer hold true, if they ever did. These days we pursue Olympic glory, for instance, with all the zeal of a Soviet Russia but without, one can only pray, the industrial levels of drug-based cheating.

But while the Americans were inventing, embracing and refining Fantasy sports in the 1960s, we remained that sexually repressed, damp island clinging on to imperial delusions of grandeur from the sanctuary of a thousand sheds.

And football, easily our greatest sporting invention, was viewed by those who could develop it – the ruling classes – as the vulgar preserve of the working man. As a result, there was no appetite to modernise it or to broaden its appeal. Football replaced classical chariot racing and medieval bear-baiting as an instrument of distraction and social policing; a perfect tool to keep the masses in their place. But it wasn't broken, so why fix it? In fact, those in charge didn't even bother to give it running repairs.

Football did have its sort of Fantasy attachment – the pools. To those born under the star of a reunified Germany, the digital age or Taylor Swift, the football pools will mean nothing, although an online version is still around today.

The pools was a betting game in which you had to predict the outcome of eight matches of your choice from the entire weekend's output of English and Scottish professional football. The scoring system involved one point for a home win, one and a half for an away win, two points for a goalless draw and the full three for a score draw, with the ultimate aim being to score twenty-four points and scoop the top prize. To do so, you would therefore need to score three points per match by correctly predicting eight score draws from a choice of more than fifty matches.

By the 1970s, the whole thing was administered by three main companies – Littlewoods, Vernons and Zetters – who employed agents to pop round your house in the middle of the week, collect your completed coupon and entry fee while dropping off next weekend's coupon, and then post your entry on your behalf.

You would then endure a disappointing Final Score on telly waiting for the result of Queen of the South versus Montrose – a match you didn't have a single clue as to the outcome of but you stuck it down for a score draw anyway – to tell you that, yet again, you'd predicted a group of games entirely incorrectly and your humdrum life was very much on for another long and tedious week.

If a match was postponed – and in those days many were because it seemed like only Arsenal had undersoil heating to thaw out their pitch – the Pools Panel would sit and decide what the outcome of a match would have been. Amazingly, at the time of writing, the panel still sits and is made up of 1966 World Cup legends Gordon Banks and Roger Hunt, and the not-quite-so-legendary Scottish international Tony Green.

Winners received life-changing sums of money – Nellie McGrail, of Stockport, won £205,000 in 1957 and, most famously, Viv Nicholson scooped £152,000 in 1961. Castleford housewife Viv vowed to 'spend, spend, spend' when husband Keith won the cash, and she remained true to that vow all the way to alcoholism and bankruptcy. On the brightish side, The Smiths' frontman Morrissey was much taken with her plight, going so far as to steal a line from her autobiography ('Under the iron bridge we kissed, and although I ended up with sore lips …') for the song Still Ill.

But that was it for football and spin-offs – the chance to win big and potentially blow it all even bigger, with the prospect of plagiarism from the world's most fey vegetarian as a side order of despair.

Would Fantasy Football have taken off had it been offered to the UK's football fans in the 1960s and 70s? Who knows. What is clear is that the powers-that-be felt no need, and had no desire, to innovate. Match of the Day, for instance, hit the nation's television screens only in 1964 – a mere thirty-five years after the BBC's first experimental television broadcasts – and even then it was under severe sufferance from the footballing authorities, who feared that ground attendances would be hit. As a result, the one match that featured on the original MOTD show was announced only once all the Saturday fixtures were under way.

With that insipid mix of cultural apathy and establishment hostility to change, it's a wonder that Fantasy Football ever took off in the UK.

Britain's shed-dwelling tinkerers did at least have a stab at developing a Fantasy version of the sport, with the earliest attempt taking place in the greatest year of England's long and frequently shabby footballing history. As a famous Nike poster once declared, 1966 'was a great year for English football. Eric [Cantona] was born'.

Non-Man United fans and Matthew Simmons might disagree, the latter being the Crystal Palace fan whose body became the canvas upon which Cantona famously created his seminal 'Selhurst Park Meltdown' work using the medium of the rage-fuelled kung fu kick.

The French forward had been sent off for reacting to the up-close-and-personal attentions of man-marker Richard Shaw by kicking the Palace defender up the arse. As Cantona left the field, he had to walk past a section of Palace fans very eager to remind him that, in so many words, a red card meant he would no longer be able to remain on the pitch.

Mr Simmons, at the time a twenty-year-old terrace regular, is alleged to have quipped that Cantona might wish to 'fuck off back to France' among other, rather more personal, suggestions involving members of the footballer's family.

The victim himself claimed that what he actually said was 'Off! Off! Off! It's an early bath for you, Mr Cantona!'

Now I'm no linguistics expert, but Mr Simmons' version of events does rather suggest he had arrived at the match, which took place in 1995, via a time machine from a hopelessly patronising 1950s film about the British working-class. Cantona will have heard many a clump of Anglo-Saxon earthiness during his time playing football in England, but I dare say 'It's an early bath for you, Mr Cantona!' was never, ever among them.

Whatever was actually said, the infuriated player slipped from the grasp of the United kitman, Norman Davies (he subsequently earned the nickname 'Vaseline' for his part in all of this), who had been given the job of leading Cantona back to the dressing room. Free of Norman's restraints, the Frenchman launched himself at Mr Simmons in the flying style, earning himself a nine-month ban from football and 120 hours of community service.

But back to 1966 ...

The other memorable footballing event that year involved England winning the World Cup, an act that inspired the next generation of footballing stars while prompting the FA to build on that achievement by overseeing more than half a century of wondrous under-performance on the international stage. And it also led to the creation of, as far as I have been able to ascertain, the world's first Fantasy Football game.

'It was just after the World Cup in '66,' explains Bernie Donnelly, a retired but decidedly sprightly schoolteacher from Knowsley, Merseyside. 'Everybody was inspired by the World Cup. I started the league with my schoolmates; me and a few friends. They've come and gone for many, many years, but I've always been there."

What Bernie hit upon was a game involving real players being used in pretend teams, with the former's actions producing points for the latter. A classic definition of Fantasy Football.

'When we first started, it was based on the old football system of five attackers and five defenders. You'd base your team on the forwards who score the goals ... we dropped the defenders pretty quickly.'

After a few years of schoolboy tinkering, Bernie finally released his fully formed version of Fantasy Football to the world in 1971. An eight-team league was set up, with managers involved in weekly head-to-head clashes in which their five-man sides racked up points for goals scored and ... that was it.

'The scoring system is all about goals. It's completely objective. Purely on goals. Nothing else. You pick five players each week and have two subs as well in case people don't play. The game is split into two seasons – autumn through to December 31 and then from January onwards – and we've got cups and a super cup competition as well.'

Bernie's game, which is still going strong to this day, in many ways mirrors the old-school Fantasy offerings from America – once a player has been bought by a manager, he remains with that team for as long as the manager wants him, often for season after season. But the boss can sell his players to opponents, giving rise to the potential for wheeler-dealing and skulduggery on a scale reminiscent of the real thing.

'If a young Harry Kane comes up, you can bid for him. If you own him, you can sell him. There's a lot of horse trading. There's always been underhand dealing – you've got the rules, but a lot of issues are at the margins. There's always grey areas and a few managers operate in those grey areas quite successfully.

'There's a lot of passion, and always has been, and managers do fall out with each other. There was a petition once to expel a friend of mine who they said was doing dodgy deals with everyone else. Managers end up not talking to each other. And they offer each other outside – that's happened once or twice.'

The one consistent feature throughout all this has been Bernie himself. 'I have to do all the admin and paperwork. I have to intervene. I have to be objective. I don't have a team. I had one many years ago but gave it up. There's a matter of vested interest. You can't do that and be the league commissioner.

'It's a democracy but really I run it as a benign dictatorship. You need to manage people and their expectations. I can negotiate and talk to people, so that's what I try to do. I've been a councillor for thirty-five years, so I must have learnt something.'

What Bernie never learnt was how to expand the game. In more than forty years of the Donnelly Fantasy Football League, it has never budged from its eight-team format and although managers have come and gone they are generally drawn from the Knowsley area. The most far-flung player of the game has been an assistant manager all the way from Manchester – a distance, via the M62 motorway, of just 29.7 miles.

'I'm surprised how long it's been going, to be honest. Could I have made a few bob out of this? One or two friends have said I should have marketed it. But no, I just enjoy it.'

That is a very British way – the joy of creation and innovation over exploitation and monetisation. As a result, the world had to wait for well over another decade for someone else – an Italian – to take Fantasy Football and run with it well outside the confines of the Metropolitan Borough of Knowsley.

Riccardo Albini, '*inventore del Fantacalcio*', clearly has a knack for grabbing what many perceive as the trivial and turning it into a mainstream concern. He was, after all, the founder of the first Italian magazine dedicated to covering video games – in 1982. Its title? Video Games. Genius.

By 1988, he was ready to test out his version of Fantasy Football, using that summer's European Championship as a dry run. By then, he'd been toying with the idea for a few years.

'In the 1980s, when I started to think about the game that later became Fantacalcio, the only stats available were goals scored and goals conceded. Knowing the richness of US stats in sports like baseball or American football in terms of representing the action on the field, I couldn't think those meagre football stats could translate into a good game.'

Riccardo's solution to the stats problem was simple and elegant and, while in no way illegal, ever so slightly cheeky – he 'borrowed' them from the newspapers.

'In Italy, sport newspapers have been using player marks or grades as a sidebox to a match review since the early seventies. And in 1985–86 they were an established and accepted way, however subjective, of evaluating a player performance on the pitch.

'The newspapers' marks are based on the Italian school marks: from 1 (minimum) to 10 (maximum), with 6 being the mark you have to reach to pass a test, exam, whatever.'

The benefits of using already published marks were clear. They required no effort to create, just to collate, and they also provided evaluations and rewards for individual players. So, for example, whereas today's games will generally award clean sheet points to every defender in a team that doesn't concede, Riccardo's version could highlight personal performance that little bit more ... personally.

'You could give a low mark to a defender for making a stupid foul in the box causing a penalty and a high mark to another one for saving a shot on the goal line.'

Most players ended up with a rating of between 5 and 7, which Riccardo believes produced 'close games and all the drama of a football match'.

After extensive testing over the 1988 European Championship and the following two Italian domestic seasons, Riccardo finally went public and launched his game in a pleasingly old school way. 'We launched the game as a book [it was 1990 and the internet was still a few years away] with the complete rules, all player marks from the previous season, some instructions on how to set up a league of friends and other assorted stuff. We published 10,000 copies and distributed them through newsstands because at the time I was partner of a publishing company.'

The beauty of that method was it involved no extra work for Riccardo. He would pocket proceeds from each book sale, while each manager would administer their own league using the rules set out in the book and the ratings published weekly by the papers.

Unfortunately, the book did not sell well – a mere quarter of the 10,000 print run. This wasn't even enough to recoup the publishing costs.

But even in this pre-internet age, the network effect came to the rescue. 'We received a lot of letters from people who'd heard about the game from friends that were actually playing it but couldn't find the book. Among these people, there were radio DJs and sports journalists, which helped spread the word just because they were playing the game and loving it. The second edition went much better and from then on we published a revised edition, which I edited, every year until 2001.

'However, the real take-up happened in 1994 when we launched a newspaper game with La Gazzetta dello Sport, which was based on the game. That definitely turned Fantacalcio into a household name. It became so popular that La Gazzetta were registering an increase in sales on Tuesday when they published the result of their contest.

'It is also important to note that in the 90s the Italian league was probably the most important in Europe and interest about football was at its peak in Italy (it went down in this century). That helped too.'

Riccardo eventually launched a website in 1998 and then sold the game on a year later to the internet arm of the Italian national daily newspaper La Repubblica. 'Luckily, we closed the deal before the dot-com bubble collapsed, but we are talking Italy not Silicon Valley, so we made some money but I still need to work to make a living.'

And that he does. Now sixty-four, the Fantasy pioneer is a contributing editor to sudoku and logic puzzle publications and he's currently planning a Fantacalcio hall of fame website.

In Italy he enjoys celebrity status, now and again at least. 'I still get asked for interviews or people ask me for autographs or selfies when they discover I created the game almost thirty years ago.'

Riccardo's game did have one, particularly Italian, quirk among its rules and regulations. Every Fantasy game allows managers to choose and tweak formations, from 3–4–3 to 5–4–1 and everything in between. In the original Fantacalcio game, in a move befitting a nation that brought us *catenaccio* – the ultimate application and celebration of the defensive arts in football – you could choose to utilise a 6–3–1 formation. Six defenders and one striker – only in Italy.

*

The story of the game's UK roots is similar to the Italian experience, but with a computer involved and no book of rules to be found.

In 1991, Andrew Wainstein decided to fuse his background in computing with a love of football to create Fantasy League. Its point-scoring system and use of computers to collate the mass of data produced by ever-increasing numbers of players mirrored Fantasy Football as it is played today.

'A friend showed me a Fantasy baseball report and I was inspired to see if I could create something for football,' said Andrew. 'I spent a while modelling a Fantasy scoring system based on the 1990–91 season stats on a spreadsheet, with the challenge being the lack of stats in football. I came up with the assist and clean sheets, whilst wanting to keep it simple and transparent as a game.'

The early days of Andrew's Fantasy life mirrored the classic British inventor's make-do-and-mend, shed-based model. Or his sister's bedroom, anyway.

'Those early days, it was done on a shoestring, just a few savings and from my sister's old bedroom in my parents' house. I wrote the software myself and was a one-man band, printing reports, stuffing envelopes, taking the postage sack down to the sorting office every Monday.'

Andrew's program collated all the data from the weekend's matches and started printing off the results after 7 p.m., following the final fixture. That took twelve hours, with Andrew eventually adapting his body clock to wake up every three hours when the printer ran out of paper.

'Soon, I took on a part-time student to help me and gradually hired a few more people, with four of us in my parents' place from 1991–94 and then into our first office as we grew further.

'Things really began to take off when we did a deal with The Daily Telegraph to run their Fantasy Football game, which of course ran through updates in the paper, with information stored on our computer. From there, things took off right away and three or four papers began running their own competitions in the same season.'

So the Telegraph game was the moment when Fantasy Football made its first move from nerdy niche to full-on national pastime. And that, in part, was thanks to the competitive instincts of press baron Rupert Murdoch, as David Pugh, the Telegraph's marketing director in the early 90s, explained.

'The most important thing going on at the time was the price war between The Times and the Telegraph. Around August or September 1993, Murdoch cut the price of The Times and I was under a lot of pressure to reach further and further into the toy cupboard to find games and vouchers to give out.' Those toys involved classic newspaper tactics to keep circulation up, albeit temporarily.

'But it started to choke off new readers,' said David. 'Why read a newspaper that was more expensive?'

Why indeed. Something had to give, and it was in danger of being the Telegraph's circulation, which at the time still resided just above the 'magic million' mark so beloved of advertisers and those with the task of selling that advertising.

In what David describes as 'a frenzied atmosphere', Telegraph execs were handed bigger and bigger budgets to come up with more and more games and giveaways to keep loyal readers on side and, maybe, attract other consumers otherwise distracted by the equally shiny, and decidedly cheaper, Times.

The big problem was that every gimmick they threw at readers had a limited shelf life. 'With the exception of the crossword, all competitions had a lifespan of three to four weeks maximum. We'd get impressive circulation improvement, but the graph then tailed off dramatically.' What David needed was something new that could transcend the gimmicky and live long and profitably.

'Two guys from the ad sales department came to me – Ed Lowe and Saul Klein – and told me about Fantasy League. I think one of them played it. Their idea was to find a sponsor to support it and underpin the costs. The big issue was to run it – the big cost was that having to publish the results took a full broadsheet page. A full page could be sold for 20–25k advertising and the newsprint alone was worth 10k. We needed a sponsor to make it work.'

Unfortunately, no sponsor was forthcoming, so the newspaper declined to run the competition when the football season kicked off in August 1993. Instead, they explored more traditional promotional avenues, with the Fantasy Football idea still niggling away at David.

'We came into '94, so I decided to run half a season of Fantasy Football. I was doing calculations based on a circulation increase of 10k for the Wednesday edition, when we would run the results. Even if it ran for six weeks, it wouldn't be too much of a burden.

'Initially, we put on about 50k of extra sales, just crazy numbers, but even putting on 30k every Wednesday was great. But the key difference was that the game didn't last a month. Once it settled down to 30k, it just kept going all of that season and the rest is history.'

David left the Telegraph in 1995 but checked back with colleagues a couple of years later to see how the Fantasy game was holding up. It still put 30,000 on the circulation every single Wednesday.

That sustained popularity, David believes, was down to the game itself, not any of the baubles that came with it. 'The initial prize was a trip to the World Cup. The essence of the thing was there was no money. It was the pride of being the best football manager in the country. We'd also give out a manager of the month jacket. There was no big money. It was a game of skill.'

There was (and still is) big money to be had, however. One man, Steve Shipley, took home £59,000 from the News of the World's Goalmine game in 1999. Not only did he win the £50,000 first prize, but also the game's second and third-place awards. In fact, he took the top six places that year and earned an extra two grand from monthly prizes as well.

More on him later in the book, but for one of the Telegraph's early winners, it was all about the glory.

Liverpool fan Jonathan Roberts won the first full season of the newspaper's game in 1994–95, a fraught affair involving a decent lead slowly eroded, which resulted in a last-day triumph by just one point. What made it even more noteworthy was that Jonathan was just twelve years old at the time.

'It was a tense finish,' he recalls, with admirable understatement. 'At the ripe age of twelve my quotes filled the weekly article and I found myself on the front page of the paper to celebrate my success – relatively mainstream for Fantasy Football – and I had a spot on the "And finally …" section of ITV's News at Ten.

'The trophy was presented to me by [Liverpool players] David James and Robbie Fowler, who'd both been in my team during the season. The manager, Roy Evans, also handed over the trophy and there was a photo of me in the front row of the pre-season team photograph. I'm not sure the winner of the FPL gets lauded in the same way these days.'

Jonathan found out for sure that he'd won only when the Telegraph phoned him up for an interview. 'Yes!' he exclaimed. 'Thank you very much.' The polite wee chap beat more than 340,000 rivals to the crown – including his father, Michael, who staggered in around the 230,000 mark. 'Jonathan took it a little more seriously,' was Roberts Sr's rather dry evaluation of the situation.

His prize included a Christmas weekend in Turin to watch Juventus play Roma. 'Lippi was the manager; Vialli, Ravanelli, Deschamps, Conte, Di Livio to name a few. Collina was also the ref, I remember.

'We also went for a two-week all-expenses family holiday in Mauritius, where we played golf and met Denis Law around the pool.'

All very nice, but Jonathan's enthusiasm still comes across most markedly when describing the Adidas Predator boots and full Liverpool kit he was given, and the £1,000 in cash that he spent on 'a new PC and the latest version of Championship Manager'.

It is perhaps not surprising that he still plays Fantasy Football to this day, describing himself as 'something of an obsessive', although he discovered the delights of FPL only in this decade.

But for a man now more forty than fourteen, his love of Fantasy remains untarnished. He still has a scrapbook detailing his

Telegraph triumph and vividly remembers the team that took him
to the top.

'The season was built on the strength of Liverpool's backline –
David James and Stig Inge Bjornebye's clean sheets, plus quite a few
Stig assists (great crosser).

'Phil Babb, of Coventry, was bought by the 'Pool during August,
so I snuck an additional Liverpool defender in (only two per team in
those days).

'Andrei Kanchelskis and [Bryan] Roy were midfield legends and
Shearer and Dublin provided the goals. Timely transfers – only six
postal transfers in those days and a 4–4–2 formation – and it became
a reality. Robbie Fowler and Le Tiss made sure I could get over the
line ... by one point come the final day.

'It was all such a novelty, but the Telegraph looked after me
pretty well.'

If only the same could have been said for another young Fantasy
gun, Irish manager Brian Haugh, who, at fifteen, had a rather different
experience in his own 1995 campaign.

'I entered the Evening Herald newspaper's Fantasy Football
competition via a phone hotline (it cost about 12–15 Irish punt back
in the day) and my mother was a bit cheesed off with the phone bill
once it arrived.

'Anyway, I kind of forgot about the team and didn't pay any attention
to it until a friend in school saw my name in the paper advising that I
had come second overall. I was taken aback and delighted, obviously,
and started looking into the prize money situation because I recalled
seeing something like 5,000 for the winner, 2,500 for second and
1,000 for third, or something to that effect.

'So happy days, quids in!'

Or unhappy days and no quids at all, as it turned out.

'However, further enquires with the newspaper advised us that
the rules, and therefore the prize money on offer, had changed over
the course of the season. Now, it was winner takes all and nothing

for second or third place. So we expressed our disappointment with this new development and advised the newspaper accordingly. What happened next really kicked things off.

'I received in the post a package from the newspaper. I cracked it open to see what goodies they had sent me. Imagine my disappointment and confusion when I laid eyes on a Sinead O'Connor CD, a Beatrix Potter – Peter Fucking Rabbit – video and a few other items that I can't even recall. Not one football-related gift in this package whatsoever; they had obviously just done a whip round in the office and sent it off to me.'

Having worked in a number of newsrooms over the years, I can confirm that that was exactly the sort of stuff that would have been lying around, unwanted and gathering dust, among the ashtrays, mounds of paper on spikes and drunken old-school hacks generally cluttering up your average mid-1990s newspaper operation.

'Well, my mother was furious at this and thought it was a pretty shitty thing to do, so she started looking into legal advice. It was established that we had a case and looked to proceed with it.'

Hell hath no fury like a woman whose son is scorned by a Peter Fucking Rabbit video, and this is what she had to say to Brian about the incident:

'We consulted solicitors. I wasn't going to have my little darling treated like that!

'The first court hearing was on October 15, 1996. Judge King thought that as you were only fifteen at the time it might have been in contravention of the Gaming Act and she had to seek advice.'

The law rumbled along even more slowly than Per Mertesacker, but Brian and his mum went back to court the following year.

'The second case was listed for February 3, 1997, but it wasn't called. Judge Collins had gone to lunch and had to be called back. Our legal team thought she might be annoyed.

'The case was heard in an empty court and she gave it all the time that maybe she couldn't have given it had she had to deal with a full court. She was really annoyed that you were dealt with so shabbily and ruled in your favour – Independent Newspapers were to pay you £1,500 when you reached the age of eighteen.

'Independent Newspapers didn't attend, but as the judge was leaving the court you called out "thanks, Judge". Our legal team was horrified. Not the done thing. The judge just smiled.

'I think you had to go back to school, but knowing you were going to come into such a large sum of money, you bought me a cup of coffee on the way home.'

Brian is keen to put the record straight on that last point – he is pretty sure there was a scone, or maybe even a Danish pastry, involved as well.

His memory of what he ended up spending the money on is a touch cloudy, perhaps not surprisingly in the circumstances. 'I'm pretty sure it funded my Leaving Cert holiday to Gran Canaria with my school friends in 1998. My first proper holiday abroad without the folks; an epic two weeks.'

Money, I'm sure you'll all agree, well spent.

I tried to get a comment from the newspaper, but they did not deign to reply. In fairness to them, it was a long time ago and I'm sure today's Evening Herald treats its competition winners a lot better.

What that shabby tale of treachery and belated justice teaches us is that, despite big backing from major newspapers, the early years of Fantasy Football had yet to mature and settle into the slick and well managed global beast that it is today.

It did, however, reach the mainstream very quickly when BBC TV ran its imaginatively titled Fantasy Football League show from 1994–96. British comics Frank Skinner and David Baddiel hosted, a number of celebrities appeared as team managers and Statto – a pyjama-clad ubergeek – was there in the background to provide the numbers and operate as the duo's comedy punchbag.

The game the show used was Andrew Wainstein's Fantasy League. 'I was involved with the BBC show,' said Andrew, 'which also brought exposure and revenue but was linked to the auction format so I think brought us more direct customers.

'Of course, there were also other aspects to the show, which made it cult viewing. It was fun to be involved with and, funnily enough, I was asked to be the Statto character and am very pleased to say I turned it down.

'I'm more of a behind-the-screen sort of person and the way he was sent up wouldn't have been very appealing to me.'

It was clearly appealing to the public, launching the career of Angus Loughran as Statto, as Fantasy Football started to embed itself into UK culture, or at least one of its sub-cultures. But in truth, the show used Fantasy Football as an excuse to exist, not as the main driver of its content. Few viewers rushed home from the pub on a Friday night to discover how glamour model Linda Lusardi's side was doing, or to marvel at the managerial insights of Wham reserve team player Andrew Ridgeley. It was all about the hosts taking the piss out of football and football players in a way not seen on mainstream television before.

So for Fantasy Football to break out and go truly mass market, both domestically and globally, two things needed to fall into place, the first of which was the rise to worldwide dominance of the internet. Because the internet changed everything.

No, that doesn't truly convey its impact on Fantasy Football.

THE INTERNET CHANGED EVERYTHING.

Better.

Newspapers ushered in the age of mass-participation Fantasy Football because they enabled players to access collated, printed and published results. To do so you just had to buy the paper. Simple.

In fact, what could be simpler? How about a publishing platform that you could access without having to pay for it? One that allowed you to play a game where you didn't have to post or phone in (at great expense) your transfers over a season? A game you could play in real time, with instant transfers, speedy updates of scores and standings, and all of it free to enter and play?

Such a system would be a game-changer, quite literally. And that's exactly what it was. When the increasingly cash-rich and globally marketed English Premier League entered the fray in the new millennium and began its own version of Fantasy Football, the landscape would never be the same again.

CHAPTER THREE

THE ONE GAME TO RULE THEM ALL

Graeme Haddow's childhood was a classic example of a Scottish boy growing up in the 1970s, obsessed with football.

'In those days, I used to collect those sticker books of teams in the English First Division and the Scottish Premier. I always got close to filling one up and think I even succeeded, maybe in '79, where I posted off for the final cards. I was very proud of the complete set way back then.

'I remember those little charts Shoot magazine gave out at the beginning of the season. You could slot the team tabs into the four English and three Scottish leagues as their league positions changed. It was the first thing I would do on a Monday, and I think that's how my knowledge of the team base grew.'

Those little charts were called League Ladders – cardboard enablers for young football addicts to interact with their drug of choice beyond the usual Saturday afternoon fix. In those days, all domestic football was played on a Saturday, with a 3 p.m. kick-off. A week was a long time to wait until your next hit. Updating your League Ladders passed some of that time.

I, too, had Shoot's League Ladders, but never had the staying power to keep updating them every week, especially as the Cowdenbeath tab never quite fitted properly and had got stuck in the lower reaches of Scottish Division Three, never to escape – a classic case of art imitating life.

Graeme and I also shared a habit of gutting the pages of Shoot for use in personal interior design projects. 'I would tear out football "pin-ups" and splash them all over my bedroom wall, updated seasonally. Quite sad thinking about it now, but thankfully they got replaced by "real 80s pin-ups" of the softer variety.'

That was a classic rite of passage back then – swapping the centre-parted wholesomeness of Everton striker Bob Latchford for, in my case, a poster of Kate Bush wearing a vest top at least two sizes too small for her. He banged in thirty goals in one particularly fertile season; she introduced me to a whole new area of star attractions up front.

Graeme's love for British football survived the distractions of that first flush of off-pitch adolescent yearning, probably due to geography.

'I was born in Bathgate, West Lothian, in 1968. My parents took the very bold and courageous step in 1974 (they twenty-eight, me six) to emigrate to South Africa.

'I grew up in a largely expat community in those younger years, and that is where my interest in football started. With a colourful blend of Scottish, English, Irish and Welsh families, football was always at the forefront of any discussion.'

Graeme settled on Man United to support as a child, Scotland's Tartan Army to follow as he grew up and … chartered accountancy as a career to pursue in Johannesburg. Football stayed with him, even through the crazy years of financial management, auditing, business strategy and taxation, and by the turn of the twenty-first century, Graeme had moved into the Fantasy realm as well.

'Myself and my old university friends back then first started playing this online game in 2001. It was called CYKI [Can You Kick It], and I think it was run by two people. We all thought this was magic and we played in the world and, more importantly, in our private league, "2MuchTimeonYrHands".

'Anyway, after two seasons the game was rebranded from CYKI to FPL. The new FPL game had the same look and feel as the old one, and in our opinion was much, much better than any other online Fantasy Football games on the internet.

'Also, it was free and very, very user-friendly. It was only a matter of time before the world got wind of this great game under the PL banner.'

How right Graeme was.

Paul Weston, of ISM, was one of the people behind the game that so delighted Graeme. The Bristol-based company had started creating Fantasy games back in 1998 and over the years they've produced them for Uefa, Fifa, Televisa in Mexico, MLS and Norway's Eliteserien, as well as an Aussie Rules version for Fox Sports Australia, rugby for World Rugby and cricket for the ECB.

'ISM first started working with the Premier League back in 2002,' said Paul. 'We were running a game for the Champions League and also our own Premier League Fantasy game called Can You Kick It. The first season had something like 75,000 users playing the game, and it just continues to grow year on year.

'In terms of the computer power involved, we have gone from running the game on a couple of servers to a large scale set-up, spinning up over fifty cloud servers over the weekend. On a Saturday afternoon at 16:40, the website is quite possibly the busiest in the country.'

It was rather more hand-to-mouth to begin with, however. 'In that first season, we were asked to use a third-party login system to register users. There were some teething issues with that, which meant the season had to start a little bit late.'

As a result, Fantasy Premier League's first-ever season was actually a thirty-two Gameweek affair, with the first set of six matches being dubbed 'pre-season' and their scores not counting. Truncated or not, it remains a season Graeme will never forget.

'Although only 75,658 played in 2003, under the new rebranded FPL, it still came down to the wire. Key players were attacking midfielders, especially Pires, Scholes, Gerrard, Kewell and Beckham. Although very expensive, Thierry Henry was a player you could NOT play without and although making your captain pick is always a dilemma, not picking Henry as captain was always risky.

'In that first season, I thought I had lost out at the end of all the games in the last round and not come first. I was devastated! But then I got very lucky off the bench. I can't remember who didn't start in my final team, maybe Damien Duff, so Gareth Barry came off my bench, as a defender. Villa lost 3–1, I think, but Barry got a "bonus" performance ... go figure!

'All I remember is that we were all in a pub together, watching all the games at the same time, and I think the overall lead changed hands nearly every minute until my sub saved the day for me.'

Graeme's team, Wee Wullie Winkie FC, ended up six points clear at the top of the table, assuring him a place in Fantasy Football legend as FPL's first-ever winner.

So how did he enjoy the lavish trappings such a historic victory must have earned him? 'Unfortunately, as it was the first season under the rebranded FPL, there was NO PRIZE! All I got was self-satisfaction, a lot of adrenaline rushes and bragging rights that I still have to this day.'

Graeme also has a printout of the final table, which he keeps, for posterity, hanging above the bar in his South African home.

'I'm still playing after all the years, season in, season out. It's much more difficult now, mainly due to the number of entrants and the ever-expanding worldwide audience.

'We still run our private league and the office banter around this is still very active and competitive. Monday morning is always FPL update day – lots of chit-chat around the weekend performance.

"For me the main attraction of FPL is that, as an avid football fan, you focus on all ten games each week and not just your favourite team. You want your FPL players to do well, albeit they play for Bournemouth, Stoke or Watford. And you're always looking out for that hidden gem in the pile.'

The real gem, as it turned out, was the game itself. And it didn't stay hidden for long. That first season's 76,000 players became 120,000 by the start of the next season, and 310,000 by the end. By 2005–06, the final figure had risen to 810,000; two years further on and it had doubled again.

Growth was large and, aside from a minor blip in 2012–13, consistent. These days, around half a million new teams play FPL every year, with the five million mark for overall players reached a couple of weeks into the 2017–18 season.

'The game is simply a phenomenon,' Paul from ISM enthuses. 'It just keeps on growing in popularity each year. Wherever we go, people are talking about who is in their Fantasy team. We often get asked if we can add some more points to their team. If they saw how badly we scored, they wouldn't ask!

'To run such a popular game has inevitably meant facing new challenges – mostly surrounding its stratospheric growth, but also regarding our own comfort with, and use of, new technology.

'Every year the game gets more and more popular,' said Paul. 'For the 2017–18 season we started with 4.8 million people playing the game, which is more than we had at the end of last season.

'In the past, people used to set up their team on a Friday afternoon, leave it for the weekend and then check back to see how many points they had on the Monday morning. Nowadays, people want to see their scores when matches are taking place.

'The mobile app is great at helping people do this. So when Harry Kane smashes in his third goal of the afternoon, suddenly everyone who has him as their captain will log in to see how many points they now have, causing a huge spike in traffic.

'To cater for this we now have to be quite creative with the infrastructure, spinning up lots of extra cloud servers ready for when matches are being played.'

It would seem that ISM have played their FPL hand rather deftly. Yes, the site does crash on rare occasions and the sheer volume of data that they have to crunch means the game doesn't always update as quickly as we impatiently feral managers would like. But FPL's easy interface and its general reliability should not be taken for granted. Personally speaking, one of the reasons why FPL is the biggest game out there is because the website is so easy to use, which makes the game so easy to play.

Not that I can let ISM off entirely scot-free. Anyone who's been playing the game from that first season will know that all the information from 2002 to 2005–06 cannot be found on the site.

'At the end of the season, when the new game is set up,' explained Paul, 'all the season's stats are archived and the summary stats are created, allowing users to see the previous years. Prior to 2006, the seasons were simply deleted when the new season was set up.'

I have a strong sense that I did quite well in one of those early seasons, but have no way of confirming it. My potential brilliance was 'simply deleted' and I am yet to be informed why this act of digital vandalism ever needed to take place. On the bright side, it means I can claim that I actually finished just outside the top ten in 2004 and there's not a great deal anyone can do to disprove it. In fact, now I come to think about it, I actually won it that year, but decided to let someone else take the glory.

One thing's for sure, all that information is rather more lovingly treated these days. It's what the Premier League themselves would insist happens, which leads on to one of the key questions about FPL: as the game is free to enter and play, what exactly is in it for the Premier League?

Kelly Williams, managing director of the London-based sports media and rights business Sports Revolution, can supply a one-word answer to that: data.

There's a general rule about the internet – if a product you are accessing online is free, then you are the product. As an example of that, there's a Fantastar service, run by a company called BlueYellow Media, which builds bespoke Fantasy sports games for companies and brands. Towards the end of their website sales spiel is this:

'Do I get an email database of registered users?'

'Yes. We'll send the user database to you upon request.'

And if we're talking databases, the Fantasy Premier League have one that's a bit of a monster. 'The database that's produced,' said Kelly, 'it's all about the data and storytelling. Where does the value lie? What people buy, where they're spending their money; it's incredibly valuable.

'When you are able to sell a car to someone, using information that a person bought their last car five years ago, they generally buy this kind of car, they earn over 100k, etc … you're not paying £2 a click for that person, you're paying thirty.

'The value is just in the data.'

So the Premier League is sitting on a digital treasure trove of information about people just like you and me. In fact, literally you and me. They have collected key information about us – our names, ages, locations, favourite football teams and so forth – and that data is worth a lot, both to the Premier League and also their key commercial partners.

Data is knowledge is power. And it's money.

'Digital media has an ultimate value because it's so trackable,' said Kelly. 'It has click-throughs: really robust ways to prove how many people have been to a site and for how long.

'There is nothing estimated about online figures. And if you can demonstrate that people are staying on a particular site for a long time, you can show the value of engagement. If you've got something that you can prove is incredibly engaging, it means you are able to associate your brand with something very personal to the person playing on it. That's a marketeer's wet dream.'

The brand itself is another key attraction when it comes to running something like Fantasy Premier League. 'For the Premier League, there's the younger demographic that we all need to attract for the future. Then there's the affirmation of the brand itself, and there's also the tremendous amount of money in e-gaming and virtual gaming. They've all got value attached.'

The Premier League's head of digital, Martin Axford, has spoken in the past about how FPL plays a major part in promoting the Premier League brand. And our addiction to using phones is at the heart of it, as he explained to the Sony Mobile blog in 2017.

'When we relaunched our digital strategy at the beginning of last season, we launched a new website as well as our mobile app and Fantasy is very much the heartbeat of it.

'The opening weekend the app had 550 million screen views and that's just in the space of three days. It's also been downloaded eleven million times over the past year since its launch.

'We know that we had to make sure the services were equipped to deliver the best and most optimal Fantasy experience via mobile. People are snacking on content more and more. They're visiting the website and the app more frequently and getting instant hits.

'We know that our fans hunger after statistics, we know that they want the editorial expertise and short form video clips and obviously that's part of the mix that we're delivering there.'

So while the Premier League is not directly taking our money through our use of FPL, its popularity and interactivity makes it a fantastic tool for persuading other major global brands – the likes of Nike and Tag Heuer for instance – to want to be part of that success story.

Then again, we shouldn't be in the least bit surprised that a body like the Premier League is seeking to monetise us all. This is, after all, an organisation that has grown very rich, very quickly, as Kelly explained.

'In 1995 the Premier League broadcasting rights were £43 million. In 2000 they were £242 million. They're £8.5 billion now. The Premier League, as a brand, it's the best league in the world.'

There are a number of reasons for that. English football's heritage, for instance, gives it an inbuilt kudos, a sort of historic heft. The country's place in the world helps as well, with selected kick-off times tapping into prime-time slots elsewhere on the planet. If you still haven't worked out why the likes of Man United and Liverpool play so often on a Sunday afternoon, it's because their games kick off in a very attractive evening slot in the Far East.

According to Kelly, the lack of a protectionist element to the league also gives it a huge global reach. 'It's not very domesticated in terms of players; La Liga have got Spanish clubs playing mainly Spanish players, whereas comparatively few British players play in the Premier League.

'They were the first to commercialise their league; they're the largest and the biggest in the world. They're number one by a country mile.'

All of that goes a long way to explaining why FPL is so popular, tapping in, as it does, to the global phenomenon that is the Premier League. So is FPL really just a way to exploit us all? Probably. But there are worse ways of being exploited, at least according to Jamie Reeves, founder of Fantasy Football Magazine.

'I think it's been so successful because it's interwoven within UK culture. The internet era has turned an ugly, confusing, paper-based game that everybody *still* loved and developed it into a sleeker product.

'This is important because it strikes the balance between being user-friendly enough for the older player, whilst also appealing to the millennial audience.'

Fantasy Football and football itself have a symbiotic relationship. The more churlish among you might even say that Fantasy Football is a parasite, feeding off its host. But those lines have become increasingly blurred by FPL, which is, after all, a game run by the organisation that runs the game that the game is about – the host and parasite as one and the same.

And if its growth has been spectacular, there is still so much more to come. 'The annual growth is impressive,' said Jamie, 'but it would be great to know more analytics. Five million plus players is HUGE, but it's clear lots are creating throwaway teams each week to chase weekly/monthly prizes.

'I think the concentration needs to shift towards improving the players' experience to increase user-retention. Compared to the US, there is almost no integration between Fantasy and mainstream media. That would help raise the profile of the game and also help with retention aims.'

The Premier League have certainly thrown increasing resources at their Fantasy brand. The website delivers more and more content, both written and video, including daily filmed updates, the weekly FPL Show and interviews with real-world professional footballers talking about the Fantasy game in which they appear.

But while Fantasy Football is seeping into the mainstream, with the occasional Fantasy Football transfer graphic flashing up on Football Focus or Soccer Saturday and TV commentators mentioning how a player's on-pitch actions can have Fantasy repercussions, we're still a long way from the American model where Fantasy Football journalists are afforded the same access as their more traditional counterparts in the media.

Kelly agrees that America sets an encouraging precedent for what FPL can achieve. 'Fantasy Football is a billion-dollar industry over there and I can see that happening here.

'We have worked hard to make Sports Revolution, as a business, future-proof, but you have to be prepared to take some risk because the speed with which things become obsolete is unbelievable now.

'But sport is one of these weird phenomena that when the world is in recession, people tend to watch more of it for the escapism.'

And she believes that the Premier League, and therefore by default the Fantasy Premier League, has a lot more growth to experience – as long as the brand itself is not compromised. 'They're only just touching the surface. Streaming is the next area where they can charge a fortune.

'Yes, they could poison the brand if they're not careful, if they do things to offend people, make the wrong choices. Fifa are a good example of that. Sepp Blatter and the money being thrown at him, issues surrounding how broadcasting rights for tournaments were handled; that can produce real discontent with the sport.

'But there are already ways in which the likes of Fantasy Football can produce revenue. We now sell ad opportunities, as in the real world, in the Football Manager game.'

If companies are willing to buy ad space – in the form of the advertising hoardings found at every professional football ground in the world – on the virtual hoardings to be found in computer games, then it's small wonder that Fantasy Football is such an effective tool for promoting its real-world counterpart.

FPL is certainly being used to help the Premier League gain an increasingly strong foothold in the lucrative American market. The 2017–18 season marked the debut of the FPL's draft game, which runs alongside the established fixed budget version.

ISM's Paul Weston described the draft version as 'a whole new game concept' because that's exactly what it is. 'Previously, people had one team which could be in multiple leagues. This game needs to have multiple teams, but that can only be in one league.

'The draft itself is interesting as people all need to be online at the same time – all getting the latest information around what players are available. The players have their own statuses tied to each individual league. We have hosted this game separately to the main game so that there are no conflicts.'

But aside from providing a new product for us fixed-salary Fantasy addicts to try, the draft version is also aimed squarely at getting draft game veterans to try a new sport, as the Premier League's Martin Axford explained to the Sony Mobile blog.

'From what our users tell us when they register we've got a number of players in every country in the world, which is fantastic. The UK takes up 40 per cent of the 4.4 million people that are playing it [the main, non-draft game] this season but then we look at Malaysia, which contributes 5 per cent of that and then Ireland, Egypt and it's very popular in the US. The interesting thing this season is that the users that are coming from the States are over-indexing within our new Fantasy draft game.

'This bears out part of the strategy we've developed and the reason why we launched draft because that's the game the States have grown up with rather than the salary cap we play here.'

The Premier League can never be accused of standing still when it comes to developing FPL. As the game has developed and matured, so it has been tweaked to give it more depth. The bonus point system and its various overhauls, the introduction of Wildcards and other chips – all these things have been brought in to try to make the game richer and more competitive.

Some purists might sniff at these innovations, claiming that they dumb down the game, making it easier for, and therefore more accessible to, the casual player. That, however, is exactly what purists do and, unless they're prepared to walk away from a game that takes up most of their thoughts during waking (and possibly sleeping) hours, they'll sniff and grumble and carry on playing anyway.

And for the most part, the changes to the game have been a success, although the jury remains out on the latest tweak – the replacement of the unpopular 'All Out Attack' chip with the new 'Free Hit' one.

But take out all the issues over data, brand management and commercialisation and you're left with a game that has endured and, indeed, thrived because of the people who play it. If they are loyal to any brand, it is to the football club that they support and the Fantasy Football team that they manage.

Unsurprisingly, the most supported club among FPL managers during the 2017–18 season was Man United, with 871,273 (17.98 per cent) virtual bosses. The least popular was Watford, with 10,712 (0.22 per cent).

When it came to naming their Fantasy team, imagination was sometimes severely lacking. Close to 3,000 FPL teams were called … Man United. A not-so-select band of 487 named their team The

Special One, while 135 trotted out the old pub quiz standard and went for Norfolk 'n' Good.

Real, everyday, living and breathing humans are what make FPL the enormous success it has become. Most of them are perfectly normal as well. Most of them.

CHAPTER FOUR

MINI-MADNESS

The very heart of the Fantasy Football experience involves competing in a league made up of a select group of fellow managers. That is the default setting when you play auction/draft games such as Fantasy League. There are only so many football players to fill each team, so that restricts the number of managers who can be in a particular league.

But in the global epic that is the Fantasy Premier League, where you're competing against millions of others for an overall ranking, the same rather more localised battles can also take place.

For such a corporate exercise in brand affirmation, FPL has a surprising purity to it. It's free to enter and the prizes, while desirable, are not what people sign up for. It would be easy enough for an organisation with the size, scope and financial muscle of the Premier League to put a price on winning its Fantasy Football game. But it doesn't.

And still the players flood in.

They're clearly not in it for the money, because no money is won. Not for first place, for second, for anywhere. Beating millions of rivals is enough for the overall winner. It's their shot at fame, glory, immortality.

As a result, the Premier League, with its global reach, official snack partner and bloated superstar salaries, has somehow contrived to invoke a Corinthian spirit long gone from the game of football itself. That spirit – a satisfaction in a job well done, in a game played for the sake of it and without need for gaudy recompense – lives on in its Fantasy offshoot.

But buried deep in that unlikely homage, something much more grubby and ruthless – and often money-driven – is alive and kicking off. It is a game within the game within the game. It is the mini-league.

If the quest for a highest possible overall ranking in FPL is some kind of Victorian Methodist Craft Fayre – all sober celebration of skills applied towards a noble end – then the mini-league is a bare-knuckle boxing tent pitched on its fringes where anything goes, winners take all and losers, now and again, get some very nasty surprises indeed.

A mini-league is Hyde to the overall game's Jekyll, the Dark Side to its Force. In footballing terms, it is Garrincha to Michael Owen. And if you don't know much about Garrincha, he was a Brazilian winger born with one leg six centimetres shorter than the other and who, so legend has it, lost his virginity at the age of fourteen.

To a goat.

But it's okay – he was drunk at the time. (Garrincha, not the goat.)

Mini-leagues come in various shapes and sizes. The mini can be misleading – there were, for instance, no fewer than 116 teams in the Chelsea Fans in Lebanon League for 2017, which is around 116 more Chelsea fans than most of us thought lived there. They primarily consist of friends, relatives or workmates, and sometimes a mix of all three. Some do it for the fun, plenty more have money riding on them and all are deeply, deeply competitive.

There's an all-women Wags League, an eight-person affair involving chess grandmasters (the trash talk in that one is quite arrogant, apparently), a league for fans of the band Mumford and Sons run by the group themselves and one in which tennis brothers Andy and Jamie Murray compete with a predictably win-at-all-costs mentality.

Fantasy manager Rob Morbin provided me with a near-perfect summary of the mini-league experience. 'Me and my mates have been in the same Fantasy league for ten years and naturally various traditions and roles have been assumed.

'Now twenty teams strong, within our midst there is the reliable last placer, no matter how bad anyone else's season is; the solitary female, who has perfected the art of mind games; the annoyingly keen one, who is predicting a double Gameweek due to Europa League fixtures three months in advance; and, of course, the League Administrator, who does all the organising, always comes close but, tragically and comically, has never won.

'He is notorious for providing live updates, much faster than you could get from BBC or elsewhere, and focuses on all the key data – "Begovic yellow, 89th minute, might lose his bonus"; "Suarez missed penalty, would've been a Sterling assist". If he never wins by the time he has his first born baby, he has agreed to name the child Fantasy.

'As all managers know, certain world events or TV shows are inextricably linked to whatever Fantasy Football incident occurred at the time. Any mention of Rocky Horror Picture Show, for example, now reminds me of coming out of a theatre matinee on a cold November afternoon to learn United had thrashed Blackburn 7–1.

'I was top of the league at the time and my initial thought was "shit, I bet Berbatov got one, and I took him out this week for Tevez". Of course, all my close rivals at the top had the Bulgarian captain for his five-goal haul. Tevez got nothing. I've never recovered.'

The mini-league almost always accepts all – a tree-hugging, social justice campaigning paragon of vegan virtue is more than welcome to join, for instance. But once they're in, they'd better be prepared to reach for the stars while residing in the gutter by a late-night Fantasy burger van from which all manner of low blows, cheap tricks and rule-bending spurt like so much toxic waste.

And if you don't believe me, here's a management consultant from Bahrain with his take on mini-leagues. You might not be surprised, once you've read about him, to find out that he asked to remain anonymous. As a result, we'll call him Bob. As in Bastard of Bahrain.

So, take it away 'Bob': 'One season, I used "buffers" in mini-leagues. Buffers are teams that are managed by less interested friends and I "co-manage" them and give them enough attention to make their team block other teams and distract attention.'

Tame enough, if a wee bit cheaty. But there's more.

'Once, I had a friend who was doing very well (he won the mini-league that year). He was newly married, so I used to change the league name and my team's name to his ex-girlfriend's name. He begged me to stop as his brother-in-law started asking questions in front of his wife like "who is Fiona?" and "why do I feel your friend is sending you messages?"'

'You know, I thought if I distracted him I'd have a better chance to win ... I know, I am a bastard. But, believe me, only in Fantasy Football.'

That's a mini-league manoeuvre right there – attempting to destabilise a friend's marriage on the off-chance that it might distract him from his Fantasy duties.

Bob's email finishes thus: 'While I am typing this, my wife is now knocking on the bathroom door. "Is everything okay? You are not playing Fantasy Football are you?"'

No, Mrs Bob, he's probably just hacking into North Korea's nuclear command centre in a bid to heighten global tensions and send his mini-league rivals scampering to a Bahrain bunker (without Wi-Fi, of course) ahead of a vital Double Gameweek. But not to worry, the season will be over soon. As will the world.

Everything, they say, has its price. Bob's biggest mini-league win has been £150. Therefore, Bob values his mate's marriage at about the cost of a Dualit 3 in 1 Coffee Machine in canvas white.

But money isn't everything in Fantasy Football. In fact, it's a mere side order to the main course that is glory, even for someone as ... committed as Bob.

'My main target is to win in my country, Bahrain. I came third in 2013, fifth in 2016, second in 2017.'

One shudders to think what Bob would do to ensure he finishes first. He does, however, touch on a key difference between those chasing a high overall ranking and the dedicated mini-leaguer.

Some five million people had teams in FPL for the start of the 2017–18 season, which makes it impossible (as well as insane) to try to keep tabs on all your competitors in the overall game. The only time managers start paying attention to their rivals in the rankings is during the climax of a season when they are in the very highest reaches of the overall table.

But mini-leagues are another matter entirely. Most consist of a manageable number of opponents whose progress you can track, so when the season gets to the business end and final placings are on the line, you can alter your tactics accordingly.

As an example, let's say Bob is first in his mini-league because his main rival had to spend an entire month patching up a marriage that was close to breaking point, for some reason or another. It is the final day of the season and Bob has checked his rival's team. He knows that, unless the chaser dramatically changes his side and takes a large number of hits as a result, all Bob needs to do is cover his rival's main moves. If they have roughly the same team, after all, they will score roughly the same number of points and the leader won't be caught.

In particular, that means trying to guess which player the chaser will captain that week. By captaining the very same player, Bob can nullify the potential swing to his rival should that captain come good and serve up a big dose of double points. It's a simple tactic that you would never use if you were merely chasing a good overall ranking, where the key driver is purely to score as many points as you can.

Conversely, if a manager is chasing the leader, they will need to try to bring in a player not owned by the leader who can score big. Such a player is known as a 'differential'.

Final-day triumphs and disasters are legion in Fantasy Football circles, but throw in the added bitterness, or delight, that comes from mini-league competition and they have a habit of sticking around far longer in the memory.

Sometimes, they even acquire their own medical term. Sort of. At least they do in Hobart, Tasmania, according to Paul, who brought in the ultimate differential a couple of seasons ago.

Paul is one of a bunch of Aussie radiographers and medical orderlies in a league called The Sorting Room, which started as an eight-manager affair but has since grown to sixteen.

'Andy led our league from Gameweeks 1 to 37 in 2014–15 and took an approximate lead of thirty to forty points into the last round. I was second, so needed to identify a player who would be a shock differential for the final round.

'I settled on Theo Walcott as he had been out injured for ten months, his last game had been in November of that season and his time on the pitch was usually limited. No one in their right mind would transfer him in!

'Having brought him into my team, I then decided I might as well make him captain and, thirty-four minutes into the final game against West Brom, he had a hat-trick and game over – he got me a score that sent me flying past Andy for a twenty-nine-point win.

'It's still spoken about as the greatest transfer ever produced and is now locally known as the Walcott Manoeuvre.'

Move over Heimlich – there's a new manoeuvre in town; although Theo would probably injure himself attempting it.

But while Bob was busy bastardising the sanctity of marriage and Paul sanctifying The Blessed Theo, Fantasy Football Scout regular Wakey was happy keeping things much closer to home.

'As I've said many times, the best way to play this game is with a (very) mini-league where all the participants live/work within close proximity of each other. There is no better way for banter and skulduggery than a league comprising just three/four/five players.

'I have many stories but a typical one, and the one that woke me up to the possibilities, was a few years ago.

'I had Rooney and my son had Robin van Persie (RVP) and he was ahead of me in the family mini-league. Rooney outscored RVP by a little bit for a week or two, so I started winding my son up about him being daft spending all that money on RVP, blah, blah, blah ... and he took the bait.

'His face was a picture on the Saturday when he realised he had done RVP to Rooney and I'd slyly done Rooney to RVP. We both captained our "swap" ... I got an RVP brace and he got a blank.

'WHOO HOO.'

Nothing says 'I love you, son' more than deliberately misleading him over a number of weeks for the sake of a few extra points in a game of pretend football. Freud would have had a field day, if he hadn't been too busy trying to shoehorn a free-scoring Bradford Park Avenue midfielder into his Fantasy side, FC Deine Mutti, for the start of the 1902–03 season.

'Playing for an overall ranking [OR],' adds Wakey, 'just can't compete with moments like that. OR is a bit colder and clinical; a mini-league is where FPL meets real life.'

Real life, said the philosopher Thomas Hobbes, is 'nasty, brutish and short'. Mini-league life, however, extends through thirty-eight long Gameweeks of nastiness. Throw in some alcohol, and it gets brutish pretty quickly, as Blame The Ref recalls.

'2015–16 season. I was checking my team with several uni mates in the room after having a few beers. I went to the toilet, leaving my account logged on. During the time that I was out, they took a twenty-point hit on my team.

'I finished at 197k that season, but worked out that without that hit I would've finished top 50k for my first year playing FPL.

'The funny thing was, I didn't actually realise that it was them until they came clean several weeks later. I thought that I'd taken the hit in my drunken state.'

Proof, if ever it were needed, that like driving, operating heavy machinery or giving your eight-year-old child that extra edge on school sports day, alcohol and Fantasy Football do not mix.

And neither does leaving your computer unattended and logged into the FPL website. I heard one tale of a particularly vengeful wife who changed her husband's entire squad for a fifty-plus points hit.

Despite the frequent (and generally correct) assertion that Fantasy Football gives all of us the chance to channel our inner football manager, the game is in no way an accurate replication of what actual gaffers have to deal with on a daily basis. All we have to do is pick a team and scour the transfer market.

Okay, so a lot of work does go into completing those two tasks, but none of it involves dealing with massive and capricious egos, carefully honing one's words in the knowledge that they will be forensically examined by a global audience, or dealing with questions from people you would hesitate to use any of your bodily fluids on in the event of them being on fire – unless, that is, you're a frequent poster on one of the internet's many Fantasy Football message boards.

So you'll never be the new Sir Alex Ferguson, however much you try. On the upside, that also means you won't be the next Paul Jewell either; the Paul Jewell who 'masterminded' Derby County's 2007–08 Premier League campaign, managing precisely zero wins from his twenty-four matches in charge.

But aspects of a manager's workload, or more accurately his arsenal, do cross over into the Fantasy world. Mind games, as shown above, are very common. And so is deception.

To quote Sir Alex's favourite Chinese military strategist, The Art of War author Sun Tzu: 'All warfare is based on deception. Hence, when we are able to attack, we must seem unable; when using our forces, we must appear inactive; when we are near, we must make the enemy believe we are far away; when far away, we must make him believe we are near.'

Or, to put it more bluntly, you can just flat out lie in a bid to confound and confuse, as Fantasy Football Scout poster Vibudh recounts.

'My friend shared this on Facebook: I once messaged my friend 90 seconds before the deadline with the message "RVP Injured WTF".

I knew he wouldn't have time to check if I was telling the truth and I was right; he immediately transferred him out for Carlos Tevez and gave him the armband. Joke was on me though, because Tevez scored higher than RVP that Gameweek.'

Deception can – and clearly does – go deeper than a deliberately misleading text, though. If you know a manager's team code, or happen to be in the same mini-league, anyone can see anyone else's FPL team. The catch is that you can see only the most recent version of that team – any changes that have been made ahead of the next Gameweek will become publicly visible only after the deadline for that round of transfers, which is one hour before the first match kicks off.

That doesn't stop managers, for want of a better word, pissing about with their line-ups, comfortable in the knowledge that their mini-league rivals will be watching such moves like a digital hawk and, ideally for the fiendishly devious pisser-abouterer, changing their own sides accordingly.

Such subterfuge, however, doesn't always go to plan, as poker player and FPL blogger Martin Coleman can confirm. 'My biggest low came when weeks of planning for my second Wildcard in Gameweek 33 and Bench Boost chip in Double Gameweek 34 were undone by my accidental failure to confirm activation of my chip.

'Mitigating circumstances were that I allowed my young children on to my desktop PC on that fateful morning of deadline day and trusted to effecting the procedure on my mobile, which I hardly ever did.

'Also, having left my activation of the chip to last, I had no changes to save, which would have prompted me to confirm. And most disastrously of all, playing mind games with my mini-league rivals, I placed all my expected biggest scorers on the bench. And score big they did – FORTY-THREE points in fact!'

As Sun Tzu also said: 'Don't forget to press Submit.'

So mini-leagues offer the Fantasy manager the perfect opportunity to keep in touch with their Machiavellian side, with often disastrous results. But in case you think that honesty is the best policy, David Rennie is here to tell you otherwise. And he's worth listening to – he led FPL for a number of weeks during the 2015–16 season, eventually finishing a hugely impressive sixth.

His Gutterball mini-league is a £10 per person entry, with payouts for the top three places. But for the 2008–09 season, the prize money was heavily skewed towards the winner (£250), with second receiving a mere £60.

'With a couple of months of the season remaining,' David said, 'I had a decent lead and my mate Iain was in second. Iain had pretty much given up but, much to my annoyance, he was gaining on me every week to the point where it got to the final Gameweek and he was within twenty points.

'We play pool together on a Thursday night and I'd made the mistake of mentioning to him that he'd been catching me. He says "I'll maybe have a look at it then ..."

'I didn't realise he still had a Wildcard left – although in hindsight it made sense since he'd given up – and I started to panic. I'd already spent the winnings, so confident was I that my lead was unassailable.'

Sure enough, Iain's fresh-out-of-the-box Wildcarded team romped home to victory on the final day. 'I ended up losing the league by a few points and had to scrape the money together to give Iain the majority of the winnings.

'Moral of the story, don't help out your enemies, and absolutely do not spend the takings of your mini-league, even when you think it's in the bag.'

So deception is vital – even when it comes at the expense of personal glory, as Charlie Donnelly knows only too well.

Charlie, whose username on the Fantasy Football Scout (FFS) website is the deeply imaginative donnellyc, won the site's inaugural Scout Cup – a big deal as FFS is populated by many previous FPL winners and was set up by Mark Sutherns, also known as the resident Fantasy Premier League expert The Scout.

'Winning the very first Scout Cup is one of the greatest things to have ever happened to me. The drama of each successful conquest, the Scout interviews, mentions of Hall of Fame. It was quite a heady mix for a fella whose imagination had stretched to surname plus first initial for his username.

'Anyway, throughout "the journey" was my older brother. Fully supportive, roaring me on after each successful round. Proud as punch. He couldn't have been more behind me.'

Charlie described his triumph as a marathon of 'crazy, energy-sapping hope the closer you get to the final'.

'Believe me, I've never been more exhausted. But the miracle happens and I win the cup. Much joy and bewilderment and celebration. My brother couldn't have been more delighted for me. Proud as punch ... but then came the punch.

'Fast forward to the end-of-season awards "dinner" for our mini-league. Hosted by my brother, all the award winners were duly acknowledged, given their trophy and a nice speech.

'My brother had won the mini-league so was duly acknowledged. But, as I found out later, "we" couldn't mention the Scout Cup win as that would alert everyone in the league to the existence of the Fantasy Football Scout website. And that would be bad for us!'

Charlie loves his brother. He is, apparently, 'the fairest, most considerate, least judgemental person' he's ever met. 'But Fantasy Football had changed him. Knowledge! Protecting the advantage was king! Don't divulge!!! He was a different person!

'I felt lost. Such and such got a trophy for being top at Christmas in a mini-league and I was the SCOUT CUP WINNER and got nothing but ignored.

'However, later that night, outside the toilets of a nightclub, a member of the league leant in against me and drunkenly whispered the question ... "are you donnellyc?"

'Oh my God! YES! YES!! I AM DONNELLYC! He knew!! He had figured it out! He had found the Scout website and, just like my brother, didn't want anyone to know. Fantasy paranoia! We were all keeping secrets from each other and I was paying the tab.

'Since those crazy days, I'm happy to report that the paranoia has calmed down and everyone is a bit more relaxed when it comes to Fantasy. The Scout website is a secret no more. But my win to everyone else in the league still is. They still have no idea.'

I suspect, donnellyc, that some of them might have an idea now.

The nature of the head-to-head combat on offer when taking on close relatives, friends or colleagues also ramps up the painful effects of the one-off moments that occur on a football pitch, which then translate into Fantasy failure.

Again, these sorts of events don't register so hurtfully when we consider our overall rankings – and rightly so. After all, our end-of-season scores in Fantasy Football are determined by every single point that we accrue along the way. So, for instance, that own goal scored by some useless plate of equine lasagne in Gameweek 4 is just as damaging as the red card handed out to your resident midfield psycho during the last knockings of Gameweek 38.

But it never feels that way in a mini-league where every point is doubly sacred, especially on the final day, because you know exactly what is needed to either fend off or overtake your nearest rival. The tales of woe that result are enormously heightened in their cruelty, misfortune and despair as a result.

Take FPL player Sanchez and his two years of mini-league hurt, for example. 'From my first season, where I led my mini-league from Week 1 to Week 37 then lost by one point on the final day, to the 2012–13 season, where I lost a £300 prize on "transfers made".'

'Transfers made', in case you didn't know, is a method of splitting teams who tie on points at the end of a season. The team that makes fewer transfers wins. Harsh, but fair enough. Until, that is, the long-suffering Sanchez rolls out the times he was denied the points that would have settled the issue long before transfers reared their arbitrarily evil head: 'There was "Balegate" (an assist for Gareth Bale that was never given, despite plenty of TV evidence to the contrary), a Juan Mata goal being called an own goal and then a final day Per Mertesacker assist that was removed as his headed pass skimmed off Lukas Podolski's shoulder. FPL overturned all of these decisions to lose me £300.

'Not that it still bugs me or anything. But I did delete my account the season after.'

And who can blame him?

Skooldaze then ups the ante by recalling the two times he was denied £500 in mini-league winnings; first when Aguero scored *that* goal for Man City in 2012 and then when John Terry came off after twenty-six minutes of the final match of the 2016–17 season – an orchestrated ego-fluff for JT in which even opponents Sunderland formed a guard of honour to clap him off.

'Even if Terry had come off just five minutes later, I would have won,' bemoans Skooldaze, who was pipped by a rival who owned Gary Cahill – the man who replaced Terry on the pitch with just enough time to claim the clean sheet points that settled the mini-league.

Skooldaze is, by all accounts, not the first person to be screwed by Terry, which is the scantest of consolations.

Mini-leagues clearly help us hone our sense of victimhood. Work mini-leagues are equally good at bringing out the creative side in many, especially when it comes to forfeits.

Adam Rubach's company in north London runs a league with no prize for the winner, but an insect-related forfeit for the unfortunate manager who comes last.

'One year it was a scorpion entombed in a bottle of vodka. The loser had to first down the shot of vodka and then eat the scorpion whole – and it was at least four inches long.

'The next year we called it the bug cereal challenge for the loser. We ordered a bag of 100 grams of crispy edible bugs, which then had to be placed into a bowl, with milk of the manager's choosing, before being consumed at the desk for breakfast on the same day our company usually sets out a buffet of fruits, yogurts and gourmet sandwiches for staff. That put a lot of us off our much nicer breakfasts.'

Vincent Fernandez, meanwhile, has a sufficiently impressive FPL record down the years – including a forty-sixth place finish in 2009–10 – that he's been in Fantasy Football Scout's Hall of Fame top fifty. But his work's mini-league remains a source of joy.

'Men and women get involved. In the early days, FPL was seen as an all-male domain in the work mini-league, but every year more and more women are joining up and are equally determined to prove their football knowledge and join in the banter.

'It's all meant to be a bit of fun, but I do love to see the knee-jerk reactions of players, who deny all interest when things are going well, and yet threaten to quit when the going gets tough.

'We labelled such outbursts as "doing a Keegan" (after his meltdown when Newcastle blew the title back in the 90s), but recently we have affectionately renamed such behaviour "doing a Radders" after one of our regulars, who quit playing for two years after blowing a 100-point lead going into the last few games of the season.

'He's back, of course. They always come back.'

Unfortunately for Radders, he came back with another bang. After rejoining in 2015–16, he had a great return and was being chased in the mini-league by a player who is German.

'Now, foolishly on many levels, the mini-league leader, English, renamed his team Spirit of '66, in an attempt to psych out the chasing German.

'With coolness of head, the German player renamed his team, in response, Spirit of 54, 74, 90, 2014, referring to Germany's way superior World Cup record. The mind games were won right there.

'The English player, AGAIN threw away ANOTHER 100-point lead. It was beautiful! To his credit, he didn't quit this time, but he's very much more subdued these days.'

International rivalries clearly add a little bit of extra spice to mini-league proceedings, as Ian Wray will tell you.

'When my mini-league started in 2003, it mostly comprised young, fresh-faced graduates. But as the years have gone by, a lot of us have risen to quite senior positions in business.

'I work in a global senior manager role within finance for a huge, huge multinational, and we have other people in the league who have risen to managing director, finance director etc positions in their respective companies.'

Ian keeps the eighty-strong league of high-flyers informed with a weekly email that includes the awarding of a virtual wooden spoon to that Gameweek's worst performer.

'But there is this one dude, from Belgium, who is really senior in the company and very serious about his work, who accumulated three of these spoons in quick succession. Ahead of our annual global leadership meeting at our head office in the USA, we went out and bought three real wooden spoons.

'I mean, this meeting was attended by all manner of vice-presidents and so on – generally, people for whom the word "football" evokes thoughts of Tom Brady and Aaron Rodgers – but we stopped the senior executive meeting at an opportune moment and invited the Belgian bloke to the front of the room to be formally presented with his spoons.

'Oh, he was fuming … utterly fuming … but the vice-presidents in the room all loved it.'

If you've ever wondered what exactly members of the corporate elite have to do to justify their salaries, now you know.

For the rest of us Fantasy plebs, mini-league forfeits tend to revolve around two dominant themes – curry and tattoos. Many a victim ends up being forced to have stuff inked on their bodies, from the Premier League logo in Twitter user @shauncoveley's mini-league to a simple 'L' for 'loser' on the lower back of the hapless @angelsleftfoot.

And as for curries, @JacobGibson's mini-league loser had to eat the hottest one in the restaurant as penance, while @RollyRollinson's crew take over their local eatery in a beautifully creative fashion.

'We have a twenty-person mini-league and each manager must attend our end-of-season curry dressed like the Premier manager in their league position. The bottom ten also buys the top ten's curry. Keeps it interesting to the final day. The race for tenth is so, so tense.'

Huddy went beyond curries, fancy dress or tattoos when deciding on the justice to be dished out to his mini-league rival. 'A newbie mate of mine was about 100 points ahead of me in our mini-league and was getting a bit too cocky. So I bet him one minute's Riverdance on the bar of his pub on a busy night that I'd catch him. He lost, and then performed the dance with alarming competence.'

Any sympathy you might have had for the loser should be quickly shelved as he clearly didn't learn his lesson. 'He wouldn't bet with me the next season, but still contrived to lose one with another mate that involved performing a karaoke Barbie Girl in full to a crowd.'

But all these tales pale when we get to the big-hitters in the forfeit stakes. I've heard of one particularly creative/evil league where the loser was forced to endure a trip from Land's End to John O'Groats, which is the most south-westerly point of England all the way up to the extreme north-west of Scotland. That involved a journey of some 874 miles (1,406km). On his own. And using nothing but public transport.

Talking of public punishments, David Rawlinson, a financial risk analyst from Manchester, England, made the newspapers for his mini-league failings. He'd finished last in his eight-player league before and ended up paying the bill at a restaurant for his 'mates' as a result. But when he lost again, they had other, rather less costly plans for him. Financially, that is.

'I was always destined to be dressing up,' he told the Manchester Evening News. 'I wasn't that nervous until I walked down Market Street a week before and saw just how many people there were.'

He had every right to be nervous – Market Street is a busy thoroughfare in a city with a population of more than half a million. And all those people don't usually get to see a bearded man dressed up as a 'sexy' nun – complete with a particularly nasty habit, stockings and suspenders – while playing a clarinet for an hour.

In case anyone felt the need to recompense David for his performance (or his outfit), his fellow mini-leaguers had scrawled two messages on bits of cardboard that they placed in front of him.

The first read: 'This is my punishment for losing last year's Fantasy Football league'.

The other was more forthright: 'Do not give me money. I am a disgrace!'

'It was crazy, it was absolutely rammed. I hadn't picked up my clarinet in about five years and it took me a good while to warm up. But loads of people, of all ages, kept stopping to watch. All the lads were watching and kept egging me on and telling me to carry on when I stopped.

'Everyone seemed to enjoy it and were taking loads of pictures. I don't take myself too seriously and just saw it as a bit of a laugh. I think I've set the bar now. It's only going to get worse so I've got to up my game.'

You can't help but wonder how things could get any worse, but I'm sure David's 'friends' will think of something.

Plenty of thought has been going into an Irish works mini-league and the punishments meted out to the losers. Before I can go into any more detail on that, a little bit of context is required.

The Chris Smalling Affair

The end to the 2015–16 Premier League season was like no other. The usual final day involves all twenty teams playing at the same time. This currently occurs on a Sunday because Sky Sports have paid an enormous amount of money to demand such things.

The key is that all ten matches kick off simultaneously to ensure that no side has an advantage. Well, no more advantage than being able to spend the billions of a kleptocrat, a porn baron, an oil-rich princeling or any other purer-than-snow individual who's managed to pass the Premier League's stringent 'fit and proper person' test to own a football club in England.

What is avoided is a team being allowed to start their match later than everyone else and who consequently would know exactly what they'd need to do based on the results from the earlier contests.

The Beautiful Game had learnt this lesson the hard way following the Disgrace of Gijon, which, to the more highbrow among you, might sound like one of Picasso's early attempts to chronicle the horrors of the Spanish Civil War but was, in fact, a football match.

During the 1982 World Cup finals, West Germany and Austria took to the field knowing full well that a German win by one or two goals would mean both teams qualified for the next round of the competition at the expense of fellow group member Algeria.

Why? Because the North African side had played their final group game the day before and, having beaten West Germany earlier in the tournament in one of the World Cup's bigger upsets, were forced to watch a sham of a match in which the Germans took the lead early and then did bugger all. The Austrians did even less, the match finished 1–0 and, by some amazing coincidence, the European neighbours went through while Algeria went home.

The crowd's reaction to this display of Teutonic efficiency was telling. Spanish fans impolitely suggested the players should kiss each other, Algerian supporters waved banknotes at them and one embarrassed German even burnt his national flag.

Fifa, however, ruled that neither side had broken any rules, so that was all right then. They then quietly introduced simultaneous kick-offs for all decisive group matches from Euro 84 onwards.

Anyway, back to the Premier League, where grubby deals between two self-interested parties have *never* taken place.

Only eighteen teams kicked off on the final day of the 2015–16 season because a bomb scare at Old Trafford meant the match between Man United and Bournemouth had to be postponed.

The fixture, fortunately enough, had nothing riding on it. In real life, at least. But many a Fantasy manager had the United keeper, David de Gea, in their teams. Quite a few others had his defensive team-mate Chris Smalling. All were therefore forced to wait two extra days for their overall rankings and mini-leagues to be decided.

The match was fizzling out, with United 3–0 up and De Gea heading for the Golden Gloves award for the keeper with the most clean sheets for the season, when Smalling struck. Unfortunately for him, De Gea and thousands of Fantasy managers across the globe, Smalling struck at the wrong end of the pitch. Into his own goal.

It was a goal with many ramifications. De Gea, obviously, had to make do with gloves made of tin, or something, as the golden ones went to his rival Petr Cech. Smalling owners endured a six-point swing, losing four of them when his clean sheet went south and a further two deducted for the own goal, which cost many, many of them their mini-leagues. And De Gea owners, of which there were legion, lost four clean sheet points which, again, cost a lot of managers mini-league money and glory.

It cost Irish Fantasy player Bernard Nolan particularly dearly. Poor old Bernie ended up bottom of his mini-league by just one lousy point because of the De Gea debacle. Unfortunately for him, his Dublin-based rivals had developed quite a taste for forfeits, so much so that their mini-league is called The Forfeit League.

Bernard's punishment was long and involved and required a passport. It even had its own website – 'Bernard's Journey of Shame'.

He was required to turn up at the airport with said passport, but no idea of where he was being sent, and then be handed a plane ticket, instructions for the day and some clothes. His brief was to fly to the UK, landing at East Midlands Airport (between Leicester and Nottingham), checking out that area's culture for a minute or two before heading off to Birmingham to complete a series of tasks – all the while dressed in a pink My Little Pony jumper and a leopard-print skirt.

'Throughout the day,' as the website explained, 'Bernard must complete annoying tasks that we have assigned and take pictures to prove he has done them. He will be doing all of this while the rest of us are in the pub, enjoying our end-of-season party – needless to say, the rest of us are all very glad we didn't lose.'

As a resident of the East Midlands, I feel the need to counter the allegation that any cultural visit to the region would be brief – the area, after all, boasts an excellent selection of motorways and more than its fair share of trees. There are also some Nando's.

Bernard survived his trip, providing photographic evidence of, among other things, his visit to Birmingham's Pride march that day, before getting home in time to be mocked by his mates in the pub.

But The Forfeit League was only getting started. The next season's losers – yep, they expanded the punishment to the bottom two – had to travel around mainland Europe in stupid clothing completing their errands, with the last one back forced to endure even more forfeits upon their return.

The league also devised a number of monthly and seasonal forfeits. As an example, Chrissy (the league's only female member) was forced to give up both alcohol and chocolate one January after finishing the previous month at the wrong end of the table. The chocolate ban was harsh enough, but Chrissy had been invited to a number of hen parties that month, all of which she had to endure stone-cold sober.

Sadly, as league member Mick O'Dwyer explained, the company for which they all worked recently underwent some 'fundamental changes', meaning the participants no longer work together, thus reducing the forfeits for the 2017–18 season.

Reduced they may be, but still grandiose:

Forfeit 1 – Christmas Carol Sing-Off

Who's in it? The bottom two at the time of our Christmas party.
How it works: Each loser will have to solo sing two Christmas carols each in the middle of a full pub for their embarrassment and the group's enjoyment. The group/crowd will vote for who is the loser of

the sing-off. The loser has to be 'Drinks Bitch' for the night. Drinks Bitch means that the person has to go to the bar anytime someone in the group asks; considering the queues that there will be at Christmas, this is not one you want to lose

Forfeit 2 – Happy Holidays

Who's in it and how it works: The bottom two losers from Gameweek 22–28 (January & February) will automatically enter the Danger Date in May. They will compete as team-mates in the Danger Date. The bottom two losers from Gameweek 29–34 (March & part of April) will join the January and February losers in the Danger Date in May. They will compete as team-mates in the Danger Date. The Danger Date will take place in Gameweek 35–38 in (part of April & May). The two teams will compete against each other, the team with the lowest accumulated total at the end will be the losers of the Happy Holidays forfeit and will be headed on their Happy Holidays.

The Happy Holidays forfeit again involves members being sent abroad to complete tasks, but with the last one back enduring further pain:

Complete Shot Roulette – Shot roulette consists of five shots and the loser must drink three out of the five shots at random (shots will be decided later by the group, not necessarily alcoholic, but no bodily fluids).

Das Boot – Just to really put the boot in, the loser will have to neck a pint out of their shoe, too.

Fair play to The Forfeit League – they take their mini-league misery very seriously indeed. But all of their shenanigans are self-inflicted, whereas real life can occasionally worm its way into the Fantasy plans of managers – particularly in draft leagues, where people often need to physically meet up to complete the annual ritual of a player auction.

One such auction took place on Sunday, August 7, 2011, at the home of Mike Pieri. Mike's Fantasy draft league, the Dwight Yorke

Cup, has been running for more than twenty years, and its members had arrived at his north London house for an evening of, as he put it, 'mirth and banter, as usual'.

That didn't last long, however. 'All of a sudden all our phones started bleeping in unison – apart from one manager who doesn't believe in them. We were getting texts and calls from wives, friends and parents. We looked at each other, stopped and listened out for the helicopters overhead and sirens in the near background – it was the Enfield riots taking place.'

The night before, a group had marched on Tottenham police station to protest about the death of Mark Duggan, who had been killed by the police. The march, initially at least, was peaceful and revolved around a perception that justice for the Duggan family had not been done.

Things escalated from there, and the area was plunged into anarchy. Missiles were thrown, shops looted and a post office burned down.

Over the next few days, similar riots broke out across north London and the rest of the country, with the initial focus of the anger, the Mark Duggan incident, sidelined and replaced by the spectacle of gangs of people essentially stealing whatever they fancied. This is not a particularly controversial or political statement to make, as footage of mobs breaking into the likes of Foot Locker, Carphone Warehouse and electrical retailer Currys was widespread and the intentions of the 'protesters' blindingly obvious.

Anyway, stuck in the middle of all this carnage were the stout members of the Dwight Yorke Cup. What to do? Keep calm and carry on drafting.

'Having one eye on the news, trying to bid and strategise during the auction became a difficult task, what with more helicopters flying overhead and by now the TV turned on so we could hear/watch what was going on. The fear of allowing a rival to outbid you was now superseded by the thought ... how am I going to get home?

'Eventually the auction ended, gone midnight as usual and with the riots still in full swing. Some managers got home, but others stayed the night due to frantic advice from those on the other end of (more) phone calls.'

The league – and its members – lives on to this day, but the same can't be said for the winner's trophy. 'We did used to have a trophy, but over the years and several attempts to bandage it up, Sellotape it and glue it back together, it got lost for ever. So if anyone ever comes across an eight-inch plastic footballer on a plinth, with a plaque stating Dwight Yorke Cup, please can we have it back?'

You heard the man. These people survived a riot. It's the least we can do.

Not so far away from Enfield is Ealing. It, too, had some trouble that August, but it's usually a fairly unrioty kind of place and it's home to another mini-league, The Ealing Men's League.

I'll stress immediately that this league has its own written constitution enshrining, among other things, the principles of the 2010 Equality Act, as well as detailing the forfeits to be undertaken should any member fail to attend the annual awards evening.

But it is the league's warm and fuzzy nature that perfectly encapsulates all that is best about mini-leagues, be they draft versions or, in this case, an FPL creation, and demonstrates why they are such enduring affairs.

League member and professional historian Paul Pambakian explained it all to me. 'Our friendship group at school were all pretty obsessed by football. The problem is, aside from one or two exceptions, none of us were particularly gifted at playing the actual game. As an academic bunch, Fantasy Football was therefore a natural place for us to live out our love for the game. The Ealing Men's League has kept us as a tight-knit group throughout the decade or so since we left school.'

Certain standard mini-league elements are in place, including a WhatsApp group reserved exclusively for Fantasy chat – any major announcements (engagements, pregnancies, etc) must be declared 'off topic' before being shared.

And there is an annual awards day. 'It's always held on the same day as the Champions League final, to ensure advanced notice, and we play golf in the day (pitch and putt in reality, but golf sounds better) before being joined by our other halves for an awards dinner.

'The trophy is presented and the champion makes a speech summarising the ups and downs of the season. Naturally, at dinner, we all wear the club tie; woven and dark green if you're asking.'

But all that pomp, ceremony and woven tie is a sideshow, disguising the deep roots that can form through a mutual love of Fantasy Football and the chance to mutually beat the mutual friends that have stayed together, mutually, through the thick and thin of real life.

'I think it's fair to say that for our group, FPL is intertwined with friendship. It's something that has allowed us to keep in touch and in competition. I'm pretty confident that without FPL, there are friends who might have drifted away from the group or dropped out of touch.

'It means that we can gather round and watch a "nothing game" with as much enjoyment as a Manchester derby, and, most importantly, it gives at least one of us bragging rights for a year.'

So, is that what we can learn from all of this – that to become a better Fantasy Football manager, particularly in terms of mini-league competition, we should savour the positivity of bonds made, and strengthened, by years of friendly rivalry?

Bollocks to that.

The key mini-league skills are clearly low cunning, high deception, borderline cheating and a fear of failure, made all the more exquisite by the knowledge that finishing last comes at a humiliatingly personal price.

The friendships, shared experiences and woven green ties that may, or may not, develop as a result are but a pleasant by-product.

CHAPTER FIVE

THE NUMBERS GAME

(Or we don't need to talk about Kevins)

I am not your typical Fantasy Football player. Yes, I love football and know a reasonable amount about it, so I have that in common with the standard Fantasy fan. And, obviously, we all share a love of the game itself. My divergence from the perceived norm comes scurrying in soon after that, though.

Numbers.

It's all about the numbers. And not just numbers themselves, but their application – stats, metrics, all that good stuff. And spreadsheets. Always with the spreadsheets. I've never used one, and never will.

This is heresy, to some at least. It is also just the way it is. My brain simply isn't wired that way. It has a modest talent for crosswords, anagrams, words in general. But not numbers.

The idea that to be a Fantasy Football fan you must be a stat-obsessed spreadsheet monkey of the highest order is a tired old cliche. Like all cliches, however, it is mired in truth. The subsequent logical leaps of detractors – that Fantasy Football is the preserve of kidult geeks across the boring, childish and socially inept spectrums – are considerably further from the truth.

But truth has never got in the way of a good insult, and the lazily spat 'Statto' conveys everything that is wrong, pointless and laughably pathetic about a life spent playing a game of footballing dress-up.

There is an elegantly simple counter-argument to such slander – it's bollocks. Yet there's no denying that numbers are at the heart of Fantasy Football, as they are in the real thing. Mathematical analysis of football is now big business and, arguably, its Fantasy versions showed the way. A game considerably less wedded to the statistics it produces when compared to, say, cricket or baseball, is now lapping up the numbers as clubs seek an edge over their rivals.

That sort of thing has been going on in Fantasy Football for a long time now. It might not quite be a case of the cart leading the horse, but it does feel as if football has finally realised what its Fantasy offshoot has been saying all along – that statistics and their application are very important indeed.

The question is, how far will the numbers take us? And how crucial are stats if you want to develop and improve as a Fantasy manager?

When I asked Bernie Donnelly – the man who invented his own version of Fantasy Football way back in the 1960s – why he played Fantasy, he had this to say: 'I love statistics. I love league tables. When I see a table, I always see a pattern. And if I don't see a pattern, it's because there isn't one to see.'

I suspect that the same could be said for a lot of the best Fantasy players out there. They have an instinctive love and understanding of numbers. Patterns appear fully formed, like ancient cities emerging from a receding ocean, to stimulate their mathematical intelligence. And numbers go even further, well beyond the mere processing of data, to entice and excite those with the numerical emotion to appreciate the purity and beauty of the logic therein.

Me? I'll give you the correct change, recite Pi to one decimal place and just about get away with the numbers round on Countdown – as long as I don't have to multiply stuff by seventy-five too much. And that's a real shame because, in an ideal world, I'd really like to impress Rachel Riley very much indeed. Or Carol Vorderman. I'm easy.

I've been writing about Fantasy Football for a number of years now, and that has required me to come into contact with all manner of stats to argue a case. I can appreciate the allure of a good one and understand the pleasure to be had from unearthing a particularly pithy one. But as a typically wishy-washy arts graduate, I've generally kept numbers at arm's length.

It's part ignorance, as I'm no great shakes at maths, and part arrogance because I don't wish to be viewed as the archetypal Statto mentioned previously.

The issue is clouded further by the fact that if I do relate to any particular kind of stat, it's always going to be one that is, to all intents and purposes, useless in Fantasy terms and bears relation to mathematics only in so far as it's got a number in it somewhere.

Take this one, for example: according to its own official website, a grand total of forty-nine players called Kevin have appeared in the Premier League since its inception in 1992. But only three Kevins graced the league in the 2017–18 season – and none of them was from the UK.

Now that's my kind of stat. A shit stat, granted, but one that begs a question – why has Kevin so fallen out of favour in this country? One of my oldest friends has that name, as does another good mate. But I don't know anyone under thirty called Kevin.

Two of the three plying their trade in the Premier League in 2017 were Belgian. Throw in Kevin Strootman, a Dutchman consistently linked with a move to England, and that's virtually an epidemic of Low Country Kevins.

Has it got anything to do with Kevin Keegan? That seems unlikely, seeing as his glory days were way back in the late 1970s/early 80s – long before the current meagre crop of Premier League Kevins were being conceived in the Belgian style.

We're all connected to Kevin Bacon, so perhaps he's the answer? But six degrees of separation are five too many when selecting a name for your child.

Kevin Spacey then? Maybe. But surely Keyser and Soze would have also been a thing among Belgian babies, and I can exclusively reveal that precisely zero of either has set foot on Premier League turf. And it's fair to say that nobody will be wanting to pay tribute to Mr Spacey in the future either.

Tracing the popularity of other names also involves a compelling lack of hard evidence. You might have noticed, for instance, a spate of Jordans in the UK for a number of years, and that's started filtering through to the Premier League. Thirty have now played in the league – the majority of them English – with the likes of Jordan Henderson and Jordan Pickford doing very nicely indeed.

Why has Jordan proved so popular? Here are my top three reasons:

- Michael Jordan
- King Hussein of Jordan
- Katie Price

But Kevin?

Apparently, the name is treated with such disdain in Germany, suggesting a person of lowly stock, that there's even a word for the cultural phenomenon – Kevinismus. That stinks of Teutonic snobbery in the same way that the word 'chav' elicits a certain disdainful reaction in the UK.

According to the book Freakonomics, a German survey asked 2,000 primary school teachers how they perceived certain names. One teacher's comment: 'Kevin is not a name – it's a diagnosis!'

That doesn't seem to have crossed the border to Belgium and beyond, however, and in Kevin De Bruyne, the Premier League is blessed with an attack-minded Belgian midfielder who consistently brings in the points.

So Kevinismus is a diagnosis that suggests positive Fantasy outcomes.

The point of that digression is to show just how poor my grasp of statistical relevance truly is. I gravitate towards whimsy which, as far as I'm aware, has never been an accepted branch of mathematics.

Whimsical Maths – Paper One

Question 1: A train is travelling in one direction at 72mph. A second train, travelling in all of the other opposite directions at once and for ever, wishes it were an elephant, dancing in fields of fairy popcorn. What is the velocity of the second train, and how much popcorn can it consume? Please show your workings.

No, in Fantasy Football, the only currency I should be dealing in is cold, hard data. Because that, according to some at least, is where the Fantasy future resides.

There's an excellent blog, entitled FPL Observatory, written by a professional poker player who identified a number of similarities between the card game and Fantasy Football. One section of his blog really stood out for me: 'The poker player stereotypes that had been around for an age were transformed over the course of a decade. The old-school competitors who believed in poker being an art, not a science, based on feel, instincts and reads, were quickly overrun.

'A new breed of maths nerd, guys using a mountain of sortable data from the millions of hands played online, began to dominate the game. Math whizzes changed the game using probability theory to their advantage.

'Similarly, I think the generation of fantasy football managers who believed that football knowledge and a "good eye" were the only requirements for success are in the process of being overthrown by algorithm builders, probability theorists and statisticians.

'Consider yourself warned if you're one of those who underestimates the relevance of maths in FPL. That geeky person who invited you to join his or her money mini-league is probably hustling you!'

The comment that immediately leapt out at me concerned the managers 'who believed that football knowledge and a good eye were the only requirements for success'. That's me in a nutshell. I was being called out as obsolete. What could I possibly do in response?

Interview the man.

Martin Coleman, it turns out, is an affable chap of my generation with an impressive track record in poker – good enough to be elevated to Supernova status by one well-known website, with companies keen to offer him sponsorship to play the game online.

His love of football and numbers would appear to have come from his father who, as a young man, was George Best's accountant for eighteen months during his swinging sixties Man United heyday.

The classic 'where did it all go wrong?' story about George could have applied to Martin's dad, as he explained: 'He was eventually sacked for nagging Georgie boy to lose his parasitic entourage.

'Nevertheless, and with predictable consequences, my dad seemed to have emulated his hero's alcohol-fuelled gambling and womanising lifestyle. And so it was he died at the age of fifty-five, an alcoholic bankrupt.'

For the record, Martin himself seems well removed from either George Best's or his father's rock 'n' roll lifestyle. When I interviewed him, the only thing he was flirting with was veganism.

I asked him to talk me through why he thought the stats guys would come to dominate Fantasy Football, which immediately showed up my ignorance of the subject. 'I very much doubt they will. I think it much more likely that the maths guys will, though.'

Surely stats geeks and maths nerds are peas in the same pod, right? Wrong. While statistics is a discipline relying heavily on maths, it isn't accepted to be an area of mathematics.

'Whereas statisticians rely heavily on intuition to compensate for the lack of precise definitions and proofs, mathematicians are trained in logic and deal only with certain truths and clear patterns, rather than probable truths and possible patterns.

'Much of what passes as data analysis in Fantasy Football has to my mind more in common with superstition than science. My first ever FPL blog was entitled So Much Mumbo Jumbo and covered my objections about the prevalence of meaningless stats in the game, so I'll not rehash them again now.'

Martin didn't want to rehash them, but I will.

First, however, here's a 'joke' he told me. I must stress that Martin has an excellent sense of humour not necessarily exemplified in what follows. I think he wanted to prove his point more than make me laugh.

'A mathematician, a probabilist, and a statistician appear on a Fantasy Football podcast. The host asks each one "what is 1 + 1?" The mathematician answers "2" and is taken no notice of. The probabilist answers "odds are 2, but I would have to run the numbers a few more times" and is also ignored. The statistician looks at the interviewer and says "what do you want it to be?" and is invited back on to the show again the following week.'

Martin Coleman, ladies and gentlemen. He's here till Thursday; try the veal. He most definitely will not.

His Mumbo Jumbo blog post railed against a reliance on stats that Martin considered unfit for purpose, with the following comment a neat summation: 'At the outset of one season, I was assured by the FPL community on more than one occasion that I was making a big mistake starting without any Chelsea players in my team, because historically they ALWAYS started strongly.

'That's the thing with statistics though, they're only true until they're not; they tell us what has happened in the past, not what will happen in the future.'

A good example of that would be Spurs striker Harry Kane and his August hoodoo. For a certified goal machine, Kane has an unhappy knack of completely failing to score during the first month of the season. This has persuaded many managers to hold off buying him until September comes around. Up to and including the 2017–18 season, it's proved to be a smart tactic, despite there being no scientific basis for it.

Mathematicians would scoff at talk of hoodoos which, Martin went on to explain, would give them an advantage over the rest of us because they 'take emotions out of the equation'.

'A dispassionate scientific approach will prevail over old-school notions of "eye test" and "gut feel", because, if nothing else, it minimises the psychological pitfalls of cognitive bias and prejudice.

'Objectivity will trump subjectivity in the long run because it is a perspective based in quantifiable and measurable facts, and not vulnerable to wider interpretations based on aesthetics and feelings.

'At the risk of sounding like a cheerleader for AI, I feel the need to point out that chess computers can now beat grandmasters. Hell, there are even computers now that can beat the best poker players. My days are numbered!'

Time for a small diversion. Again.

Martin's mention of 'cognitive bias' brings us on to another scientific area used to explore and explain Fantasy Football – psychology. I am a dullard in this field as well. My levels of understanding are at the 'pop' end of the scale. And not classic pop that stands the test of time, but Agadoo or anything by Vanilla Ice – pop that makes you fear for the very future of mankind.

A while back, the Fantasy Football Scout website published an article from member Ludo entitled The Psychology of Fantasy Football. It's a great read, which I will summarise here while imploring you to seek it out for yourself (via the link in the Addendum). And to continue the poptastic theme, it also has a sub-heading – The Scarcity Heuristic – which could have been a deeply pretentious band spun off from any number of 1980s art school shoe-gazer combos.

Ludo starts by explaining an example of cognitive bias thus: 'Some Fantasy managers will captain a player from the final match of the Gameweek, not because they believe this fixture boosts performance, but to avoid the trauma of an early captain fail.'

Yep, I understand that one. A lot of us will have done it.

Moving on to confirmation bias, it is '… the tendency to find information that confirms our current beliefs, at the expense of other views. We often fall for this when looking at statistics, where we ignore those that don't fit our theories, and focus on those that confirm them.'

You've still got me, Ludo, and you're backing up Martin's comments.

The scarcity heuristic, it turns out, is equally understandable: '… the more difficult it is to acquire an object, the more valuable we perceive it to be. In Fantasy Football, this can be observed when we overvalue expensive players and undervalue cheaper options.'

And on the article goes through gambler's fallacies, omission bias, groupthink and many more. It really is a great read and, for reasons of not wishing to completely plagiarise, I urge you to dig it out for yourselves.

The point is that many Fantasy players have a tendency to let emotion, or other unscientific notions, guide them through their choices. And, as Martin stresses, those of a mathematical bent will not fall into that trap. Probably.

'An understanding of probability is a key component of both Fantasy Football and poker. More often than not, the player considered most likely to score a goal in any given PL match is priced at odds against to do so by bookmakers, meaning they deem it more likely he won't score than he will.

'By way of example, Alexis Sanchez, the top points scorer in FPL for 2016–17, failed to score in twenty-one of the thirty-eight games he played in, which is roughly 55 per cent of the time. In fact, he only provided an assist from those twenty-one games on six occasions, meaning in fifteen games (39.5 per cent) he scored no attacking points whatsoever.

'Let's assume, however, that we "know" Sanchez will score in half of the games he plays over the next three seasons. It would be well within the normal distribution of goals predicted by standard deviation for him to go eight games in a row without scoring – especially if those are the Gameweeks that I own him!

'Actually, a sequence of eight blanks in a row over the course of 100 games can be expected to occur around 17 per cent of the time. Likewise for eight scoring games in a row.'

'Standard deviation' has always struck me as being a bit of a contradiction in terms, much like 'fun run' or 'young Conservative'. And by the end of my interview with Martin, I feel none the wiser, but better informed on the subject of maths. This is entirely due to my shortcomings, not his, and as I start to drown in mathematical minutiae, I have to reach out and grab on to a more general point to save myself from going under.

Does the potential primacy of maths as a Fantasy tool mean that, to be a successful player, we will all have to become considerably more numerate and considerably less, well, human? Will there be some kind of geeky arms race in which Fantasy players will be compelled to learn increasingly complex mathematical notions just to keep up? Will there be any place left for footballing insight?

Peter Blake isn't so sure that numbers will become the only game in town. His blog, Mathematically Safe, is his take on an 'obsession with playing Fantasy Premier League (FPL) and trying to gain an advantage using analysis'. Its name derives from the title of the Half Man Half Biscuit song from the album Trouble Over Bridgewater, because he believes that 'if you can't find a HMHB song or lyric to narrate whatever you are doing, you're just not trying hard enough'.

That's a bold claim. Whatever I'm doing happens to be trying, as a self-confessed mathtard, to explain the power of numbers to people almost certainly better informed than me on the subject. Is there anything worse than that? There is surely nothing worse than washing sieves, with the possible exception of being Garth Crooks.

Does that work for you, Peter? It should do, what with it being from Lock Up Your Mountain Bikes, as I'm sure you're aware.

Obscure references to criminally underappreciated Wirral songsmiths aside, Peter has good news for those of us who struggle with the more scientific approach to Fantasy Football. When I asked him whether the rise in software aimed at giving Fantasy managers the edge would lead to a time when the game would become more of a tech battle than a human one, he was not convinced.

'I don't think there is a danger in that; the greatest algorithm in the world can't account for a bad tackle that forces your captain off at half-time. Footballers aren't machines, they are susceptible to environmental, emotional, psychological and physiological factors that we are unaware of that can impact performance.

'Ultimately all we can use the algorithms for is to increase our probabilities of success, but you will still get some decisions wrong. Some will get more wrong and some lucky person will get them all right, but ultimately that may not even matter when a player out of your price range scores a hat-trick.

'We can work with probability, but fundamentally you still need a lot of luck to get enough decisions correct to win because some things over the course of a ninety-minute game are unpredictable.

'In my opinion, that dichotomy that exists between what should happen and what does happen is what makes football great to watch, and the never-ending battle to control and predict the chaos is what makes FPL such an addictive game.'

So the romance of football lives on and the numbers will be kept firmly in their place. Or, to put it to Peter's Half Man Half Biscuit test, even men with steel hearts love to see a dog on the pitch.

And that place should be as close to our hearts and minds as we can make it.

'I don't believe that fundamentalists on either side will prosper in the long-term,' Peter says, referring to the battle between stats and football knowledge. 'Good players to my mind are the ones that intake a lot of data from multiple sources, which can include watching players on the pitch, listening to managers in press conferences, utilising communities' collective knowledge (the "wisdom of the crowds" approach) and, indeed, statistical analysis.

'Data and numbers are basically meaningless if you do not know how to utilise them; I use statistical analysis to inform my decisions, but the numbers I look at are not selected randomly but because they can be used to prove or disprove a hypothesis.

'The starting point of that hypothesis will often be a triangulation of multiple data "feeds" and stats will be used to validate the theory. Equally, big data analysis can give you a good steer on what to look for of importance in the other data.

'Stats can lie though – as can all the other data feeds – and hypotheses can be incorrect, which is why it is not a good plan to rely on only one source of information.'

Relying on one source of accumulated and applied data can, however, get you really quite far. A team at Southampton University decided to try to create some software to advise Fantasy players on the best players to pick. They were, and still are, led by a Dr Ramchurn.

In the interests of full scientific disclosure, that's ...

Dr Sarvapali D. (Gopal) Ramchurn,

Associate Professor (Multi-Agent Systems),

Agents, Interaction, and Complexity Group,

Electronics and Computer Science,

University of Southampton, UK.

In the interests of humanity, Dr Ramchurn generally goes by Gopal.

He and his team created an algorithm robust enough to form the basis of a predictive tool which, in turn, was robust enough to be tested not just by academics in a lab, but by genuine, living and breathing visitors to the Fantasy Football First website.

'Algorithm' is a word used by many but not necessarily understood by all, one of the all being me. At the risk of sounding like the technofool that I most assuredly am, I asked Gopal to explain what exactly an algorithm is. His analogy was comfortingly everyday enough for me to grasp.

'An algorithm is a series of logical steps. You follow these steps to generate some kind of outcome; a very structured way of executing some calculations.

'For example, making breakfast. You put the oil in first, crack the eggs and then cook them for five minutes. It's a description of a process from start to finish.'

I'd personally look at four minutes for those eggs but, you know, science.

Anyway, the tool Gopal's team created basically ended up doing what we, as Fantasy managers, do every week – sift through the data. In our case, the data will involve players, prices, teams and fixtures (both immediate and future).

Apparently, with 500 or so players available to buy in the FPL game, that throws up the potential for more than 10,000,000,000,000,000, 000,000,000 combinations across price brackets, matches etc, per week for us to consider. A lot of those combinations will immediately fall by the wayside because you hate a particular player, you can't afford most of the obvious ones and that co-worker with the lovely smile is heading your way and you've yet to reveal your crippling Fantasy addiction to them, so it's time to shut down your web browser and pretend to get on with some work rather than pretend to get on with some work while playing Fantasy Football.

Gopal's tool, which doesn't fancy anyone and doesn't care who knows about its Fantasy issues, also uses data from past performances, of both individuals and teams, over a number of seasons to suggest the optimum player to bring in for upcoming Gameweeks.

In early testing, the tool finished well inside the top 1,000 out of hundreds of thousands of teams in the Daily Telegraph game, which was impressive. Gopal also had his software try out various other games, including FPL, so if you ever check out your team's overall ranking and notice The Squad Room just ahead of you in the standings, you're being beaten by a machine. To be fair, you wouldn't be alone – in the 2016–17 season, it finished in the top 80,000.

Pleasingly, when Gopal talks of his software's most recent FPL performance, it sounds just like any other Fantasy hard luck story. 'We were doing very well until the last two weeks as we didn't have Harry

Kane and didn't have the Bench Boost. We were in the top 40k, then we went to 80k.'

A top 40,000 finish would have been significant as it would have put The Squad Room in the top 1 per cent of all FPL teams. Even so, a finish well within the top 3 per cent is not to be sniffed at. It also suggests that the vast majority of Fantasy managers would benefit from using the software, making it a potentially commercially viable prospect. But there's a long way – and a lot of money – from potential to actual.

To create software that learns – one of the bedrocks of artificial intelligence – and can act wholly independently of humans is the ultimate goal. 'Understanding the subtleties of the game – if we could do that I think it would be almost human. If we did have the team to do all this analysis, I think we could get very close to beating everyone at this game.'

But it's a big if and, for now, the software very much requires the human touch. 'However refined and beautiful the algorithm, you're always going to need a certain amount of human input, an informed judgement from a human.'

Among the judgements Gopal's software struggles with involves players new to the Premier League – because they don't have the history built in that helps drive future predictions. The changing nature of each football club is another.

A good example of the latter is Man United. Under Sir Alex Ferguson, the club had a particular identity and a shedload of trophies to show for it. Under David Moyes, that identity became confused and the trophies considerably more thin on the ground – at least when compared to the 'Moyes Out' banners trailing behind the planes in the sky. Similarly, Louis van Gaal and Jose Mourinho further reshaped the club in their image, meaning all that historical data is no longer a constant and easily transferable thing because a Ferguson United would have travelled to, say, Arsenal with a clear and generally well-executed plan to destroy Arsene Wenger's psyche, whereas a Moyes United would go to the same place and park the bus. We, as football-loving humans, instinctively recognise this. Machines do not.

Ironically, the real-world applications for these Fantasy algorithms have the potential to be far more important. Gopal's predictive tools can, for example, be used to help deploy drones to the exact area they are needed most following a major natural disaster.

But as a Fantasy Football tool, at least for playing the FPL game, the software has its limits. Gopal is still looking for funding and is quietly confident that new versions concentrating on American football's NFL and the daily Fantasy sports games now flooding the European market could prove considerably more commercial.

For now, however, in a battle of Man v Machine – or more accurately Man v Machine Helped By Man – we fleshy carbon units are still winning. Or at least the top 2 per cent are.

This is good news. The danger of overly accurate predictive tools is that they would take the fun out of the game. By minimising the chance of error, you're minimising one of the key Fantasy Football drivers – the chance to prove your knowledge is quantifiably better than someone else's. If we all ended up getting our answers from a machine, then we'd all be only as good as that machine – one of the reasons purists bemoan the current state of Formula 1, for instance.

But there is no doubt that the correct use of statistics can massively improve our chances of success in Fantasy Football. The big question is how much weight you give to them when compared to other analytical tools that we humans take for granted, tools such as the 'eye test' – the simple act of watching a football match and reaching certain conclusions about a player based on their performance.

Why? Because the stats can lie. Or, more accurately, a lazy reading of the stats can lead you to faulty analysis.

As a ridiculously simple example, if you see a statistic declaring that a certain player had four shots from which he scored twice in a match, you would understandably conclude that here is a man in excellent form who very much needs to be considered for inclusion in your future plans.

But if you'd actually seen the match in which those stats were created, you would have come to a different conclusion when you witnessed his first goal resulting from an incredibly fortunate rebound off the side of his face and the second involving tapping in a cross which, if he'd left well alone, would have gone into the net anyway.

Fantasy Football Scout columnist Prokoptas is all too aware of the vexed issue of stats v eye test – he writes about the former, but is happy to acknowledge the importance of the latter.

His real name is Edwin Dickinson, an anatomist working in Leipzig at the Max Planck Weizmann Centre for Integrative Archaeology and Anthropology, with his research surrounding digital methods of modelling the musculoskeletal system across primates. This, let's face it, is just a grant-winning way of describing 'monkey business', but back to the matter at hand.

'FPL is a game of projecting future performance, and we are simply weighing different criteria more or less heavily than one another in making those projections.

'But even if the decision-making process is sound, the range of possible outcomes always includes total failure. That doesn't invalidate the process itself, or mean that you were wrong – you just decided to hit on fourteen and drew a nine. I think that holds true both for the eye-test, statistical projections, and any combination of the two.'

So how does he believe statistical analysis can help when examining, say, a well-owned striker's current goal drought? 'Football is a complex game that involves hundreds of factors we could never hope to quantify or to observe during the game (perhaps there is a robust and direct causation effect between hours of REM sleep the night before a game and expected assists, but I'm confident I'll never discover it).

'The more we observe of a team playing together, and the more astutely we can handle performance statistics, we can begin to improve our ability to project performance a little.

'But random events will always occur that defy our expectations and projections. We have to accept that they will happen and undermine all of our careful calculations. But if we can cover the highest percentage of likely outcomes, then we should do okay in the long term.

'So ultimately, we simply prefer different weightings of data in determining the optimal process, which is as it should be, or else we'd all trot out the same side every week!'

Fantasy Football pioneer Riccardo Albini, if you recall, struggled to find relevant statistics in football when he was devising his Fantacalcio game in the 1980s. In the end, he used the marks given to players in each match, as dreamt up by newspaper sports reporters, as the base for each player's score in his game.

That was then. Now, he acknowledges that football stats have come a long way, although he is concerned that they have come rather too far.

"I believe that the future – at least in Italy – is to give up newspaper marks and use stats. Of course everybody thinks that, but stats could be difficult and complex and to me no one came up yet with an easy but interesting scoring system.

'The problem is that some companies think that the more [stats] the better. But I believe less is more. Nowadays there are either too many numbers to read or one single number, like the Opta Index, for example, which you don't know how it came about.

'I think you should use a few clear-cut stats, maybe losing some performance nuances, because to enjoy the game you need to be able to understand easily the relationship between the index and the performance stats. Otherwise how are you going to look for the players you need in your Fantasy team?'

That's not to say you can't excel at Fantasy Football when relying almost wholly on statistics for help. But to do so, you need an expert eye, a lot of time and that wholly unscientific factor – luck.

Take the experience of Simon March, who won the FPL title in the 2014–15 season. Simon's triumph, on the face of it, was a stroll in the park. He went into the final Gameweek with a thirty-four-point lead and ended up winning by twenty-one points. In a contest in which some people have found out that they've won only following an agonising wait for the post-match allocation of bonus points, such a victory looks, on paper, to be a stress-free affair.

But in the same way that football is played on grass, not paper, Fantasy Football is played in the mind. And the mind plays host to all manner of irrationality.

Simon was in amongst it almost from the get-go. He was in the top 100 by November, the top ten on Boxing Day and leading the pack by Gameweek 24 in early February. Having to defend a lead for fourteen whole Gameweeks was a tall order made taller still by circumstances entirely beyond Simon's control.

'Maintaining a lead is a very different challenge to chasing one. You can no longer just play your own game, you have to be conscious of what the people chasing you are doing.

'I had a spreadsheet of the other teams in the top ten that I filled in every week so I could identify the danger players while trying to identify some opportunity to gain on them. At that point, it had definitely become a bit of an obsession; I was reading everything I could on Fantasy Football, I was even dreaming about it.'

It was enough, you would have thought, to make a grown man paranoid. Unfortunately for Simon, there was plenty more where that came from.

'Weird things start to happen when you're leading Fantasy Football. I started seeing my name mentioned in blogs and hearing it on podcasts and I even got interviewed by a national newspaper. I kept getting alerts that people were trying to hack my email account, which I don't think was entirely a coincidence, and there was even a campaign among the top fifty players to all change their team name to my name. A few of them did and I definitely freaked out for a moment when I saw my name down in fifteenth place!'

Simon's final-day experience will be familiar to anyone who has been in that welcome, but oh so unpleasant, situation – lots of waiting, pacing, fretting and pacing. And pacing, anguish, doubts and pacing.

And pacing.

For Simon, the fact that he was living in Singapore at the time made matters even worse. He had to spend the entire day waiting for the final matches of the season to begin, which they did, for him, at 10 o'clock at night.

A full day's pacing meant that kick-off was a blessed relief. 'In two hours it would all be over, either way. But that relief didn't last long as just about everything that could go wrong for me in that first half did.

'The player placed fourth in the world at kick-off, who had started forty-three points behind me, had captained Diego Costa, who hadn't even started the game. However, his vice-captain, Theo Walcott, raced to a first-half hat-trick. Goals and assists seemed to be flying in for him and, meanwhile, my team, including my captain Sergio Aguero, were all doing exactly nothing.

'It was the nightmare scenario that I'd been torturing myself with for the past three months playing out in reality. At half-time, should everything have stayed the same, he was going to overtake me.

'I started to question what I'd done wrong to deserve what was happening and I honestly very nearly didn't bother following the second half. I started to tell myself that winning Fantasy Football was a nice dream, but it wasn't going to happen so I should just get used to it and get on with the rest of my life.'

It has always been specious to say that Fantasy Football is the closest thing to being a 'real' football manager. There are similarities, of course, the main one being the long and lonely hours spent setting up a team that you then have to send out and watch, pretty much powerless, as they crash and burn in front of your eyes.

But where the two worlds diverge most markedly is at half-time. While the downcast Fantasy manager can only sit and wonder whether hemlock is available over the counter at their local pharmacy, the real boss can go about inspiring his troops in the dressing room, employing every tactic, from inspirational speech-making to throwing a boot at the squad's prettiest player, to turn things around.

After fifteen minutes of infamy, Simon returned to his virtual dug-out for the second half.

'Then, in a moment, everything changed. I refreshed the page of the forum I was using to follow the scores and the page was filled with one-word posts all saying the same thing: "Aguero!". My captain had scored!

'I can't fully explain what happened next. I just remember a lot of jumping around and yelling. My poor neighbours, who had only moved in the day before, must have wondered what the hell they'd let themselves in for! I doubt anybody in the world celebrated that goal like I did.

'On that same forum, somebody put into words exactly what I'd finally started to believe: "Aguero goal; March wins."'

And so it proved.

'I was on my feet nervously counting down the seconds as the games finished, blowing an imaginary final whistle from about 7,000 miles away. Then I spent ages trawling through the top fifty teams in the world just to check nobody had caught me. I think I wrote a post on a Fantasy Football forum thanking everyone for their support, and sometime around 3 a.m. I went to bed.

'I woke up the next day, immediately reached for my phone and saw the game had updated and, there I was, number one at the end of the season. I'd made it.'

How Simon made it produces a strong case for playing the game by the numbers. As mentioned already, Simon was living and working in Singapore when he claimed his FPL crown. That meant he approached the game in a singular way.

'One thing that has surprised a few about the season I won was that I watched almost no football at all. Maybe two matches the whole season. That's not to say I don't enjoy watching football, I do, but given I was in Singapore, which is seven to eight hours ahead of the UK, most games took place very late or in the middle of the night.

'So I immersed myself in the stats as a way of feeling involved in football while I was out there. Surprisingly, I think the emotional distance that not watching much football created probably helped me manage my biases and make more ruthless, data-driven decisions. I'm one of those people who actually quite enjoys looking for patterns in piles of data so it suited me okay.'

There's that word again – 'patterns'. And some compelling evidence that you can excel without using the 'eye-test', or generally immersing yourself in the world of football.

Simon's stat-driven season of success does come with a rider, however. 'While I'm not suggesting people give up watching football, I think controlling your personal biases is one of the less spoken-about aspects of doing well in Fantasy Football. The game is littered with so-called rules and "logic" that quickly become accepted as fact and, unchecked, these can quickly ruin your game.'

And he's honest enough to acknowledge that you can plan all you want, process as many stats as your brain can handle and watch football until the cows come home and your partner leaves it, but luck will always play a part.

'I remember very late in the season, maybe Gameweek 36, one rival had got to within a few points of me on the Saturday. He'd taken a punt on Alexis Sanchez as captain over Sergio Aguero, who was my captain and, probably, the objectively obvious choice. Both were yet to play and I remember looking at his team and thinking that if Aguero doesn't score a hat-trick today, he's going to catch me.

'Aguero then went and scored a hat-trick, with two assists for good measure. When I look back on the season, it's moments like that that stand out. And they also underline how much luck was involved.'

So, if you have the eye for it, look for patterns in the data – those telltale figures that point to a perfect statistical storm in which a certain player is likely to score. Form, fixtures and the underlying metrics that suggest a higher probability of bonus points being awarded are, to the expert, obvious places to be looking. They should become obvious to lesser Fantasy managers such as myself as well.

According to some, the stats don't lie. Others put them the wrong side of damned lies. The truth, as with so many things, is probably to be found somewhere in the middle. But you ignore them at your peril. And with Simon March's eye and a smattering of luck, they might take you very far indeed.

CHAPTER SIX

THE GLOBAL GAME

By the time the 2016–17 season was done, there were more than four and a half million teams in the Fantasy Premier League game. As the 2017–18 season developed, that figure had jumped to five and three-quarter million. Well over two million of those were run by UK managers, a million and a half from England alone.

Even when employing my differently able mathematical skills, that meant more than three million managers outside the UK were playing a game based on the domestic football calendar of a damp outpost of a European continent with which its people had decided to sever formal economic and political ties.

One of the supposed claims of the Brexit brigade – and I use the word 'supposed' advisedly here as there was a remarkable and depressingly steamy mound of disinformation to be found on both sides of the argument – was that we could thrive in our brave new post-EU world by exporting marmalade and our expertly blended ranges of tea.

There was never any mention of one of the nation's truly global successes – FPL.

Every manager that has an FPL team must enter the name of the country in which they live, meaning that they all have both an overall ranking and one for their country's league as well. This, in turn, means that someone with the time and inclination can scour the FPL website to find out how many teams are registered to each country. Writing a book about Fantasy Football handed me the inclination, so I also found the time.

Some of the figures I unearthed boggled my tiny, stat-lite mind. For instance ...

It was very easy to lapse into an A-Z cliche and declare that FPL was hugely popular from Australia (128,000-plus teams) all the way to Zimbabwe (7,000).

Bhutan (population 784,000) had 2,750 teams – that's one for every 285 people – whereas Belarus (population 9,498,000) had just 1,559. Which just goes to show what the state-run firewall of a not overly benign dictatorship will do to your Fantasy prospects.

There were 3,565 registered teams from war-torn Syria and more people played FPL in Nepal than Northern Ireland. The same was also the case in Iran, compared to some quite well-populated place that went by the name of China.

Norwegians seemed particularly keen on the game, with nearly 110,000 registered users, which, again applying my 'maths', amounted to one in fifty of the population.

But Norway had nothing on somewhere called the French Southern Territories. I confess that I had never heard of this place, but surmised that it was probably some territories, in the south of the world, owned by France. I was partially correct.

The French Southern Territories, or Terres Australes et Antarctiques Francaises (TAAF) as the French would have them, consists of five islands. They are:

- Kerguelen Islands, a group of volcanic islands south-east of Africa and sort of halfway between that continent, Australia and Antarctica.
- St Paul and Amsterdam Islands, north of Kerguelen.
- Crozet Islands, south of Madagascar.

- The Scattered Islands, which should lie at the very end of a quest in Narnia, but actually float around, in a dispersed fashion, near Madagascar again.
- Adelie Islands, the French bit of Antarctica. French sovereignty is not recognised there, presumably because of some strident penguin independence movement, so Adelie isn't officially part of TAAF.

Discovering this wonderfully faraway and obscure set of territories was, to me at least, interesting enough. Finding out that there were no fewer than sixty-nine FPL teams there … you can imagine my delight.

That might not sound like much of a number, although it will be enough to force a snigger in the more childish among you. But it's a massively tumescent one when you realise that the population of TAAF is 310. In the summer. In the winter, just 150 hardy souls, consisting of visiting military personnel, officials, scientific researchers and support staff, make TAAF their gaff. So nearly half the population were playing FPL, according to my calculations.

My research was diligent, taking in as it did more than just a quick look at Wikipedia. I wanted to talk to the Fantasy hotbed that was TAAF and pick its windswept and actively volcanic brains. I needed to know why FPL was such a thing there, although I could imagine that the long, cold days, the harsh environment and the nationalistic penguins might have quite a lot to do with it.

But TAAF was French and, I think it's fair to say, the French don't readily take to English pursuits.

Where to start? I tried an EU department called Octa – Overseas Countries and Territories. Or Pays et Territoires d'Outre-Mer. Or Landen en Gebieden Overzee. Or even Oversøiske Lande og Territorier.

Octa was supposedly something to do with TAAF, and I received a polite reply from a charming chap (I smoothed the way by telling him I'd voted Remain) called Nicolas Ferellec, who couldn't help, but suggested I contact the TAAF administration direct at a website address he kindly forwarded.

Nothing doing there either, presumably because they were too busy thinking of ways to stifle penguin-based dissent through the standard French medium of cooking and eating them. So I started thinking a bit more laterally, discovering a US-based Antarctic cruise company that ferried a few hardy tourists out to TAAF's various bleak and remote islands.

They, too, remained silent, so I tapped up a friend of mine, a scientist who occasionally played cricket against a team from the British Antarctic Survey, to see if his polar opposites might know of a person I could contact. They didn't, although I did learn that if you ever play the British Antarctic Survey at cricket, some of them take it rather too seriously indeed.

Aside from actually going there myself – for which I had neither the time nor the budget – I was left with only one choice. I would have to go on Twitter.

What I found there was very Twitter. There were frequent references to the place, mostly coming from accounts supposedly written by satellites passing overhead. Obviously.

Samples included the whimsically lyrical takes of SuitSatAdrift (@SuitSatAdrift) ...

I'm 406km above French Southern Territories right now. The Milky Way's a broken saucer on a cold stone floor.

And ...

Hello French Southern Territories! The bustle over Port Louis, French Southern Territories reminds me of mornings on the ISS.

While the gently self-aware FengyunAdrift (@FengyunAdrift) went for ...

I'm so over Port-aux-Francais in French Southern Territories. I mean I am like literally over Port-aux-Francais.

And ...

Beneath me right now: French Southern Territories. Don't waste an anti-satellite missile on me, no, no.

I must confess that I found it all quite charming, if entirely pointless and borderline insane, which is actually a neat summation of Twitter itself, if one disregards the death threats and the racism.

But Twitter wasn't finished with me, or the French Southern Territories, just yet ...

Happy #420 in Amsterdam Island, French Southern Territories! #420PM Smoking some #Volatile Crosswalker or Kerguelen in French Southern Territories: By now they should have the raving munchies in Kerguelen.

And ...

Hot Teen French Southern Territories educated show on webcam. Hot Teen French Southern Territories mind freckles on webcam.

Do those hot teens 'mind freckles' as in look after them? Or do they just not like them? I wasn't going to click the link to find out, however tempted I might have been. And as for an educated webcam show, was that to PhD level? Part of a degree in professional genital manipulation? I will never know.

My personal favourite of the whole bunch came from an especially deranged account called Animal Tech Cop (@animal_tech_cop) ...

French Southern Territories' Police are Using Hippopotamuses to Eliminate Reprogenetics.

And ...

French Southern Territories' Mayors are Training Seals to Take Out Industrial Agriculture.

And even ...

French Southern Territories' Comptrollers are Teaching Elephants to Stop Composite Materials.

Animal Tech Cop's seventy-two followers are fed some interesting stuff, it has to be said. Although probably not nearly as interesting as the stuff consumed by the person who decided the account – a bot 'tracking the rise of animal-human collaborative policing of technology' – was a good idea in the first place. That person, for the record, is Greg Borenstein (@atduskgreg), a technical game designer at Riot Games.

The upshot of all these Twitter travails was that I was none the wiser, nor better informed, about TAAF and its legion of Fantasy fans.

And then something happened, again on Twitter, that perfectly explained my utter failure to solve the Fantasy mystery of the French Southern Territories and, indeed, demonstrated how stupid I'd been about the subject all along.

The Irish blog, FPL Hints, is a fine Fantasy Football resource. And in May 2017, its Twitter account attempted to fill the sorrowful void created by the end of an FPL season by running the Alternative World Cup.

In a nutshell, FPL Hints asked its followers to vote for a number of quite obscure world locations, with these places grouped together in head-to-head match-ups. The winner of each tie would progress through the competition until only two were left to do battle in the final.

That final took place on June 4 between Christmas Island and Heard & McDonald Islands, with the former running away with it and securing 63 per cent of the Twitter vote.

In my book, this was thoroughly deserved simply for the fact that Christmas Island's capital is Flying Fish Cove – the sort of name even a Disney executive would have considered too outlandish, too arrrr-Jim-lad-piratey-bollocks, to use in an incredibly successful film series based on a theme park ride.

But why was this even a thing? Well, for starters, boredom needs to be faced head-on by a lively mind. And the main reason for the vote was that Christmas Island, as the winner, would now be the preferred location for FPL Hints' many fans when they came to create their Fantasy team for the new season.

Because – and I knew (but forgot) this fact all along – you don't actually have to live in a place to claim you're from there when you set up your FPL team. In fact, you can even change your alleged location week in, week out, if you so choose. A friend of mine once made the mistake of allowing his young son access to his FPL team account and the little scamp changed his team's country of origin every single time he was online.

This fact has major repercussions for some of the stats I threw at you at the start of the chapter. It doesn't entirely invalidate them – I'm sure, for example, that the vast majority of FPL managers who claim to be from Norway really are. But you or I could just as easily declare on the FPL website that we are Norwegian when, in reality, I am most definitely not and, if I'm being honest, I'm not sure you are either.

By the start of the 2017–18 season, there were no fewer than 1,450 FPL managers plying their Fantasy trade on Christmas Island, which has a population of 2,072 people and precisely zero radicalised penguins, although the red crabs have been stirring.

This figure, as we now all know, is not entirely true. As in it's not true at all.

Then again, the good people of Christmas Island itself, as in members of their official tourist board, heard about FPL Hints' contest and ended up pledging to give a prize to the manager at the top of the country's Fantasy Premier League table on, appropriately enough, Christmas Day.

The contest to be the Christmas Island number one took on an added element of intensity as a result. What would the prize be? An all-expenses-paid trip to the island itself? Honorary citizenship? The right to drive a flock of crabs through the streets of Flying Fish Cove? The speculation was almost as fevered as the competition, with long-time league leader Martin Coleman – yes, our professional poker man from the previous chapter – pipped to the crown during the very last round of fixtures before Christmas Day itself by FPL Fly, a self-confessed FPL addict who had recently overcome testicular cancer and who described himself on Twitter as 'half the man I once was'.

FPL Fly's triumph earned him … a Christmas Island crab fridge magnet.

All of these shenanigans had a major consequence for my Fantasy expedition to the French Southern Territories. Because, as I should have realised from the very start, there were not sixty-nine FPL teams out of a winter population of 150. And not even out of a summer one of 350. In fact, there were probably no FPL teams on those far-flung islands at all; just sixty-nine Fantasy managers having a bit of a laugh at, as it turned out, my expense.

But I'm okay with that. It's absolutely fine. It took me a while (and you a thousand words or so) to realise what a monumental waste of time the whole TAAF fiasco turned out to be, but as they always say, travel is about the journey, not the destination. And that journey kept me pleasantly amused until it was time to venture elsewhere on the Fantasy map.

How about Assam? That sounds exotic enough. A north-eastern state of India with a population of thirty-one million or so, it's perhaps most famous for the tea it produces.

When I was handed an FPL story with an Assamese twist by a chap called Jay, I was delighted. But the fact that Jay is as British as fish and chips and chicken tikka masala meant I had to move on, although I will mention in passing that his puntastic FPL mini-league, Gheorghe Hagi Pudi Susu, is the classic infantile phrase that an Assamese toddler will say to their mum or dad when they need the loo.

Interestingly enough, Jay also confirmed that another 'classic' gag thrives in continents far and wide too – the deliberately embarrassing father. 'My dad, bless him, when I went to uni would text me asking "Hagi korila?" – effectively asking if I'd been to the toilet that day.

'He's only just stopped asking these stupidly personal and irrelevant questions recently. I'm thirty-five, married, with a six-month-old daughter.'

Suitably culturally enriched, we move on further east and down a bit to Koh Samui – Thailand's second largest island. It's a beautiful destination, perhaps best known for its Full Moon Party, and one chosen by hundreds of couples worldwide as a venue for their wedding. As a result, Koh Samui also has a professional wedding celebrant who goes by the name of Johnny Paterson.

Johnny is a semi-retired Scottish ex-pat in his fifties with an infectiously positive outlook on life – hardly surprising when you live on a tropical island and get paid to turn up at people's weddings. I must confess that when I saw the term 'wedding celebrant' and learnt of Johnny's roots, I might have lapsed into lazy stereotype mode and presumed that here was a man who was paid to go to people's weddings and, well, get drunk and probably pick a fight.

Far from it. Johnny actually officiates at these weddings, which are non-denominational ceremonies that usually take place on the beach. It's not exactly a bad gig, as Johnny readily admits. 'It's a hugely rewarding experience and it always restores my faith in human nature. Amidst all the doom and gloom that nightly news shows beam out, I'm constantly reminded that real love, tenderness and inner beauty exist – in abundance.'

He has some stories to tell, as you might expect. One involves a groom who drunkenly tattooed his soon-to-be-wife's name, Marie, on his arm the night before the wedding. Except that he actually got the name Maria instead, and she was his ex-girlfriend. The groom ended up, as Johnny put it, 'wearing the wedding cake that night', although the marriage did endure, apparently.

Johnny also recalls the see-through outfit worn by another bride, who worked in the 'exotic dance' trade, which attracted a large crowd of men to what was meant to be a private, two-person ceremony.

Most weddings go without a hitch – even when Fantasy Football manages to worm its way into proceedings. And it does.

'I marry couples from all over the world and I can usually spot a Fantasy Football fan. Usually I meet couples a day or two before the ceremony date to chat through the details and I have to be truly careful to keep on track if the conversation drifts towards Fantasy Football.

'I've had quite a few stares from brides, and I've had a few grooms who've written their own vows, which include promises about the amount of time they spend on Fantasy Football.

'It's rather funny on the day, but I do warn grooms that their new wives will remember those promises and they really need to be sure that a) they can keep those promises and b) if she's not a Fantasy Football fan laddie, is she really the right one for you?'

Johnny's own wife seems okay with it. He's in the Irish Times mini-league – named after an island pub, not a newspaper – and often stays up late to watch Premier League matches as Koh Samui is six hours ahead of the UK. But he makes sure he discharges his family duties at the same time.

'My two granddaughters (aged five and seven) live with my wife and me, they have done since they were born. The girls will sit with me and watch the early football match, which is brilliant and a source of great joy for me. As I'm at home much of the time, I'm close with the girls anyway and it's a great feeling for me to spend as much time with them as possible. And my wife gets a break from them – at that age they can be somewhat demanding in many different ways.

'I don't think they are in love with the game yet, I think it's the fizzy pop, crisps and chocolate I sneak them that may be the greater motivation at the moment, but I live in hope.'

If Fantasy Football crops up now and again in what passes for Johnny's 'job' (all that heat and happiness must be incredibly debilitating), it actually led to employment for another Fantasy obsessive.

Ivan Hadyan is in his mid-twenties and lives in Indonesia. Ivan is probably better known among Fantasy's Twitter brigade as Andrey Arshivan, a talented graphic designer with a decent track record in FPL – he finished 5,678th in the 2014–15 season.

He admits to being clueless about the game when he first started – he even captained Bolton goalkeeper Jussi Jaaskelainen once, so that's some compelling evidence right there – but stuck at it and began producing weekly graphics of FPL stats on Twitter. That ended up forming a large part of his design portfolio and he landed a job at Pandit Football, a major website in Indonesia, as a result.

In fact, work and Fantasy sports seem to go together really rather well. Any number of studies in America have shown that the benefits of allowing employees to dabble in their Fantasy pursuits in work time – especially as part of an office-based mini-league – far outweigh the occasional, shall we say, lapses in productivity.

Scott Peterson, an FPL fan from Pittsburgh, hits his local, Piper's Pub, to watch Premier League matches, but it is at work where he really reaps the benefits. 'While I enjoy the Fantasy game for what it is, I've found that it has benefited me in other ways. When I've met with English clients, they are surprised that I know so much about the Premier League and that's usually a plus for me.

'Most of all, however, I feel that being a part of the game has, in some small way, made me a more global citizen since I'm more plugged into a game that the whole world loves.'

That line's a keeper – whenever anyone questions why you'd wish to spend so long on a game of footballing make-believe, just tell them you're trying to be more of a 'global citizen'.

You'll be hard pushed, however, to better the claims of Maciej Onoszko to that particular title. A Polish-born Canadian resident who works as a markets reporter for financial media company Bloomberg News, he couldn't be more global if you covered him in maps and forced him to work as a 1970s drinks cabinet.

Maciej finished 798th in FPL's 2015–16 season and is sufficiently obsessed with the game that he has separate Twitter accounts for his professional and Fantasy lives.

'2011–12 was my first season. But the first two seasons were just practice. I *really* started playing in 2013–14 – that's when I started paying closer attention to player and team stats, fixtures and started longer-term planning.'

Maciej is in little doubt that the financial world in which he immerses himself for a living bleeds into his Fantasy hobby. 'Managing a portfolio is a careful process, to which you have to give a lot of thought. You're planning your decisions carefully, you assess all the pros and cons. Sounds familiar?

'You also need to make sure your portfolio is balanced. You may want to have some risky assets like stocks in there, but also safe ones like bonds to protect your capital in case the risky ones lose money.

'FPL is exactly the same; you want the "safe assets" that guarantee points and some differentials who don't always pan out, but will do wonders for you if you get them right.'

The similarities between Fantasy Football and financial management don't stop there, either. 'People in markets depend on data, on numbers, they are the foundation for all decisions. But markets aren't about the numbers only, they're even more about trust.

'Again, it's the same with FPL. You have a budget to invest and you want to choose the best players. You look for the players with the best stats, but then you also want them to look good on the pitch. You want to be sure the player actually backs up the stats with the potential to score FPL points.

'And then you think – is he really worth the 8.0m or 9.0m or 12.0m? No way! There are better options that are cheaper. And so on.'

And perhaps the area in which the two worlds collide involves that most human of preoccupations – not wishing to miss out. 'Oh boy, there are no bigger bandwagons than in financial markets. Except in markets we call them bubbles.

'The mechanism is exactly the same as in FPL – you see the player doing well, suddenly everyone talks about him, you get excited too, you have the fear of missing out, you buy and … it doesn't end well.

'My point is that portfolio managers and managers of FPL teams go through exactly the same kind of thought processes.'

So the wants and needs that drive international money markets are really no different to those that inform our Fantasy choices. And the same habits crop up whether you're a journalist in Toronto or an IT professional in Kenya, which is precisely what Brian Moseti is.

'After the conclusion of a day's games, say Saturday, I will "stalk" my opponents' teams to perhaps see how they had fared. I will make fun of my friends whenever they had a captain fail, especially a triple captain fail. Ha ha. Good times.'

Or a lab technician in Uganda, like Ivan Kasagga. 'A poor Gameweek equals a reduced love towards eating. A good one, the opposite.'

Or an operations manager for a gas and oil company in Cameroon, like Stuart Pask. 'Trying to identify trends and patterns in a game that are often overprinted by human performance is interesting to me, so I guess that is how I am still hooked. Addictive when you guess right and you score differential points and you get green arrows, then when Aguero gets sent off ... not so much.'

Fantasy Football is a unifying experience while the real thing, with its tribal nature and long standing and often incredibly bitter rivalries, can be painfully divisive.

In all, some 252 countries, principalities and regions are represented in FPL, although, as the company that runs the game, ISM, admits: 'We suspect that some people say they are from other countries when they are actually living in Bracknell.'

That confirmation, once again, of my French Southern Territories lunacy was fine. I'd moved on by then. To Australia.

Some countries' attachment to FPL is rather more obvious than others, and it doesn't come much more obvious than the English-speaking, sports-mad former colony that is Australia. Football (real football, not the Aussie no-rules version) has never traditionally been a big spectator sport there, but that's changing. And there's always been a large fan base for the sport among ex-pats.

As a result, well over 100,000 FPL managers call Australia their home, including Julian Zipparo, the Sydney-based brains behind a team called Ranieri's Ghost that came very, very close to winning FPL in 2013.

Julian led that year's campaign for around half a season despite not watching a single match. 'Of course it lasted till the second last week and after the bloody national newspaper here in Australia covered it, and then it completely consumed my time and effort.

'And I did start watching games ... and I fell at the final hurdle. Sigh ... anyway, it's a good pub yarn for me.'

The newspaper report into Julian's success – published before his near-miss – couldn't be any more Australian if it tried, which was particularly apt for a rag called The Australian.

The headline reads: 'Our man in the big league shows 'em how it's done ... in his sleep', before going on to proclaim: 'Yep that's right, Australia currently boasts the greatest football mind in the world. You bewdy!'

Julian himself is quoted as follows (and, yes, it is improved by reading it in an Australian accent): 'I've been a football nut my whole life, but I don't have Foxtel and obviously the games are on at two o'clock in the morning. I enjoy the stats side of it; I comb over all sorts of dorky statistics about the game and watch the highlights online every once in a while.

'I started out playing to beat my bloody mates at work and all of a sudden I was top of the table and getting Facebook friend requests and emails from completely random people from countries you'd never even think to go to.'

Julian got national coverage as a heroic failure, but by then Australia had already had two winners of the FPL title – and back-to-back at that.

First came John Frisina in 2007–08, before Jason Moultrie, a geologist from Mackay, Queensland, won the following year. Jason's victory was historic – the first (and currently only) manager to win by virtue of making fewer transfers than his nearest rival. And when I say 'nearest', it means the top two that year both finished with 2,256 points and transfers-made became the tie-breaker.

Jason won a trip to London, along with his friend Duncan Thomson, to watch Chelsea take on Aston Villa. Duncan clearly earned the trip as it was he who first introduced his mate to FPL two seasons before

Jason's victorious campaign. And as Aussies let loose in Pommyland, where do you think they went? The pub, of course.

Earlier in this book, we met Sal Browning, the senior exhibitions co-ordinator at the Museum of Science and Industry in Manchester. Sal recalls a drunken night out at her friend Anna's leaving do.

'It was a Wednesday evening and we went to a pub that was showing the Champions League quarter-finals first leg, as I wanted to see the Arsenal v Barcelona game.

'Cesc Fabregas – it was back in the day – looked like he'd got injured and I shouted to my friend how whack this was as he was in my Fantasy team and I might have to substitute him or transfer him out.

'From this comment, a random bloke spoke up and said was I talking about the official FPL game? I said of course, what other game is there?

'So we got talking and it turned out he had won the overall thing the year before! He was called Jason, and his friend was Duncan and they were in the UK (they were Australian) claiming their prize of free VIP tickets to a game of their choice, with travel.'

Jason's all-expenses-paid trip, it turned out, included a significant outlay on hospitality that evening. 'We had a great rest of the night with them,' Sal goes on. 'All seven of us, including my other half Damian, ended up in an indie club dancing, singing and drinking cocktails until the early hours. The guys from Australia paid for all our drinks and it's gone down as a legendary night.'

As well it would.

The cultural, historical, linguistic and alcoholic ties between the UK and Australia make the popularity of FPL Down Under easy enough to understand. But closer to the game's home, the take-up is even greater, with some of Europe's more northerly countries leading the way.

CHAPTER SEVEN

OUR FRIENDS IN THE NORTH

Finland is incredibly proud of its FPL prowess. I mean, how many other countries have used their London embassy website to tell the world of their Fantasy achievements?

None. That's how many.

'Finland's best kept secret' was the headline on a 2010 embassy story written by Tiina Heinila, who proclaimed that 'there is one thing in football where Finland is on top of the world – the world's biggest Fantasy Football manager game Fantasy Premier League'.

The article includes a graphic showing the top three countries, by average score per manager, in that season's FPL. Finland came top, with their 17,015 managers (out of a population of around 5.4 million) each averaging 1,793.5 points. That beat Hong Kong's 9,956 Fantasy bosses into second place by a chunky 28.7 points.

Interestingly enough, yet more proof of the FPL-managers-choosing-bogus-places-to-claim-residency-in phenomenon came with the third-placed country – step forward the 503 managers 'from' South Georgia and the South Sandwich Islands. That doesn't sound so much, 503. Until you realise that the actual population is thirty.

Back to Finland's FPL supremacy. For those thinking that these figures are from 2010 and a lot could have happened in the meantime, well, the Fantasy Football Fix website did some calculations following the 2016–17 season to determine which country had the best average rank among its FPL managers. The winner, with an average overall rank of 1.42m was, yes, Finland. England came in at 1.74m, Australia 2.00m and the USA 2.25m.

Anyway, the embassy piece goes on to quote one Mikko Kuronen, a UK-based Finnish football correspondent, as to why the Finns are so good at Fantasy Football.

'My theory is that many Finns are long-distance supporters of English football clubs and that the Premier League is, in a way, considered to be the domestic league by many – instead of the Finnish one.'

That all sounds reasonable, but it doesn't properly explain any Finnish Fantasy finesse because the same is true of both Norway and Sweden – ask a Norwegian which team they support and they'll invariably mention an English side first and a domestic club after that.

'One big reason behind the Finnish enthusiasm,' the article continues, 'might be that YLE, the Finnish equivalent to the BBC, has long traditions of showing English football on national TV. In the 1980s and early 1990s, the English First Division was about the only game in town for those interested in international football – and thus the Saturday kick-off established itself as the highlight of the week for many Finns.'

That was a curious thing about the early 1990s. While Finns were lapping up English football live on TV, fans in the UK had to make do with highlights packages from their own league and full matches only from Italy's Serie A.

'Since then the whole culture of football following has changed,' the article goes on. 'With internet and pay TV, there is not much difference whether one follows the Premier League from Finland or here on the spot. In fact, it is not possible to see as many televised live games here in the UK than it is in Finland.'

Here again, the same could be said of their Nordic neighbours. It's clearly a factor in the Finns' success, but not a unique one. In fact, Mikko comes up with only one truly Finnish explanation for the country's FPL supremacy: 'Thoroughness. When Finns set their minds to something, they tend to do it well. Many Finnish fans also seem to know their football trivia, even to the point of being a little bit annoying.'

And Finland has one more thing to boast about – possibly to the point of being a little bit annoying. It is the FPL legend that is Ville Ronka.

'Legend' is an overused word. Its dictionary definition is: an extremely famous or notorious person, especially in a particular field. And in the particular field that is FPL, Ville Ronka is both extremely famous and notorious.

The fame is simply explained. In nine FPL seasons, Ville has only once finished outside the top 20,000. For the sake of completion, and because it's wildly impressive, here is the complete list of the Finn's finishes:

Season	Points	Rank
2008–09	2,078	4,266
2009–10	2,466	569
2010–11	2,225	362
2011–12	2,243	1,631
2012–13	2,248	4,668
2013–14	2,534	90
2014–15	2,332	277
2015–16	2,319	1,450
2016–17	2,267	21,905

The first obvious question to ask is: what the hell happened in 2017? The second one is: Ville Ronka – man or woman?'

The answer to both is … nobody knows.

And that's why he/she is as notorious as it/they are famous – even to Fantasy players as good, or maybe even better than him/her/them.

Peter Kouwenberg, who I mentioned a good deal earlier in this book, is one of a select few managers who have been good enough to replace Ville at the top of Fantasy Football Scout's Career Hall of Fame – a league table that tracks the FPL performances of the best managers over all the seasons they've been playing the game.

Peter's take on the Finnish enigma? 'I agree entirely that he is a legend, although I only know as much as anyone else.

'I would still argue he is the best player out there, but has been hurt by the fact that point hits over patience proved the way forward in the season I overtook him and the guy (or girl?) is a machine in terms of his cool approach.

'The guy doesn't make knee-jerk decisions – he must have it nailed to the chair. And he never blinks. As I say, I still consider him the better player; just unlucky that recklessness has been rewarded recently.'

Ville is a popular boy's name in Finland – the second most popular in the country according to some websites, with 0.17 per cent of the population going by it. The problem is, as with countries, there's nothing stopping FPL managers choosing an entirely bogus name, and sex, for themselves. All you need to register an FPL team is an email address – the rest is up to you.

So while Ville Ronka probably is Ville Ronka, he could also be a she and not Ville Ronka at all, just someone who has called themselves Ville Ronka for reasons known only to themselves.

The only thing we know for sure is that Ville's team, Timppikset, was the most consistently successful one of the past decade, until that 'awful' finish in 2016–17.

Does that tarnish the legacy? A touch. But it hasn't halted the speculation regarding the mysterious maybe-man himself. Far from it. When I idly tweeted that I envisaged Ville Ronka inhabiting a Finnish castle amid the fluttering of Fantasy bats, I was surprised to receive a number of replies, both on Twitter and via email.

'I always imagine a bald woman in a cloak working in a billionaire's laboratory' was my favourite theory, as proposed by Twitter user FPL

& I, while FPL Acid chucked in the rumour that he 'only cobbled a team together to beat his son', and an anagram bot liked my revelation that Ville Ronka could be rearranged to spell Evil Lo Rank.

I also received a poem, from one Esther in Bedworth, which deserves a full run-out:

Ville Ronka,
Willy Wonka?
Total stonker!
Or a big fat plonker?
No one knows because why?
Because he's a mystery,
Like my Nana's gravy,
That she won't let us in the room to see
When she's doing it

And Southbound Jack sent me a limerick:

There once was a Ronka called Ville,
Who made all the others look sillier,
He comes from Helsinki,
Or somewhere else in Finland I thinky,
Nobody seems to know reallier.

I'm no judge of poetry, so I'll leave you to decide on the virtues of the works above. But, if nothing else, they demonstrated the curious fascination this Finnish enigma exerted on more people than just me, extending well beyond a dodgy/laureate-standard poem or two.

Entire topics on Reddit have been devoted to the man, his methods and history. One of the oldest Fantasy Football websites, Fiso, has a long-running thread entitled 'Let's Catch Up With Ville'. It's been going for more than two years and, at the time of writing, had amassed 2,163 posts discussing the manager's moves, tactics and general genius.

And bogus Twitter accounts, purporting to be from the man himself and offering 'expert' advice to anyone foolish enough to be sucked in, have sprung up and been slapped down on more than one occasion. These accounts have usually been created by the same person who I will not, as the saying goes, grace with the oxygen of publicity in these pages.

I had to find out more. And in my fearless quest to try to discover who Ville Ronka truly is, I would like to say that I left no stone unturned. Unfortunately, that would be a lie, mainly because a chap called Adam Levy got to the stones before me and then contacted me with his findings.

Adam found a Ville Ronka on the LinkedIn website. 'This Ville Ronka has, since 2016, been studying applied sciences at a university in Helsinki,' he wrote.

Could he be the one? Adam began cross-checking by taking a look at Ville Ronka's FPL mini-league, IVU vs Hari.

'One of the members was at the same university for two years when LinkedIn Ville Ronka was there. Going on through the other names in the mini-league and … ah … stalking around a bit, there are three people who are, or were recently, at another university, which is also in Helsinki, and they were also doing "applied" kinds of subjects.

'I appreciate the "evidence" may be too circumstantial, if not too weird! But if you wanted to follow it up, the Ville Ronka on LinkedIn is a "connect" request away.'

He was indeed, and it would have been remiss of me not to try it. But I had a sense of certainty that I would fail because, let's face it, you don't become an international man of Fantasy Football mystery by coughing up your identity to a random stranger on the internet, particularly one who is keen to put them front and centre of a book. No self-respecting shunner of publicity would. They'd be kicked out of the Enigma Club if they did, and that's an organisation damned near impossible to join in the first place, what with the chairman consistently turning down his own membership application.

And what would actually be achieved if Ville Ronka finally stepped out of the shadows? What we already (sort of) know about him would be confirmed – he's probably a he who's probably from Finland. He's a relatively cautious Fantasy Football player who eschews excessive transfer hits and plays the long game. And he's a bit of an addict, because he signed up for the Norwegian Eliteserien Fantasy game over the summer of 2017 to cope with FPL's summer withdrawal symptoms.

Do we really need to know more? Wouldn't the revelation that he's a twenty-something science graduate with a desk-based job in the tech sector who's saving up for a house while pursuing his passions for cold beer, hot birch saunas and the extreme metal musings of Impaled Nazarene, wouldn't all that just strip away the layers of mystery that made him so interesting in the first place?

There's a Ville Ronka on Instagram who likes dressing up in camouflage gear while holding an assault rifle. Another owns a construction company in the town of Lohja. A third was the guitarist in an early 1990s prog rock band called Nova Scotia. Could any of them be The One? I could have asked them, I suppose. But I wasn't entirely sure I wanted to.

The American clergyman Harry Emerson Fosdick once said that 'I would rather live in a world where my life is surrounded by mystery, than live in a world so small that my mind could comprehend it'.

Thanks to the internet, the world has never been smaller. Thanks to Ville Ronka, some mystery still remains.

Moving west, there's no mystery when it comes to Norway and Fantasy Football – the two can't keep their hands off each other.

As already mentioned, one in every fifty Norwegians has an FPL team, and its domestic version of the game, Fantasy Eliteserien, is almost as popular. It's run by Norsk Toppfotball (NTF), the league organisation for the thirty-two clubs playing in the two top leagues, Eliteserien and OBOS-ligaen, in Norway.

NTF's marketing manager, Martin Ygre, was blown away by the instant popularity of Fantasy Eliteserien. 'Our initial goal was

20,000 players during the 2017 campaign. We had over 60,000 before Gameweek 1, and have now surpassed 71,000 players.

'The popularity took us by surprise, and it is a confirmation of the high interest in Norwegian football and Eliteserien, including among the younger generation as over 60 per cent of the players are between sixteen to thirty-four years old."

The game is mainstream. Eurosport promotes it live in-studio and produces vodcasts, while the VG newspaper runs articles on its website and features on its web-TV shows Runden and Foppall.

But the influence of England on all this is never far away. Fantasy Eliteserien takes place during the FPL-free summer months, thus dragging in the addicts who need their Fantasy fix all year round. And another key reason for its popularity, according to Martin, is that it is 'based on the same framework, rules and regulations as FPL'. In fact, it is even designed and run by the same company, ISM, that is behind FPL.

This should probably come as no surprise, as Norway has kept English football close for a long time. The Norwegian national lottery company, Norsk Tipping, started its version of the football pools in 1948, with the majority of the matches on the coupon English ones. Norwegian TV broadcaster NRK showed the first match from English football – on a show called Tippekampen – in 1969.

These days, a trip to England to see a football match is virtually an annual pilgrimage – some 93,000 fans travelled over in 2014 – and the Norwegian fan clubs of the likes of Man United and Liverpool are huge. Around 42,000 people, for instance, belong to the United fan club's Norwegian branch which, some wags might argue, is probably more than follow the club in Manchester itself.

This is not some kind of parochial interest in seeing Norwegian stars doing their thing on an English stage either. Long gone are the heady days when Tore Andre Flo, Ole Gunnar Solskjaer, Stig Inge Bjornebye and John Arne Riise headed up a sizeable contingent of domestic talent earning their living in the Premier League. For the 2017–18 season, only Bournemouth's Josh King was a regular starter.

But with that kind of historical connection, it's no surprise that Norwegians have taken to FPL in such numbers. 'Fantasy Football is widely popular in Norway and has become a typical topic of conversation among many Norwegians interested in football,' Martin explained. 'Over the past few years, the number of articles, podcasts and vodcasts about Fantasy Football have increased in Norway, sparking discussions among fans on social media, blogs and forums.'

And when you've got your closest neighbours heavily involved in FPL as well (and in the case of Finland, quite happy to boast about it), that adds an extra pinch of spice to the Fantasy stew.

'I don't think the "Norwegian temperament" is a thing; however, we enjoy a bit of banter between the Nordic countries,' Martin continued. 'We can get quite competitive and make fun of each other, especially with our Swedish neighbours, *sota bror*.

'We have our own sets of similar jokes and puns across the countries, the only difference being which country the joke is about. The Nordic rivalry gets real intense during competitive tournaments, especially within winter sports and football.

'That being said, we have Norwegian players at the very top of FPL; last year a Norwegian player even led the FPL for a number of weeks. So Finland – be prepared to lose your title.'

It's not exactly the infamous 'Maggie Thatcher, your boys took a helluva beating' goading of England by Norwegian football commentator Bjorge Lillelien, but this is Fantasy Football we're talking about here, and it is an entirely more civilised pursuit.

The one surprise, perhaps, is that this mass of Fantasy managers from Norway is yet to produce an FPL winner. One did, however, come rather close.

Knut Hebaek, a fifty-year-old teacher from Kjelsas, a suburb in the north of Oslo, led the 2016–17 season by Christmas and stayed top well into the new year. In fact, by Gameweek 23 – close to two-thirds of the way through the campaign – he wasn't just leading, he was threatening to run away with the title.

His team, Hebknut, had built up a forty-seven-point lead over the second-placed side and an even more daunting sixty-six-point margin separated him from the chasing pack.

There was, however, a bit of an issue.

Knut prided himself on accumulating points consistently, eschewing 'bandwagon' players who happened to be the latest flavour of the month and instead sticking with picks who brought him steady returns over time. He was a Fantasy tortoise plodding, albeit rather briskly, past all manner of FPL hares.

But he had succumbed to the charms of the game's chips – and in particular Triple Captain and Bench Boost – early in the season. In essence, the tortoise had watched the hares speed off into the distance as the race began and caught and then passed them by stealing, at knife-point, the bicycle of a passing olive salesman.

This, if you carefully study the text of the original ancient Greek fable, is exactly what happened in Aesop's tale, with the hares eventually winning the race when they jumped into a passing minibus with a mile or so to go.

Okay, so the tortoise analogy, much like Knut's chips, only takes you so far. He had a good reason for blowing those chips way before anyone else, though. Because he had no idea what he was actually doing. At least not at first. He admitted as much in an interview with the Stavanger Aftenblad newspaper.

'I've understood very little of what's going on. People who are a bit younger than me say that my performance is useful,' he declared with pleasing dryness. And while that might have been so much Nordic understatement, it was true that Knut's time at the top came in only his second FPL season. His first came to a very premature end when he gave up after failing to work out how to make substitutions. 'I was unable to finish the team and was not aware when I was going to swap players.'

Knut was persuaded by his teenage son to give it another go, although the challenge was one heavy on the irony. 'No, he thought I was going to drop off right away,' Knut told the TV2 website, 'and then I was determined to show that he was wrong. That was the "fuck you" in me talking. Now I'm so far in front of my son that I can hardly find him on the list.'

He was in the top 2,000 by the end of Gameweek 6 and hit the top spot by December in what was, to all intents and purposes, his first ever FPL season.

Beginner's luck? To an extent. Although he had a certain footballing background to draw from as he had played the game professionally for Kjelsas. When I asked Martin Ygre for the English equivalent, he came back with the following: 'Kjelsas are now in PostNord-ligaen – the league below OBOS-ligaen [Championship] and Eliteserien [Premier League]. So, similar to League One in England?

'Geographically, Kjelsas are located in our capital, Oslo, a couple of kilometres outside the city centre, so any smaller English team in or around London could suffice as a ground for comparison.'

I'm thinking Charlton Athletic, if we're going for a League One team. Although Brentford, currently in the Championship, might be a better example.

Back in Norway, Knut was using his ex-player expertise, a tendency to go for gut feeling over stats, the 'eye test' of watching lots of football, and his love for Liverpool to guide his selections. And when it became clear that he was on for a season like no other, he even started picking Man United players.

'I can cheer when Manchester United score now … as long as they're losing.'

Unfortunately, Knut's early profligacy, when he blew those chips way before any of his contenders, finally came back to haunt him. The problem for anyone playing FPL for the first time is that everything is fresh, everything a surprise. Many of these surprises, for Knut, were pleasant ones. But one was not.

He had no idea that Premier League fixture pile-ups led to late-season double Gameweeks in FPL. Seasoned campaigners knew this and, as a result, saved their Triple Captain and Bench Boost chips to maximise the potential points from players with two fixtures in those frantically busy end-of-campaign Gameweeks.

By the time those double Gameweeks came around, Knut had been caught. Once they were done, he'd been passed. He ended up finishing seventh, a full sixty-two points off the top spot he'd made his own for a large chunk of the season.

But still, seventh in your first (proper) FPL season was a momentous achievement, and it made Knut something of a minor celebrity, appearing in national newspapers and on television as a Fantasy Football-mad nation – and fans from further afield – rode the wave with him.

'I received questions from people from places like Cairo and Athens, wondering what to do in Fantasy, and several strangers also made friend requests on Facebook.'

For a self-styled 'Fantasy amateur', it was a hell of a ride.

So what of Sweden in this Nordic narrative? Well, they had more than 55,000 teams registered for the 2017–18 season, well up on Finland's 20,000-plus, way down on Norway's 110,000.

But seeing as their population is close to double that of either of their neighbours, Sweden's FPL claims were not the strongest, either for overall participation or historic excellence. Could they bring anything else to the Fantasy party? Hell yeah.

As part of my research for this book, I asked people to fill out a questionnaire, including one section regarding any information about Fantasy Football players who also worked in 'interesting professions'. The examples I gave were 'sex worker, high court judge, vicar, or maybe a combination of all three'.

A reply I received from one Johan Stromberg, a forty-nine-year-old doctor and author from Klagerup, Sweden, went way beyond that.

'In my own mini-league I have at least 3 medical doctors, 2 professors, 1 drug-dealer, 1 psychologist, 2 farmers, 1 architect, 1 film producer, 1 arborist, 1 interior designer, 2 semi-famous musicians, 1 professional hunter, 2 malaria researchers, 1 pool guy, 2 polish handymen, my wife and one member of ABBA.'

I was blown away. I mean, the tabloid press had always insisted that all the Polish handymen had come to England to STEAL OUR JOBS, and yet here was clear evidence that at least two of them had actually gone to Sweden instead.

Oh, yeah, and ABBA.

Back I went to Johan, wondering who that 'one member of ABBA' might be and whether I could ask them some questions.

'If you don't mind sending me your questions first I can relay them to my father, Benny, and ask him on your behalf?' came the reply.

The internet is many things to many people, although most of them are porn-hungry cat-lovers with an Amazon habit. But it is also a wonderful tool for connecting complete strangers from across the globe, with one party then promptly hoaxing the other. The idea that I had just stumbled across the fact that Benny Andersson, one quarter of one of the biggest pop bands of all-time, was an avid Fantasy Football player was just too good. And maybe too good to be true.

A quick dip into the life and loves of Benny Andersson rather suggested the latter. The composer of some of the late twentieth century's most popular songs was engaged once, married twice and had three children – two boys and a girl. None of them, not even the daughter, was called Johan.

Game over?

I thought I'd better dig a little deeper and came across an obscure publication called Thoroughbred Daily News. Despite the massive and obvious temptation to pepper this section with piss-poor ABBA puns – and Mamma Mia, it was hard to resist – I have chosen to rise above that shit. The same could not be said for Thoroughbred Daily News, as the headline for a 2011 article, 'The Name of the Game – ABBA's Benny Andersson' made abundantly clear right from the get-go.

And in that piece I found the following sentence: 'By 1981, Benny met and subsequently married Mona Norklit, who worked as a producer for Swedish television. Ms Norklit had previously been married to, and had a son, Johan, with the vet and horse breeder Berndt Stromberg.'

Kerching!

The article went on: "'I was going to be Johan's stepfather, but I wanted there to be a good way for me to maintain contact with his real father, Berndt," recalled Benny. "So I decided to have a horse in training with the Strombergs. It could be fun, and a good way for the families to stay in contact with each other.'"

So there it was. Johan was on the level. Benny really was his father. And he was a Fantasy Football manager to boot.

Although ...

A little bit of me – the paranoid, hope-for-the-best-but-expect-the-worst bit – could still conceive of this being a massive wind-up. It was, after all, easy enough to claim to be someone, set up an email address in that person's name and then let the fun begin.

Two things then occurred to ease my tortured mind. The first was that Johan himself was so damned interesting that even if Benny turned out to be a figment of his clearly lively imagination, what he was telling me about himself was a decidedly superior second prize.

The second was the clincher – he invited me to join his mini-league. The one with those Polish handymen STEALING SWEDISH JOBS.

The LMCC Open (it's an obscure reference to a family in-joke, apparently) contained Johan, his wife, Ludvig Andersson (who I took to be the youngest son of Benny and Mona), and, of course, Benny himself. Benny's team, ISOLDE BULLS, has been active in FPL since 2006–07, with a best finish of 207,565 in 2010–11.

Sadly for me, Benny was proving elusive. He had a piano album coming out and was also involved in some film projects, apparently. He was, I was told by Johan, very busy, although I did notice that he had managed to find the time to Wildcard in Gameweek 3.

I wasn't bitter, though. I was too busy enjoying Johan's snippets of information about his own Fantasy experiences. 'Fantasy Football definitely has increased my knowledge of otherwise rather obscure characters on the pitch and given me a much deeper familiarity with most players' faces. In fact it so much increases the enjoyment of the game that I nowadays find myself bored with football without it.

'Let's face it, I'm an addict. And a sober alcoholic, in fact. FPL has all the hallmarks of a great drug, with few physical side-effects on top. I probably spend at least five hours a week on it. The period leading up to the first Gameweek, at least double that.

'As I said, I'm not so much obsessed as addicted, perhaps. It didn't help in my previous marriage, although it wasn't the crucial factor.'

For a man from a country famed for its people's inherent stoicism, otherwise known as a dislike of unnecessary emotional displays, Johan was being refreshingly open.

So I asked him about his relationship with Benny.

'My experiences "acquiring" Benny as a father are generally very good, but also deeply personal and would probably require a whole book to meaningfully explain to anyone else – which I one day may, or may not, try to do.

'So far, and to this point in life, it is obvious that I, to say the very least, consider myself extremely fortunate. Some people would even call it blessed, but I guess that would have to be in a musical rather than any religious kind of way.'

And, of course, the relationship had to include reference to Fantasy Football. 'Playing, and consistently beating him, at Fantasy Football is a completely different so called "ball game", however. Or, more to the point perhaps, always having a reliable and mutually exciting topic of discussion.

'If you are not already playing Fantasy with/against your own father, I strongly suggest you start doing that. If at all possible. If you already do, you will know what I mean.'

My father, alas, is long gone. But I still knew what he meant.

Johan then informed me that he had written a book, and that it used Fantasy Football as a plot device. He went into more detail about it in a long and pleasingly wordy email.

'As anyone whose unfortunate ancestors never were dominions under the Empire, or who himself wasn't lucky enough to be born into the Commonwealth, can attest, I too have always been smitten by the splendid allure of British culture, among which good sport must come at the very front.'

Great start. And the follow-up was one of the longest sentences I'd ever read.

'Spending the better part of my career as an expatriate and somewhat sovereign, albeit rather solitary, Scandinavian Samaritan in the former British protectorates of Tanganyika and Zanzibar, and having led rather a cosmopolitan life among the elites of Europe and America in between postings, now finally back again at the family farm and on home ground again, so to speak – and since early childhood and through it all addicted to English football – I would strongly argue that the Premier League is of equal if not superior importance than the local national leagues, even in some of those corners of the world that Britain would definitely not otherwise consider within her immediate sphere of influence.'

Johan then went into a shorter story about Drop water bottles, which turned out to be relevant when he started talking about his book.

'In Bezoar, my yet-to-be-published book, George Weah water bottles play a small but nevertheless very important part in my alter-ego's hunt for the spurious antimalarials that were, and still are, threatening Zanzibar and the rest of mainland Africa.

'A certain Doctor Henry Hartman soon finds himself entangled in a dark web of counterfeit life-saving medicine, Chinese ivory smugglers, crooked local police officials and other local mujahedeen, Cuban agents, corrupt Zanzibari politicians and even some not so bona fide pirates, as he simultaneously also tries to uncover the astonishing life story of a geriatric and minuscule but still very resourceful African guerilla commander, General Rastaban, who he meets with one of those empty bottles of Weah's last Drop in his hands.'

Johan continued to outline the plot of his book, bringing in two of Sweden's more iconic/ironic twentieth-century historical figures – the second Secretary General of the UN, Dag Hammarskjold, who was shot down and killed in Northern Rhodesia while flying on a peace-keeping mission, and Baron Bror von Blixen-Finecke, professional hunter and husband of Karen 'Out of Africa' Blixen. Even Che Guevara and his failed revolution in the Congo got a mention.

But I had been promised Fantasy Football. And I got it.

'Dr Hartman, as well as several other of the book's characters, do however find time to make their transfers and captaincy selections in due order, and as in life, at least also in the original version, it was through the private league chat-function that the author first re-established contact with the by now long-disappeared doctor . . .'

I don't know about you, but I'm so buying that book if it ever comes out.

The LMCC Open includes a team called Kibubu, managed by one Stuart March. His team is also in the Chester Golf Club's mini-league. That's the Chester in England. How did he end up in a mini-league of Swedes?

'Stuart is an old friend and retired British serviceman from Chester who, among many other things, installed my swimming pool in Dar es Salaam, Tanzania, where he's been making his living the past twenty-odd years or so.'

At the time of writing, I'm riding high enough in the ABBA-tinged mini-league to be beating Stuart, Johan and Benny.

And if I ever had doubts as to the veracity of Benny being an FPL nut, I had no such issue with another international figure, one Prince Abdullah bin Mosaad of Saudi Arabia.

Because I met him.

CHAPTER EIGHT

THE PRINCE

I've never been a big one for royal protocol. I've had no reason to be, what with me being as common as muck.

My brain is full of other stuff – lots of it football, some of it American state capitals and one stubborn little spot that contains nothing but Graham's law of diffusion, a fact that refuses to leave despite its consistent lack of applicability in any area of what passes for my life.

So when I knew I was going to meet a straight-up, bona fide prince of a realm, I needed to work things through, boiling stuff down to a few key scenarios in which I could make a right royal first impression:

- The Groveller: 'May I humbly thank You, Your Highness, for Your most generous, indeed gracious, beneficence in agreeing to talk to me. I am barely worthy of Your time. In fact, I must go. I am not worthy. I AM NOT WORTHY!!!' (I then throw myself to the floor and attempt to kiss his feet.)
- The Cultural Appropriator: 'Prince Abdullah bin Mosaad, may your tribe increase! *Zay el aasal* [you are sweet like candy to my soul]. I don't mean that in a ... you know, not like ... in ... oh bugger.' (I leg it.)

- The Overcompensator: 'Prince, eh? I've seen worse.' (I playfully punch him in the face.)

All the usual things you don't even think about when going to meet someone new – amount of eye contact, firmness of handshake, ear hair visibility levels – were suddenly in play. And all the usual things you do think about – appropriately unstained clothing, minty-fresh breath for that ring of confidence, ear hair visibility levels – were ramped up to the max.

None of these scenarios involved rolling up to his London home thirty minutes late due to a combination of personal incompetence and a Google Maps fail.

Did he care? Nope. He just got on with watching the football.

And that was what struck me about HRH Prince Abdullah bin Mosaad bin Abdulaziz Al Saud – he was, genuinely, just another Fantasy Football fan. Except he had more money than most.

Money, it turned out, was a subject on which he was ... not touchy as such, but definitely keen to stress a key fact about. Yes, he acknowledged that being born a prince in Saudi Arabia gave you a bit of a leg-up in life. You know, the little things like your garden having a grass football pitch in it – a bit of a big deal in a place known as the Desert Kingdom – which most of the future Saudi Arabian national team came to play on after school was out for the day.

But Abdullah's personal fortune was exactly that – personal.

Stereotypes involving Saudi princes tend to revolve around the silver-spoon birth, the expensive English public school education, the piety at home and the impiety at various Mayfair establishments. These tropes speak of privilege, entitlement and a life lived surfing carelessly on a slick of black gold.

Abdullah was not cut from such cloth. He gained an engineering degree in Riyadh. He married, stayed married and had seven kids. He set up a paper business, the aptly named Saudi Paper. Tissue paper was the product of choice, as it happened, because it was the only type he could afford to buy as his initial budget was so threadbare.

He did the usual entrepreneurial start-up things. He got rejected by banks. Lots of them. Being a prince, it turned out, was not so useful when dealing with financial institutions because if the whole right royal venture went belly up, they weren't entirely sure they could even ask for their money back, let alone demand it.

He put in the hours – sixteen to eighteen a day. His whole life was work; weekends, evenings, the lot. He lived with his in-laws to save money and brought the same cost-cutting ethos to the business side of things. If he needed a hot-shot lawyer to negotiate an international contract, he instead hired the cheapest one he could find and led the negotiations himself.

As he told Campden FB, a magazine for 'business-owning families of substantial wealth', being a prince in the business world was a double-edged sword. 'It comes with benefits. For instance, if you are twenty-two years old and want to see the Minister of Industry, I think it is easier to do that if you're a prince. If you want this done or that done, it has some benefits and some disadvantages.

'I think being a prince can be a curse if you don't quickly grasp that being a prince is not enough to have a good life. You have to work as hard. You have to do something. Nothing big will be handed to you.'

The business grew and diversified into recycling. It went from national to continental. And then Abdullah took it public.

'That's when I saw how much it was worth, how much I was worth,' he told me. 'And when I saw that, I knew I didn't want to work like that any more. I'd spent all my time working and now I wanted to enjoy the money.'

What would you do if you won the Lottery tomorrow? Or maybe double-crossed that international drug dealer you'd met on the school run and then escaped with all their cash?

If you're a sports-mad Fantasy Football nut – and let's face it, most of you probably are – you know what you'd do. Sure, you'd probably make sure your close friends and family were taken care of, or at least the ones you actually like. You might even give some away to charity. But most of it would go on jetting around the world gorging yourself on the best sport this planet has to offer.

That's exactly what Abdullah's hard-earned money went on.

He's been to countless Super Bowls and Champions League finals – his first was Liverpool's 'Miracle in Istanbul' win over AC Milan in 2005 – and once undertook a mad twenty-four-hour round trip from Riyadh to Dallas and back again just to see his NFL team, the San Francisco 49ers, in action. They won by a couple of touchdowns that day and it was, by his own admission, one of the happiest trips of his life.

He watches sport in his homes in Riyadh, London and Beverly Hills, the latter a mansion formerly owned by Cheers and Frasier star Kelsey Grammer and in which the likes of David Beckham have been entertained.

He is, essentially, living our dream. If, that is, the dream also involves buying a stake in Sheffield United FC.

When I turned up, fashionably late, at his house, which is not so far away from the FA's headquarters, I was shown downstairs by Selahattin, a very smiley and approachable Turkish guy who had arranged the interview. He has been variously described as the prince's friend and business associate. In an ESPN interview, he merely said he 'brings projects' to Abdullah, whatever that might actually mean.

I only found out later that this was Selahattin Baki, currently a board member at Sheffield United and formerly someone with a bit of a past involving his beloved Fenerbahce and the Istanbul club's more – let's just say fervent – supporters. He'd been a member of KFY (Kill For You), a group of Fenerbahce ultras. He'd even appeared on Danny Dyer's Real Football Factories television show back in the day, using choice phrases such as 'non-stop action' and 'sometimes knives start talking' to demonstrate his youthful tastiness.

All of that led to fellow Sheffield United board member Jim Phipps issuing a comment positively dripping with understatement. 'The prince chose Mr Baki based on his love and knowledge of football, and based on a judgement about his ability to add value to the work and deliberations of the board. This judgement remains unchanged.

'The prince is aware that Mr Baki is a fervent supporter of Fenerbahce and that, in younger days, the fervency of his support may have overcome his better judgement.

'Indeed, Mr Baki has built a reputation as a well-regarded, law-abiding businessman and has earned his place as a trusted adviser to His Royal Highness.

'His passion for the game, bridled by wisdom gained through experience, is an asset to us.'

I must stress that I'm not condemning Selahattin based on past indiscretions – when I was younger, I was hooked on Aussie soap Neighbours, so who am I to judge? If anything, I brought the subject up to demonstrate the prince's ability to see the potential in a man that others might have balked at, given his ... chequered past.

And the wonderfully dry tone of the Sheffield United board member's comment to the press was decidedly relevant because understatement, it turned out, was a bit of a thing with Prince Abdullah.

I'd insisted on interviewing him at his house for two reasons. The first was professional – interviewees tend to be more relaxed at home. The second was, if I'm being honest, personal – I wanted to see what a Saudi prince's London house was like.

I was flirting with those Saudi stereotypes when I imagined what I would discover. I was thinking thirty-seater cinemas buried three storeys down ... diamond-encrusted swimming pools ... gold-plated butlers.

What I got was a big, but otherwise unassuming, London house that genuinely felt like a home. What I didn't get was a guided tour. Time was not on my side. I was thirty minutes late, after all.

Selahattin welcomed me in with a Turkish story about people falling off a roof that I didn't wholly understand, but took to be an attempt to inform me that my tardiness wasn't an issue. He then showed me to the basement; a spacious room involving two enormous sofas, one barefooted prince sat in a very large chair and an entire wall plastered with huge-screen TVs upon which three different games of football were being played out.

I sat across from Selahattin and next to a man called Jan van Winckel. Pleasantries were exchanged and any awkward silences filled with ease by the Burnley v Newcastle match occupying the biggest of the big screens at the end of the room.

I had Burnley's Stephen Ward in my Fantasy team. Abdullah had Newcastle keeper Rob Elliot and midfielder Matt Ritchie in his. We wanted very different things from the match, but were immediately united by our disparate Fantasy causes.

'I have some relatives that are passionate about the Italian Serie A, but because of FPL they are now more interested in watching the Bournemouth versus Burnley match than any from Serie A.'

Abdullah spoke often to my couch-mate Jan, seeking clarification on football matters. He turned out to be the technical director of the Saudi Arabian Football Federation. He'd also been asked to help out with international scouting for Sheffield United after Abdullah had bought a 50 per cent share in the then League One club.

In short, he knew his stuff. But then so did Abdullah. In Fantasy terms, at the very least. He finished 194th in the 2012–13 FPL season and reckoned he might have had a shot at winning it if not for some unfortunate captaincy decisions after Christmas. He also has two other top 10k finishes to his name and his aim, every season, is to try and win the thing.

'Part of the reason I bought Sheffield United is my love for English football and the EPL. My dream is to take SUFC to the Premier League and a big part of my love for the Premier League came from Fantasy.

'Without Fantasy I'd still watch the EPL, but not like now, where I need to watch every game simultaneously, on multiple screens at my homes.'

When he's in the USA, he is almost childlike in his excitement when the football is on. 'The time difference means the games are on early. I'll wake up at two or three in the morning, before the games, because I'm already thinking about them, getting excited for them. I'm extremely passionate about all sports, but especially football.'

His passion for American football extends to his Twitter handle, @Saudi49er. In past interviews, he readily admitted that if he were truly as rich as some believe – he's definitely not a billionaire, 'just' a multi-millionaire – he'd have bought the San Francisco franchise by now.

When he's not watching proper football on his many screens, he's consuming the American version and plays NFL Fantasy Football as well as FPL. In the US version of the game, he's known as an inveterate trader always on the look out for ways, and players, to improve his teams. He's also developed a knack for spotting talent just before they turn potential into points.

When I asked him which version of Fantasy Football he'd stick with if forced to choose between FPL and gridiron, I expected him to go Stateside. That game, after all, is more involved and complex. It suits wheeler-dealers, and Abdullah has certainly done some good deals over the years, like buying a half-stake in Sheffield United for the appropriately princely sum of one whole British pound.

He didn't have to think before replying. He went for football. Our football. FPL, he said, was the better game because it was simpler and purer.

'What I love in particular about Fantasy football is it's a competition with five million other people. It is thirty-eight weeks of engaging fun, all the while trying to improve one's world ranking.'

Abdullah certainly has history when it comes to football. The boy who once kicked a ball round his grassy garden with future Saudi international players grew up to become president of the country's biggest club, Al-Hilal – the kingdom's equivalent of Man United, but without the rain and the exorbitant price of a pint, for obvious reasons.

Now he's joint owner of Sheffield United, which is not even the Yorkshire equivalent of Al-Hilal.

The nominal fee he paid came with a pledge to invest rather more in the club on an ongoing basis, although fans' hopes that this would turn the Blades into the next Man City were quickly put in their place. As Abdullah pointed out, the likes of City are in essence owned by a country – the UAE – whereas he is not, and never will be, a fully-fledged nation state.

At the time of the deal, in 2013, they were stuck in League One. When I visited his house four years later, the Blades were mixing it at the top of the Championship, edging ever closer to Abdullah's dream of Premier League football.

His tenure at the Yorkshire club has been marked by a certain caution, a strategic frugality that has involved the recruitment of players based on their suitability to the team, and to the structure as a whole. Abdullah's money is not an exercise in conspicuous consumption, of eye-catching, fan-pleasing purchases designed to stumble upon football's fool's gold – instant success. He made that much clear in an interview with the Sheffield Star newspaper just a few days before we met.

'Most people assume because you are a prince, you are born with a lot of money. Some are like that but I had to work hard for mine. So when I spend it, I want to spend it wisely. Honestly, though, I am really now a fan.

'We cannot waste money. If we spend money, it can only be to improve the team. We have to run the best financial operation, have the best people.

'There are obvious things on the football side because everyone wants to keep driving forward. But there is also the commercial side, ticketing and the fan experience.

'I love movies and there is one called The Firm. Somebody in that said "I am paid to be suspicious when there is nothing to be suspicious about".

'We can only relax when we are in the Premier League.'

Not that he lacks ambition. When I asked him which players, money no object, he'd buy for the Blades should they ever be promoted, he went for Harry Kane, Dele Alli and Sadio Mane. But even that spoke volumes for his overall plan for Sheffield United. Not for him the superstars, the Messis and Neymars. He wanted team players with their best years ahead of them and a proven track record in English football already in the bank.

His Fantasy methods are rather less conservative. Nobody pays him to be suspicious in the Fantasy Premier League.

'I have always enjoyed finding the player just as he hits a good run, the player who comes into form, before everyone else sees how well he's doing and jumps on as well. I have football knowledge and I am thorough, but I describe my Fantasy self as a gambler.'

His one golden rule sounds obvious, but is often hard to adhere to in these days of squad rotation. 'I don't like owning any non-starters. Other than that I'm flexible.'

In yet another life, he was once the Saudi Minister of Sport, a globetrotting businessman and bureaucrat. His loves are alliterative – family, films, food and Fantasy – with a taste for Arabic poetry thrown in to interrupt the stream of f-words.

But these days, he's as much a sports-mad couch potato as anyone around his age (early fifties) with probably a quarter of his time and a fraction of his wealth.

'Watching sports is part of my daily schedule, be it NFL, the Premier League, Saudi League or the Champions League. I love tennis and following my favourite teams – Barca, Roma and Zamalek.' The last one of those, by the way, is an Egyptian side.

The day before I met him, the NFL was back in London, with the Minnesota Vikings taking on the Cleveland Browns at Twickenham.

Abdullah wasn't there. He was in his basement, watching a packed Sunday of Premier League action before starting his usual American football shift later that night.

He puts in the Fantasy hours, an extremely dedicated 'eye tester' who looks and learns, looks and learns, mixing the pleasure of watching football with the serious business of improving his overall rank.

Being a football club-owning prince affords him both the excuse and the time to hone his FPL skills. The lifestyle has other Fantasy benefits as well. One of them involves having a fully-qualified football coach to hand – my couch-mate Jan van Winckel.

Jan has known Abdullah since 2002 and has been, among other things, the head coach of the Swaziland national team, an assistant coach at Club Brugge and the Uefa Pro Licence instructor for the Belgian Coaches Association. He's worked with the Argentinian coach Marcelo Bielsa, who he considers to be the best coach in the world, and with players such as Eden Hazard, Dmitri Payet and Ivan Perisic.

These days, he also deals with such stars in a Fantasy context. 'Prince Abdullah introduced me to the game two seasons ago and created a mini-league to teach me how to play the game. He is a much better player than I am, however.

'I still try to figure out whether it was one of the best things that happened in my life or one of the worst!

'What I do like is that Fantasy Football brings back the fun to watch a football game. Because of my profession I try to see as many games as possible, but it used to be more a job than an entertainment. Now I can combine both.'

So does he think all his coaching expertise informs his Fantasy play? 'Yes, I believe it does. I think I understand better how players are using their squad and when they are rotating. Pep Guardiola, for example, is using a lot of team tactics of Marcelo Bielsa. He is an admirer of Bielsa and consults with him sometimes.

'I used to assist Bielsa and it gives me a better insight into Guardiola's rotation strategies.'

That, in itself, is Fantasy gold. The 2017–18 season was, after all, a bit of a nightmare for managers desperate to tap into all those lovely points flowing from Pep's Man City line-up, but consistently frustrated by the coach's insistence on chopping and changing his starting side week after week.

Real-world coaching skills, however, are not overly applicable to Fantasy Football. 'Coaching or managing a football team is about training and practising. The game is nothing more than the outcome of the training process, while Fantasy Football is looking at the underlying statistics, although football is also rapidly changing.

'We are currently collecting literally hundreds of thousands of pieces of data on each player during each training session. We transform these into Key Performance Indicators, but the interpretation is much more important than the collection of these data.

'In this sense I always use the DIKW model in which we all collect Data, Interpret them, add our Knowledge to them and finally use our Wisdom/best practice to gain a competitive edge.'

So Abdullah has time, dedication and an internationally regarded football coach on his Fantasy side. His cup is full to the brim. And it could be about to run over.

Should Sheffield United make it to the Premier League, he will happily pick their players, or the maximum of three he's allowed, for his FPL team. It remains to be seen if any of them are actually any good in a Fantasy context, but at least he won't have to fret about whether they're going to play, or get shafted when one of them picks up an unannounced injury.

In the past, he's also readily admitted to using his ever-growing footballing contacts in the pursuit of Fantasy goals, telling the Daily Mail: 'I remember once when George Gillett owned Liverpool, I called him to see if I could find out if Steven Gerrard was going to play because he was in my Fantasy team. I said to Gillett "can you find out if Gerrard is playing?" He said he'd do his best.

'It's useful to know what's going on. I have many friends who can give me information about players and, hopefully, I'll have even more in the future.'

When I asked him whether he would exploit his Premier League clout for the same Fantasy ends if, without wishing to tempt fate, Sheffield United ever made it to the top flight, he promptly came back with: 'I hope I don't, but I can't assure you of that.'

It was a typically open, honest and only half-jokey reply from a man who might be a prince, but is equally obsessed with, and dedicated to, Fantasy Football as the rest of us FPL idiots.

He just happens to have more houses, TVs and noughts at the end of his bank balance than your average Fantasy manager.

CHAPTER NINE

GET A LIFE

'Get a life.' 'Do grown-ups actually play that?' 'Bet his missus is playing away.'

The reaction, on the internet at least, to stories about Fantasy Football and the people who play it, is depressingly predictable.

To be fair, based on the levels of vitriol and sheer blind hate that are displayed by default on the online charm schools that are Twitter and the comments below newspaper stories, such abuse is actually rather tame. And, as with all insults, they tell you more about the neuroses of the person slinging the mud than anything else, particularly the ones that equate Fantasy Football to being cuckolded.

The 'get a life' comment is also decidedly revealing. What is actually so wrong with a life spent, in part, on a harmless game that involves a measure of thought, skill and analysis? We all need a hobby, and Fantasy Football is one of the least objectionable ones out there; certainly when compared to crystal meth, Nazi cross-stitch or subjecting random strangers to personal attacks on social media.

Granted, there will be a few of you reading this book who really should devote a little less time to the game and rather more to family, friends or jobs. But most strike some kind of happy balance, albeit one skewed slightly towards studying the stats of a particular footballer who hasn't scored for the past four matches despite firing in more shots than any other midfielder in the 5.5–6.5 price bracket. That one's due a goal, he really is.

But is thinking that, or actually bothering to find out such rarefied information, a genuine indicator of a life either spiralling out of control or trapped in some kind of tedious triviality? I mean, what exactly does someone have to do to satisfy people that a life is being got? Where do you even go to obtain one in the first place? Is there a shop? What's the refund policy? Does Amazon do it cheaper? And can your life be left with a neighbour until you get back from work?

We can't all specialise in healing the sick and the lame, alleviating child poverty or reimagineering Wheel 3.0 for the post-digital age. Or spending our time sat on a computer trolling the world and his cheating wife. Fantasy Football is winning nobody a Nobel Prize any time soon. Nor is it curing cancer or promoting world peace. It's merely giving a large number of people from across the globe the chance for a bit of distraction from the planet's ills. And they do that through the medium of being even more bothered about a game involving twenty-two very well paid humans running about in shorts while millions of considerably less well-paid fellow humans shout for, at or against them.

Fantasy Football players do have lives. They merely elect to spend part of them forgetting, for however brief a moment, that terrorists keep blowing people up, the bills need paying and we are all but tiny specks of dust fleetingly caught in the sun's warm but unforgiving light.

That doesn't mean such a person can't find the time to attend, say, their second child's school concert. It's just that, like the rest of humanity, they'd probably rather be elsewhere than listening to a group of 'musicians' murdering Let It Go on their irredeemably screechy violins. And if they manage to sneak in a couple of minutes' research into the run of fixtures involving their latest budget striker transfer target while the aural slaughter continues, then who are we to judge?

And grown-ups DO play Fantasy Football. Lawyers and politicians, engineers and IT professionals, actors, presenters and sports stars – all are happy to mix a bit of fantasy into their real lives with no discernible problems whatsoever. Well, I might have heard stories of doctors who maybe, just ever so slightly, delayed surgery to change their team, but the rumours were never completely verified so I'll just leave them here for the time being.

George Bernard Shaw once wrote: 'We don't stop playing because we grow old; we grow old because we stop playing.'

Fantasy Football gives us the opportunity to reconnect with our inner child; the one that felt the elation of a goal or the despair of a defeat to its very maximum. Football, or any game for that matter, was more important back then, our reactions to it more visceral.

Years of context – of tests to pass, money to earn, births, marriages and divorces to experience – all of it dull that importance, and rightly so. But being reminded of our youthful certainties and their emotional extremes is not a bad thing. If only death and taxes are inevitable, at least Fantasy Football offers us a knowingly frivolous diversion along the way.

When I asked one Fantasy manager whether he thought he was obsessed, he seemed proud that he had once made a transfer 'in the queue for Thunder Mountain'. That's not just an example of someone feeding their inner child, it's someone trying to give the little bugger type 2 diabetes. And he didn't care.

That, in an age so quick to judge, is refreshingly childlike, as is the experience of actor Ian Houghton. 'I've been close to missing an entrance a couple of times during a Saturday matinee when waiting for a full-time whistle to confirm a clean sheet.

'My ex-wife could never understand the attraction of Fantasy and often accused me of avoiding reality at all costs. But that's part of being an actor too, I suppose.'

Feyzi Ercin, a lawyer from Istanbul in Turkey, is equally candid about his obsession with the game – one that made him FPL's leading Turkish player in 2015.

'An average of ten to twenty dreams a season involving fantasy stats and actions … Going to bed with a three-hour time difference on Monday with your captain playing, waking up for the loo at 3 a. m. and finding yourself on your mobile checking all stats … Awakening to the noise of neighbours at 5 a.m. and instead of going back to sleep, finding yourself thinking "why don't I check some websites and gain some time now?" … Logging on every single day at work, first thing … I am surely obsessed.'

But is it harmful? Feyzi thinks not.

'I play Fantasy Football because football was the greatest game on earth until money, capitalism and Uefa/Fifa destroyed it. And because role-playing is fun and this is the greatest role-playing game in history where, technically, you are THE manager indeed. A combination of football and role-play cannot be bettered in any game, methinks.'

Work, he readily admits, has suffered, but his personal life has been enriched. 'Job-wise, if I had shown the same passion and energy to what I do as a profession, I would be rich by now, but such is life. And it has been very positive in my personal life. It allows my spouse to see the child in me and allows me to see their generosity and patience. It creates transparency.'

I wouldn't personally recommend justifying your Fantasy Football obsession to your significant other by imploring them to 'see the child in me' because, in most cases, that child will be sent to bed without any dinner. But Feyzi's enthusiasm is infectious, and the healing powers of the game should not be underestimated.

Take the case of Mohammed Fouad Khan. 'It was the season Liverpool were on the up with Sturridge and Suarez, and Sterling later joining the show. Early in that season, I was driving my best mate's car and unfortunately had an accident. We stopped communicating and stuff. This was around November. At that point in our mini-league he was in the top three and I was mid-table.

'I'd known him from grade one, we went to the same school. Fantasy Football is what our friends chat about every time we meet, tease each other on blunders, mind games into buying players etc. We used to talk a lot about transfers and captain picks every week whenever we chilled, but until April or May that season we didn't meet.'

A lifelong friendship ruined by a prang involving a black Honda Accord coupe? Not if Fantasy Football had anything to do with it. 'Basically, we finally met for footie after the season ended. I finished ten points or so behind him. We both started talking again.'

Lovely. The circle complete, the relationship mended. And how did they approach that whole crashed car thing? Shouting? Fighting? Recrimination?

'I remember clearly one of the first things he asked me was why didn't I sign Sterling near the end of the season.'

You can look at that story in one of two ways. A pair of grown men ignoring the messy realities and hiding behind their mutual love of Fantasy Football could be deemed childish. Alternatively, a willingness to embrace what they share, rather than be divided by past troubles, is decidedly mature. I know which camp I'm in.

In the interests of balance, however, it would be remiss of me not to mention that an average Fantasy obsessive's life is somewhat removed from the redemptive example above. It is a far grubbier affair, to be frank.

Unless a major international football tournament is taking place, June is the Lost Month – a washed-out, empty shell of a period in which NOTHING HAPPENS. After a season of mainlining the purest Fantasy junk your dealer can supply, June is unadulterated cold turkey.

If you've got children, you can't even go on holiday because the little money pits are still at school. This brings us neatly on to July, a month that has one major thing going for it – it isn't June. July, for many, *is* the time to take the kids on holiday because August is when the football season starts. Your July holiday, however, can clash with the day when the new FPL game opens its doors, allowing managers a first look at the players' new prices for the season ahead.

Premier League teams also start their pre-season, affording us all the chance to see new signings and up-and-coming youngsters who could, if identified and tracked, provide us with cheap or surprise packages to start our Fantasy campaigns on the front foot.

As a result, combining holidays and Fantasy Football – even in the relatively kindly month of July – can be a trying affair. For all concerned.

If you have a partner who's driven many, many miles out of the way just to find the merest whiff of someone else's Wi-Fi so they can fanny about with their team while overheated children succumb to dehydration in the back seat and tempers fray like a two quid shirt off the market, I can only say this – you are not alone.

Entire holidays might not have been planned around the internet connectivity of a particular tourist region, but you can bet that certain journeys were. Ever wondered why your other half has suddenly developed a burning interest in that Victorian pumping station 83.56 miles away from your woodland yurt during the family's 'back to nature' vacation? And why did they spend so long in the toilet when you finally got there? If you didn't know already, you do now.

Holidays aside, July is, to many, the best of Fantasy times. It's like a newborn child – all wonder, hope and potential without any of the crashingly inevitable disappointments yet to come. Okay, so Child One could have been the Girl Who Brokered World Peace but ended up drinking sheep dip and punching that goat with the wonky eye when you went to the inner-city farm. It will, rest assured, be completely different with Child Two.

So it is with every new Fantasy campaign. August arrives and brings with it the new season. Nine and a bit months of joy. Or, more precisely, a week or two of joy and months and months of what-ifs, what-could-have-beens and that time when you rage-transferred out a striker the day before he went on a goalscoring spree not seen since the last time you did exactly the same thing and completely failed to learn from it.

July's meticulous planning, much of it spent furtively on a toilet in a third-rate tourist attraction, turns to dust sharpish.

The forward who scored eight goals in three pre-season matches goes six straight hitting nothing but a post, three corner flags and a man dressed as a nun eight rows back behind the goal.

Your most expensive signing scores a hat-trick on international duty and you acknowledge your own brilliance at building your entire side around him, licking your lips in anticipation at that form being translated into so many points for you when he returns to domestic duty. You captain him the next week and even watch the match on the telly, allowing you to see the precise moment when he breaks his leg in three places in super slow-mo ultra HD 5G clarity.

You uninstall WhatsApp to quieten the increasingly shrill braying of mini-league rivals who seem to take such delight in your misfortune. They phone you up instead. You stop taking their calls, so they start visiting your house. You seriously consider moving and telling absolutely nobody about it when, in reality, all you actually need to do is stop playing Fantasy Football.

But that is never going to happen.

Depending on which hemisphere you happen to frequent, the nights either draw in or stretch out. Leaves fall/grow, temperatures fluctuate, but football remains your constant. Shelves remain down, relationships atrophy and careers gather dust because all you can be bothered about is why the footballing authorities think scheduling all those bloody international breaks was ever remotely a good idea. Just when you were turning around your disastrous start to the season, you get a ten-day break with no Fantasy Football whatsoever. It's unfair, unjustifiable, inhuman.

You react by petulantly playing your first Wildcard.

It bombs.

Christmas looms, so you get your shopping done, online, during a four-minute break from updating your spreadsheet examining the range of defenders in the 4.5 price bracket that offer the best chance of earning you bonus points from their average-per-match clearances, blocks and interceptions.

The New Year brings with it the usual battle not to play your second Wildcard on the 'e' of Auld Lang Syne.

Instead, you immerse yourself in the prospects offered by the new players who arrive in the January transfer window, settling on that exciting young striker who's been Belgium's top scorer for the past two seasons. He promptly gets sent off for headbutting the opposing team's mascot – a multi-horned human/animal hybrid thing with a leeringly stupid grin who the fans voted overwhelmingly to be called Facey McFaceface – that had been blatantly goading your man for missing two penalties on his debut.

But just when you decide to fake your own death and start afresh milking llamas in a Peruvian commune overlooking the Licancabur volcano, all those months of scheming, studying and playing the long game finally kick in.

You Wildcard before a Double Gameweek and gain more points in a week than you managed in the whole of October, outscoring 5.49 million people worldwide for good measure. WhatsApp is reinstalled and used to its maximum trash-talking potential when you Bench Boost during another Double Gameweek and move into the top three of five of your fifteen mini-leagues, two of which come with a decent cash prize.

The season ends with honour intact, a bit of the folding stuff in your hand and another pleasing sum won in a side bet with a relative who had been taunting you for months with the sort of foul and abusive language not normally associated with a churchgoing widow in her mid-eighties.

And you finally learn from previous years' mistakes by stockpiling cans of soup and back issues of Fantasy Football Magazine in preparation for a month spent locked up, shivering and alone, in June's Fantasy void.

Get a life? That's quite enough of one for many Fantasy managers. Away, they've just found a lovely campsite with award-winning Wi-Fi reception right next to a nuclear power station that is just the perfect place for next July's family holiday ...

Away from the global, free-to-enter obsession fest that is the Fantasy Premier League, it's not so much a case of getting a life, but completely transforming the one you had.

Remember the man who took the top six places in the News of the World's Goalmine game? His name is Steve Shipley and his 1999 success changed his life quite dramatically.

As with many newspaper games, the version in the (now defunct) News of the World allowed people to enter multiple teams. It was, and remains, an economic no-brainer for the newspapers to do that – most offer free entry to the casual player with a team or two, while serious managers with the time and inclination have to pay for the privilege of entering tens, if not hundreds, of slightly different line-ups.

Steve was a student at the time. He'd studied maths at Warwick University before moving on to a software engineering degree, and then a PhD in computer science, at nearby Coventry. He'd already got a bit of a track record heading into 1999, winning £3,000 for a third place in the News of the World's 1997 game and finishing just outside the money the year after that, pipped to a prize by his very own brother.

'I did, however, win a £2,000 monthly prize that season. This meant that I had the funds to have a really serious crack at the 1998–99 News of the World competition, which was important considering I was a student. Having twice come close, I knew that I had a good chance of scooping the big prize with enough time, effort and money, and I was determined to make it happen.'

The internet had arrived by then, but most people only ever took trips down the quaintly termed 'Information Super Highway' on work systems, so Fantasy games remained decidedly old-school affairs involving phones calls and print articles. As a result, Steve's commitment to winning was mind-boggling.

'I spent over £1,000 on the competition, entering and managing over 100 teams.

'Back in the days before competitions had made their way on to the internet, entry could be both costly and time-consuming. In order to enter a team you'd have to ring a premium rate number and enter a three-digit code (and confirm it) for each player. Then you'd have to give your personal details; 50p per minute seems a lot now, let alone twenty years ago.

'Transfers were yet another premium rate number and, in the News of the World, tables were only published sporadically so, if you wanted to check where your team was placed, that would be another premium rate number – this became more important towards the end of the competition when trying to work out who your competitors had in their teams.'

The past is a different country, but 1999 retains an air of familiarity. As an example (and in ascending intellectual order): the Beckhams got married, Jar Jar Binks took his first shot at ruining Star Wars for everyone and Spongebob Squarepants put down a deposit on a pineapple under the sea.

And in football, it was all about the Scottish game. For Steve, at least.

'That season, no striker in England really stood out from the crowd so Henrik Larsson of Celtic, with twenty-nine league goals (including three hat-tricks) and five cup goals was the must-have player, and my gamble to have him in virtually every team paid off.

'The same was true of Rangers' free-kick and penalty-taking midfielder Jorg Albertz (twelve goals and one hat-trick) and Chelsea midfielder Gustavo Poyet (eleven goals).

'By the penultimate weekend of fixtures (the last round of the Scottish Premier League plus the Man U v Newcastle FA Cup final), I knew that I had an extremely good chance of nabbing the top prize, although having fallen just short twice you don't want to count your chickens.

'That week went well and come the final week (just the Rangers v Celtic Scottish Cup final), I was just about home and hosed. As it turned out, with a fair number of Scottish-based players in my teams, those final two weeks propelled me into all of the top six places for the first time.'

He ended up, thanks to a couple of monthly prizes as well, winning £59,000 that year – a decent return on an investment of £1,000 and most of your waking hours.

Steve had recently married and his wife was expecting their first child. The money paid off a chunk of his mortgage, but it also got him thinking.

'Coming towards the end of my PhD, I started to look into what I was going to do next with my life. A bit of money in the bank, reduced the urgency to find a "real" job and I decided to see if I could make my in-depth football knowledge pay in the world of betting.

'I read up about all things betting-related before dipping my toe in the water. I started with spread betting and, remarkably, I was successful from the start. I branched out into other sports and later moved on to fixed-odds betting. With the advent of betting exchanges, I migrated on to those. Things went so well that I have so far managed to avoid the "real world of work".

'The Fantasy Football wins had a major, major impact on my whole life.'

Steve's story is, arguably, the ultimate example of the inner child breaking out and making it in the adult world without the need to compromise. It's many a football fan's dream to win money from their Fantasy hobby. A great number also like a bit of a flutter on sport in general. Steve has carved out a living from both.

But before you indulge in a bout of petty jealousy, Steve's also a Leeds United fan, so football hasn't always been good to him.

Things were considerably worse than that for another newspaper winner. In fact, Shaun Woodford's Fantasy experience didn't so much change his life as save it.

Shaun, from Northumberland, had been hooked on Fantasy Football since his first attempt at the game during Euro 96. Like other early adopters, he didn't have the internet to take the administrative burden. In fact, he didn't even have a phone at home.

'I remember entering by using a street payphone, entering codes for each player, which cost about £20 per team. The early years were just a bit of fun – it wasn't until many years later I would become the player I am now, obsessed with trying to win big money.'

He concentrated on The Daily Telegraph and The Sun's games, coming agonisingly close to cashing in on the latter's Euro 2012 Dream Team offering.

'I was second and third in the main game at the semi-final stages, but both my teams relied heavily on Portugal getting to the final. The semi-final was 0–0 and Spain beat them on penalties, which blew both my teams away. If it had gone in Portugal's favour it would have been almost impossible for anyone to catch me with only the final to play. So close but so gutted! I blame Ronaldo for not taking a penalty.'

That near-miss proved to be the start of a downward spiral for Shaun as he endured what he described as 'the most difficult two to three years of real life'. He lost three jobs, due to a redundancy, a workplace fraud in which he was the victim, and then illness. And when his partner also lost her job, the debts began to mount up and they ended up homeless.

'My partner, the kids and myself were evicted from our home as we couldn't afford the rent payments and had all of our possessions taken away to storage by the local authorities.

'All four of us were given a bedroom to share in a homeless hostel. Drug addicts and alcoholics all shared the property with us and the council told us we'd get rehoused within a few weeks. Five months later we finally got a home after borrowing money for a deposit from family to rent privately.'

They moved into their new home two days before Christmas and, having spent months living out of one suitcase, began unpacking all the belongings that had been kept in storage during their time in the hostel.

'Every item of clothing and furniture was mouldy. The beds were mouldy, the TV broken, everything was ruined. So not only did we have to start from scratch to build a new home, but we accumulated thousands of pound of debt over this rough time. I had car finance, credit cards, owed rent, money owed to family, all of it building up – almost 10k of debt hanging over my head with no idea how to get out of the mess that my life had become.'

Shaun's plan to turn things around didn't go down that well with those around him.

'As summer was approaching, I told my friends and family I was going to play to win The Sun Dream Team's Euro 2016 game. But they all said the same: "Shaun, it's a waste of time"; "Shaun, you can't afford it"; "Shaun, don't be daft".'

Having gone so close in the same game four years earlier, he ended up having to rely on Portugal again. 'I suppose the heartache of getting so close four years earlier helped me with this as I learnt from some mistakes that I made.

'On the night of the final, I had a team in second place with mostly French players and another about ten places behind with mostly Portugal players, so I was thinking I could hold on to second. But when

Portugal scored and keep a clean sheet, it sent my lower team right up the table to win by one point.'

Shaun won £25,000 – enough to pay off all his debts, replace the things destroyed in storage and 'treat the family to a couple of holidays, which is the least they deserved for what we went through.

'I have probably said too much, but I like to tell it not so I get a pat on the back, but to inspire others. And to show that even when your life has hit rock bottom and you don't know how you will ever get your life back on track, just keep going and never give up.

'And most important of all, no matter what your dreams are, you must always pursue them and always believe in yourself no matter who doubts you.'

It's a high-risk strategy, and certainly not one I'd personally recommend to anyone unfortunate enough to find themselves in the same trouble as Shaun. But for such a trivial and childish pastime, Fantasy Football clearly has the power to help people not just to get a life, but completely transform it.

I've played the games at which both Steve and Shaun have excelled. But my attempts were always woefully amateur, single-team efforts that didn't cost me any money but never stood a chance against the multi-team jugglers who work their way through dizzying combinations, spending huge amounts of time and some serious money to win big.

A lot of their tips and tricks are, however, entirely transferable to the slightly less high-stakes world of the Fantasy Premier League.

Shaun, for instance, takes his work before a game seriously. Very seriously.

'My preparation for my Euro 2016 campaign took a couple of weeks. I dedicated two to four hours per day to each team for the two weeks prior to kick-off.

'Take Switzerland, for example. I would read three different magazine previews of them, individually searching each player's domestic season, looking up national team results for friendlies and competitive matches to try and work out their most likely line-up.

'I'd then find out who takes corners, free kicks and penalties. How many pens did the team win? What sort of style do they play? Who creates the most chances per game. Do any players often get subbed early? Who picks up too many bookings? Is it worth picking a Swiss defender on the cheap etc?

'So after doing this for every team, I could create a shortlist of players.'

To be the best, you have to beat the best, which apparently means spending an inordinately large amount of time studying Swiss defenders. Needs must, I suppose.

As for Steve, he describes himself as a 'meticulous' Fantasy player, but not a cautious one. 'I don't think you can be that cautious when you are trying to beat so many other players.'

And for him, there is one golden rule by which he abides. 'I'd say the overriding rule would be to have a very clear idea of the rules of the game, notably the scoring system and which matches count (Premier League/FA Cup/League Cup/Champions League/Europa League).

'Most importantly, know the transfer system. It's the smart use of transfers that will make the biggest difference to your chances of success.

'Some competitions allow transfers to be made in between games on the same day. If your life circumstances mean that you aren't in a position to complete such transfers, then enter a competition that has less regular transfer windows, otherwise you'll be putting yourself at a serious disadvantage.

'If you do enter a competition with extremely regular transfers, it's a bit like playing chess in that it's important to plan two or three moves ahead, particularly if points are given for a player merely making an appearance.'

So a successful Fantasy manager is one that plans and plots in great detail and knows that to win any game, you need to know the rules inside out in order to exploit them to the maximum.

Funnily enough, in a chapter about lives obtained, diverted and transformed, that's great advice for getting on not just in Fantasy Football, but life itself.

CHAPTER TEN

PERSPECTIVE

For every exception, there has to be a rule.

Talk to past winners of the Fantasy Premier League title and they'll all tell you the same thing about the final day of the season – it's hell.

Nerves, expectation, an entire day spent pacing up and down listening to, or watching, matches that have the potential to bring to glorious reality the spoils of nine months of feverish Fantasy work.

Or just spoil it.

Winning the FPL crown, it would seem, requires a brutal confirmation of the no pain, no gain dictum.

And then there is the exception.

His name is Matthew Martyniak, a physiotherapist in his forties from Preston in Lancashire. Matthew won FPL in 2012–13 by two points – a margin so painfully small that your average elite manager (if average is the right word) would have lost weight/hair/marbles and more as their day of torture unfolded.

Not Matthew.

'Probably what sticks out in hindsight the most on that final day of the FPL season was actually how calm and at peace I was within myself considering the circumstances.'

There was a blatantly obvious, and yet infinitely complex, reason for that.

'From what I know now but I did not really understand at the time, I got this inner calmness, peace, and possibly clarity too from the previous five hours that day.

'That final FPL Sunday, I was up at around five in the morning to climb a fair-sized mountain called Mount Krizevac, in English "Cross Mountain", which is beside a beautiful little village called Medjugorje, in Bosnia and Herzegovina.

'It was Pentecost Sunday, a special Christian feast day that celebrates the coming of the Holy Spirit, which is God Himself living in us, with us, and through us.'

Yep. You read it right. On the final day, Matthew had Van Persie, Bale and God on his side. And before I get slapped down for trivialising another man's faith, here's another quote from Matthew:

'No, my faith has not informed my playing of Fantasy Football, although having a team with Moses, Gabriel Jesus, Eden (Hazard), Christian (Benteke/Fuchs), and Angel (Rangel) may have crossed my mind. I don't pray for FPL points. Prayer does not work like that!'

Religion ... religion in a book about Fantasy Football ... really?

Time to get all the cards out on the table. Full disclosure. I am not a religious person. But I have met many people of many faiths in my life who have been, so very obviously, good people. And they all share a common thread of wonder and curiosity and doubt as to the world in which they live that is balanced and nourished by their faith in a power above and beyond their own petty concerns and transient physical existence. They seek understanding of the world, while acknowledging their personal naivety. They are open and thoughtful, and if they are certain of anything, it is of their faith and precious little else.

Such people do not use that faith to judge or belittle or hurt. They seek to understand and to help and be judged themselves through their actions. Matthew, as far as I can see, is such a person.

And on the Sunday he won his FPL title, his faith had led him on a pilgrimage up a mountain and back down to earth to help out at

Cenacolo, a place of rehabilitation for people with addictions – drugs, alcohol, pornography and anything else that the world can throw at us and to which we succumb.

'That final FPL Sunday morning at the top of Cross Mountain, I asked, with faith in prayer, to receive the Holy Spirit and the free gifts and fruits it brings to us – such as wisdom, knowledge, understanding, love, joy, peace, kindness, patience, to name a few.

'Something "strange" immediately happened to me and the area around me during my prayer. It is difficult to explain what happened, and it is impossible to measure or quantify, only faith can explain it.

'I suppose the immediate calmness, inner peace and clarity that I had were the visible, or external, signs of the Holy Spirit working within me.'

If you've had enough of The God Stuff already, that's fine. Move along. There are other chapters ahead which are completely faith-free and might contain some blistering passages detailing the sins of the flesh. Or Richard Dawkins. I don't know. I haven't written them yet.

But this chapter is all about Matthew, and Matthew is a Christian. He deserves to be heard on his terms and that is what he will get, whether you agree with what he believes or not.

'Around the time of booking the pilgrimage, I broke into the overall FPL world top three for the first time.

'I noticed that the pilgrimage coincided with the final week and weekend of the FPL season. Although it was five months away, I had a good feeling at the time that it would be a special week, but I wasn't to know at the time how special it would be, and in what way.'

Matthew's pilgrimage involved, as mentioned, helping out at Cenacolo, a centre with no doctors, psychiatrists or social workers to help people overcome their addictions. The idea of the place revolves around community; a sharing of space, work and learning that can help rebuild the individual self fractured by addiction. It involves a simple, uncluttered life of cooking, cleaning, gardening and tending to animals. People also learn new skills, learn new languages and help with new building projects.

And, yes, they pray. As Matthew put it: 'The community life with prayer leads them to faith, then this leads them to love, and this leads them to serve others. Then finally it leads them to a new life that is free from the slavery of their addictions.'

Matthew's pilgrimage was also a personal one, an attempt to escape, however briefly, 'the noise and distractions of the world and all its problems and to enter into a quiet place of prayer and peace, a place internal as well as external'.

That, when you're painfully close to winning the Fantasy Premier League, sounds like a pretty good idea.

'When all the afternoon Premier League games were taking place, I was literally a world away from it all. No phone, no radio, no television. There was nothing or nobody around to tell me what was happening in the world of FPL and how my team was doing.

'The lack of FPL communication, however, was actually a good thing. Not just to keep myself peaceful and relaxed, but more importantly, so I could give my full and undivided attention to where I was at that present moment in time without any distractions.'

The distractions would have been enormous. Because while the Premier League title had long been done and dusted – Alex Ferguson's Man United won the league at a canter that year – the FPL fight went all the way to the final whistle and, as it turned out, beyond.

Matthew's two-point margin of victory only transpired after bonus points were awarded following the completion of the last matches of the season. When United were picking up their trophy and the Old Trafford turf was littered with that outsized winning confetti you only ever see at sporting events, when all that stage-managed kerfuffle was going on, Matthew was not on course to win the FPL title.

If he'd known that, he would have been in bits. Instead, where he was gave him a perspective on the whole thing that clearly lives with him to this day. 'Although that final Sunday was the day I won the FPL title, that day was the day I actually met the real winners in life, who were the people who had overcome addictions.

'Sadly addictions are real, not fantasy, and many people around the world suffer from some kind of addiction, but thankfully, with the right help, love and support, there is a way out for all sufferers, a new life free from addiction.'

That might seem twee, or the sickly stuff of a birthday card message. But in Matthew's case, it's from the heart and, to be fair, he had some first-hand knowledge on which to base his comments.

What he didn't realise at the time was that addiction was about to blight his own life – from the most unlikely of sources.

But before we get on to that, it's time to leave God on the bench for a while and geek out at Matthew's winning season.

'As I mentioned earlier, through prayer that morning I had a lot of inner peace and calmness, and I am sure this aided my FPL thinking in a positive way.'

Okay, so God has immediately insisted on getting into full kit and making an appearance, like an infallible John Terry, but Matthew's FPL experience was actually a lot more to do with something of a footballing false prophet – a player by the name of Gervinho.

Arsenal fans will have instinctively flinched at the very name. For the rest of you, here's a brief guide to/refresher of the Ivorian forward's Premier League history.

Gervinho joined the Gunners fresh from helping Lille to the French title, racking up twenty-eight goals and fourteen assists across two highly successful seasons. His two years at Arsenal were rather less stellar, managing just thirty-one matches – he played more in his final season at Lille – and scoring a mere nine goals.

And the less said about his hairstyle the better.

His misses, including a horrible open-goal affair against Bradford, became the stuff of bitter legend for Arsenal fans as a once bright, if mercurial, talent lost his confidence and, eventually, his place in the side amid rumours of him being bullied by some team-mates.

Things picked up quite markedly for Gervinho when he moved to Roma and, the last time I checked, he was earning a reported £165,000 a week, plus a £130,000 goal bonus and a £50,000 appearance fee, in the Chinese Super League.

So let's not feel too sorry for a guy who once allegedly blew the chance to sign for Al Jazira in the United Arab Emirates by demanding a helicopter and a private beach as part of the deal. Instead, we can celebrate his part in Matthew's Fantasy Football success.

'FPL, like in real life football, is full of what ifs, buts, and what might have beens. They are both unpredictable at the best of times, and that is probably one of the main reasons why we like them and why they go well together.

'And of course, no matter how meticulous your FPL preparation is, once the players cross that white line on a match day anything can happen. So yes, luck, fortune or even destiny does play a huge part in determining outcomes in FPL.'

Matthew's destiny had a name, and its name was Gervinho.

While plotting his strategy for that season's upcoming Double Gameweeks, he realised he needed a midfielder at a certain price. He wanted Arsenal's Theo Walcott, but couldn't afford him. And then – to the surprise of no one who knows anything about Theo – the England man got injured on international duty.

Matthew's profession came in very handy at that point – as a physiotherapist he recognised that Walcott's injury was likely to keep him out at least until the first Double Gameweek, 'even though Arsene Wenger wasn't giving any clues away at the time'.

So, in a move both bold and bonkers, he plumped for Walcott's team-mate Gervinho instead. 'I took a punt on him against popular FPL community opinion at the time, and rightly so, as this was Gervinho after all!

'Thankfully he did start Gameweek 32 due to Walcott's injury and he chipped in nicely with an assist and two bonus points.'

With the benefit of hindsight, getting an assist and two bonus points should have been a signal for Matthew that it was time to cash in and sell his Arsenal man on. Gervinho, after all, was to consistency what Cruella de Vil was to animal rights. But Matthew stood by him.

'Then, as I hoped and expected, Gervinho started the first Double Gameweek 33 fixture against Norwich at the Emirates. This was an enticing fixture for him to get a few goals and to keep his place in the team for the run-in.'

Oh ye of too much faith ...

'In the first half I remember watching him go around the Norwich goalkeeper only to fail to score into an open net! Norwich went down the other end and scored, Gervinho was then hauled off at half-time and Walcott, who was fit again, replaced him.'

An assist and bonus points one match, an inept and ghastly miss the next was Gervinho's Arsenal career in microcosm. Time then for Matthew to get rid and move on, right?

'It was the Double Gameweek 37 – a big one in FPL. There were quite a few teams, mine included, bunched together within a few points of each other at the very top of the overall rankings. A rampant Arsenal side were at home midweek to the new – and possibly hungover – FA Cup winners, Wigan Athletic.'

But Matthew had seen sense by then and sold Gervinho, right?

'Although Gervinho never really got a look-in after the Norwich game, I was hoping that he would play some part in the match and get me some valuable points against a Wigan side that looked there for the taking.

'My first sub on the bench that day was Shaun Maloney of Wigan. He'd been a good pick for me and he was having a decent end to the season, but I didn't trust him, nor trust Wigan away at Arsenal that evening.'

Matthew was at work when the match kicked off and remembers being unusually nervous, 'not just about the game, but in knowing that at any moment my FPL title-winning dream could be over'.

He checked his phone. Gervinho was on the bench. No surprise there, and Matthew still had the chance of his man coming on for something to cling to as the match progressed. He got on with his work and waited for an hour before checking his phone again.

There had been a goal. For Wigan. Shaun Maloney was the scorer.

'Oh no, I thought, this is not going to plan!' Matthew said, revealing a level of understatement not seen since someone on the Titanic reckoned 'that iceberg might be best avoided'.

By the time he got home from work, the match was reaching its conclusion, with Gervinho in Matthew's virtual team but still on the real-life bench, while Maloney was on his virtual bench but playing and scoring in the actual match.

Having spent the first eighty minutes of the encounter urging Wenger to bring Gervinho on, Matthew put his radio on and listened to the last knockings of the match, fervently hoping that the Arsenal manager would keep him right where he'd been all night.

'This was probably the most agonising and nerve-racking moment of my Fantasy Football career. It was either a one-point last-minute sub cameo from Gervinho or an invaluable six points from Maloney.'

This is the Fantasy experience in a nutshell, albeit with the stakes unusually high.

Generally speaking, a Fantasy manager's lot is similar to their real-world counterparts because both scheme, strategise, select and then have to watch as others attempt to put their plans into action. But real managers have one more trick up their sleeve – they can bring players on or take them off. And last-minute substitutions have a nasty habit of wrecking all manner of Fantasy plans.

'Thankfully, Arsene Wenger had less trust in Gervinho than I did and kept him on the bench. The thirteen points in total I had gained from owning Gervinho – his seven from GW32 and his zero playing in DGW37 that gave me Maloney's six points – were crucial in the end to me winning FPL. But they weren't exactly as I'd planned.'

And while Gervinho scrapes by on his weekly wage wondering whether he'll ever get that private beach he so needs, Matthew still mulls over the time his man changed the course of FPL history in the most Gervinho-like way possible.

'But I can't help thinking, even to this day, that what if he had scored that open goal versus Norwich in DGW33? Things may have been very different, but whether that be good fortune or bad fortune, I will never know.'

In a bid to put Matthew's mind at rest, I now declare that Gervinho was always going to miss that open goal. The sun rises, the sun sets, cats miaow, corporations avoid paying tax and Gervinho misses open goals. It is as nature or, dare I say it, even as God intended.

It wasn't, of course, just Gervinho who won it for Matthew. He was, for instance, an early adopter of Swansea's Michu, who scored a lot of points for minimal money, while he stuck by Robin van Persie when many others had cut and run, captaining the Dutchman for one Double Gameweek and gaining thirty-two points as a result.

But it seems entirely fitting that Gervinho – a player who tested the faith of all and sundry during his time at Arsenal – should be considered so vital by a man of faith. And an FPL-winning man of faith at that.

Matthew had been playing Fantasy Football for years and was another who remembered the pre-internet chore that was phoning through your transfers in the Daily Telegraph game. He'd been running as high as seventh in that competition one year, ending the season seventieth overall – his best ever Fantasy Football finish until the big one came along.

So it wasn't like he didn't have any experience of knowing what it was like to be right up there, competing with the best at the sharp end of a football season. It's just that whatever experience he'd managed to glean simply wasn't enough.

'That 2012–13 season was different to any other that I had played before, as from Christmas onwards until the end of the season I found myself in the unfamiliar position of being in the FPL overall world top ten. The second half of that season I had to take the seriousness and competitive nature to another level – a level I never knew I had.

'This new level of seriousness I had for FPL that season actually had a negative effect on my family, my friends, my work and myself. I couldn't focus on anything else properly other than FPL. It was very draining mentally and physically. When the season was finally over I said to myself and to some friends ... 'that's it, no more, that's me done with Fantasy Football'.

'I just wanted my life back.'

Matthew's pilgrimage to Medjugorje, and the Cenacolo centre there, was not a one-off. He returns every year. He's also visited a similar centre in England and frequently travels to Lourdes in the south of France both as a pilgrim and also as a volunteer healthcare worker.

So the life he sought to regain was one of selflessness, not the selfishness of so much time and effort spent on a game of virtual football management that had brought him a measure of personal glory and fame.

Did Matthew become the one and only FPL winner to quit the game and decline to defend his title? Was he genuinely 'done with Fantasy Football'?

Quite the opposite.

'After winning FPL during that summer of 2013 I decided to carry on playing it as I still liked the game, and also, I had a FPL title to defend.

'I thought though that from then on FPL could not be any tougher than my winning season, and that I would certainly not take it as seriously any more as I had achieved the ultimate goal in FPL.

'I was very wrong.'

It's important, again, to put all of this into context. We're not talking about a Fantasy obsessive – although by this stage Matthew clearly was just that – who lived and breathed the game and nothing else. His life wasn't totally defined by Fantasy Football. Far from it. He had helped so many others and yet could not help himself.

'The following two seasons were actually much harder, much tougher and much more draining, and as a result, it was affecting my life to the point where FPL was taking over even more. Fantasy was becoming my reality, and in turn, reality was becoming less real, or a fantasy even. As the competitive nature in me took over again, I wanted to win it again, or if not win it then at least defend my FPL title well.'

He did just that, achieving two consecutive top 1,000 finishes – the stuff of dreams for most of us rather more mortal Fantasy players. The problem for Matthew was that it just wasn't enough.

'From a fantasy point of view this may sound good, but from a reality point of view it really wasn't. I was mentally and physically drained by it all. My mood, my actions, my thoughts in reality were being directly affected by my Fantasy life, my FPL team and its results, whether they were good or bad. It wasn't healthy for myself and those around me. I seriously started to question if I had an addiction to the FPL game. I also started to enjoy FPL, and football in general, less and less.

'I wanted to quit the FPL game many times during those two seasons, but my pride – and possibly an addiction to staying in the race until the end of the season – kept me going.'

I'm not an expert, but there doesn't seem to be much 'possibly' in that idea of addiction. Matthew wasn't enjoying what he was doing any more, but he kept on doing it anyway. Results that previously would have been seen as a high were now merely pale imitations of that first big hit, that best time. Matthew was trapped in a spiral of diminishing returns and it was having an impact on his life, his family and friends.

Or, put another way:

1: Experimentation.
2: Regular use.
3: Abuse.
4: Addiction.

Matthew's addiction expressed itself both socially and internally.

'At friends' and family gatherings for example, especially over the weekend whilst the Premier League and FPL was in full flow, I was hardly ever present, even if I was physically there. My mind was a world away – in the FPL world. I wasn't interacting normally, such as listening, speaking, acting, behaving, with those around me, those who I love and care for most dearly.

'I was putting off a lot of things that needed doing, or never even did them at all – those things that are important, that are in reality, such as helping and being there for family, friends and others.

'As a result, those around me became frustrated with me and I became frustrated with them, as well as myself. I just wanted to be on my own with FPL, with no distractions – which is what I thought everything outside FPL was becoming.

'Internally, I struggled as a result of my actions. The love, joy and peace I used to feel and share with others was draining away from me. It was being replaced by emptiness, sadness and restlessness.'

You don't have to be physically dependent to be addicted. Gambling, for instance, is so obviously all in the mind, but that doesn't lessen the addiction of all those that suffer it. And you can laugh off all of this as something that will never happen to you and I'm sure you're absolutely right.

But it did happen to Matthew. A ridiculous, fun, trivial game – a literal fantasy – took hold of him and changed what he was. Yes, this is Fantasy Football we're talking about. It's not crack or alcohol. Nobody's house was robbed to fund the next hit. Nobody was abused. Families weren't torn apart and nobody died.

It doesn't change a thing. Matthew was stuck in a miserable circle from which he couldn't seem to extricate himself. I dare say there was a good deal of self-loathing involved as his mood, and therefore his actions, became increasingly dependent on factors that were – despite his best efforts – ultimately beyond his control.

There is no doubt that there is a ridiculousness to this, that there are far more debilitating and damaging addictions out there. But ironically, unlike football, there isn't a league table for these things. You don't get relegated from the Premier League of Class A addiction to some kind of Championship, where lesser addictions duke it out for the right to be taken seriously again, perhaps coming up against faded giants of the addiction world (Laudanum? Absinthe?) who still remember the glory days when everyone knew who they were and couldn't help but use them.

If you're addicted, you're addicted. And Matthew was addicted. He needed help because he couldn't help himself. The source of that help, as it turned out, was there all along.

'By the summer of 2016, it was time for me to have a serious reality check and take a good look at my life and the things that matter the most – the things in reality and not fantasy. My family, friends, neighbours, my work, my community, the church, and of course God and His will for me.

'I had a decision to make. It was either to quit indefinitely playing FPL, or if I was to carry on playing then I would have to go back to my roots to why I started playing it in the first place, which was for the fun, enjoyment and friendship that hobbies and interests give you, which is the healthy aspect.'

Matthew underwent what he described as 'FPL detox': spending more time in prayer, with family and friends, focusing more on his work – including voluntary work – and spending less time and effort on FPL.

'I do not take Fantasy Football as seriously now and, as a result, I started to, and still do, enjoy the game again. More importantly, I am in a healthier place within myself and with those around me, and I enjoy life more now.'

I should point out that Fantasy Football, even when Matthew was at his lowest ebb, was never completely a negative thing. He set up a mini-league that runs every season to raise funds for charity, and he has always been generous with his time when people have sought to tap into his obvious FPL expertise.

He was more than happy to provide hints and tips to me for this book. But his contribution won't be a specific, entirely Fantasy-related, nugget of wisdom.

Matthew brings perspective to this particular table. He brings a need to remember why you started playing the game in the first place. And he is living testament to the fact that however strong or grounded or together you might be as a person, however much real life you might be fortunate enough to lead, Fantasy Football can and does have the power to shape and change that life – and not always for the best.

So remember to take a step back now and again. See it for what it is – a game to be played and enjoyed in conjunction with, but never as an alternative to, reality. Fantasy can help us escape, but we should never allow it to entrap us. Well, at least for no more than nine months of every year.

But this is Matthew's story, so Matthew will finish it off.

'The pressure certainly wasn't off after winning the FPL. It was actually greater than before, especially the following two or three seasons. Some of the pressure was good in regard to it helping me do well at the FPL game, but some of the pressure wasn't so good and, as mentioned earlier, it became unhealthy.

'Now things are much different. For a start, I know I will not win the FPL again. If I thought I could win it again, I would need to put more time and effort into the FPL game like before, which I am not going to do. I have had my moment of FPL glory, and it is more than I ever imagined or dreamt of when I initially started playing Fantasy Football just for fun.

'If I am to continue playing FPL, I am going back to my roots and playing it just for fun, enjoyment and for the friendship with others, that is the amazing FPL community.

'Just enjoy it and do not take it too seriously. And don't let it take over your priorities in life at the expense of yourself and others around you.'

CHAPTER ELEVEN

THE DUEL ON A SUNDAY

At times – and if you're not paying full attention – it can be hard to differentiate between Fantasy Football and the real thing.

Not in terms of the players, obviously, although the pros can, and do, dabble in the pretend stuff. No, where the two worlds collide is in the media, and none more so than on the final day of any given season.

Websites run detailed breakdowns of the campaign as it has unfolded. Tactics are dissected, line-ups examined, all possible outcomes considered. Managers are interviewed on radio and television. People whose own teams have nothing left to play for but a bit of pride and a negligible position change here and there start to ally themselves with the protagonists still battling it out for the ultimate crown.

And that's just in the Fantasy Premier League. The global circus that has sprung up around the FPL – the websites, Twitter accounts, the bloggers and the podcasters – all have their say on the final day.

They, after all, have been a part of the whole story in a way that the traditional media covering the real thing have not, and can never be. Every Fantasy Football pundit, every writer, presenter and self-styled guru, has been in direct competition with those managers blessed to still be within touching distance of the title.

Through thirty-seven Gameweeks of effort and anguish, they have fought and then followed them, watching them disappear into the distance and to a points total of appropriately fantastical proportions. Until only the select few are left.

This is the story of a duo who went head-to-head on the final day of FPL's 2016–17 season.

BEFORE

Like so many other media outlets, the Fantasy Football Scout website ran a lengthy preview of the 2016–17 season's final day. I should know, because I wrote it.

Here's something I prepared earlier:

The Fantasy Premier League title race – unlike the real thing – is going to the wire.

The top two are separated by just a pair of points heading in to Sunday's final round of fixtures after both managers put in barnstorming Gameweek 37 performances to distance themselves from the chasing pack.

Third-placed boss Roope Liimatainen is some 33 points back and with a sufficiently similar line-up to the leaders to suggest his race is run. Spare a thought also for Conor Barwise – he's a point behind in fourth and having to juggle his Fantasy commitments three days into a family holiday in Italy.

The pair will need to radically alter their teams, with the inevitable hits that entails, and go big on differentials if they are to have any hope of glory now.

Sixth-placed Mervyn Glasgow is in the same boat, but has to get a mention here as he's currently top of the Fantasy Football Scout league. And just four points behind him comes our leading site member, Billy Ketsu, so there's plenty to play for there on the final day. Top work, gentlemen.

We'll have a look at the prospects for the FPL Cup final later, but for now, it's time for the Big Show.

The Tale Of The Tape

Uwais Ahmed (Fahad's XI) v Ben Crabtree (FC Crab Dogg)

The crash-bang-wallop end to Gameweek 37 propelled Uwais Ahmed from third to first thanks to his captaincy of four-goal drama-machine Harry Kane. Previous leader Ben Crabtree also had the Spurs striker, but saw his double-figure lead at the top eradicated in one fell Kane-shaped swoop courtesy of Uwais' gutsy armband call.

__Uwais__ – best finish 5,768 in 2011/12. Playing since 2008. Arsenal fan.

He was in the top ten this year from GW22, slipping out to 12th in GW24 and then leading the pack for all but two weeks from GW29.

__Ben__ – best finish 353rd in 2011/12 and also managed 1,369th the season before that. Playing since 2009. Everton fan.

Top ten (straight in at four from 12th) in GW28. Has never led by the completion of a Gameweek – highest has been his current second position.

And on went the story into ever-greater depth about the pair's moves and misfires over the season – their captaincy choices, their favoured formations, the players they'd stuck by and the gambles that had bombed.

Uwais, it emerged, was probably the more conservative of the two. He had made fewer transfers over the course of the season and played the game in a thoughtful, considered fashion that would have had the purists nodding in approval.

Ben was more of a maverick, taking more transfer hits and breaking one of the golden Fantasy rules – he allowed his real-world footballing allegiances to dictate a part of his Fantasy policy. Everton fan Ben played the entire 2016–17 FPL season without ever picking a Liverpool player. If you think you can hear a faint sound right now, it's those purists grinding their teeth over that.

But actually, these last men standing had more in common than just a love for, and demonstrable skill at, playing Fantasy Football.

Both were thirty-one years old and lived in the north-west of England – Ben in Liverpool, Uwais in Blackburn, Lancashire. Both had white collar jobs – Uwais was a buying co-ordinator in the retail sector and Ben a supply chain procurement planner.

And neither could be accused of hiding from life behind a keyboard. Uwais was a self-described 'people person' with a strong sense of his identity coming from a love of family and a close circle of friends, while Ben was a quietly composed individual with a hint of a twinkle in his eye and, at the risk of lapsing into stereotype, more than a hint of a Scouser's dry wit.

Ben's season had started, in his own understated way with words, 'better than normal'.

'I entered the top 10,000 within a few weeks and managed to stay around there, hitting 2,000 at some point. I'd been this high before, but generally didn't start this well. I know that at the start there aren't many points between thousands of positions so my focus was still purely on winning my mini-leagues.

'I managed to keep the high position and stretch my mini-league leads so reached a point after halfway through the season that I didn't have much to play for. A high overall rank is nice to get, but there's an extra enjoyment in checking your rivals' teams for who they've bought and how well they've done that week.

'There were a few thousand teams above me so I didn't feel I was competing against anyone in particular.'

When Uwais described his start to the season, the similarities between him and Ben were, once again, striking.

'I start every season the same way. As friends, we have a private league known as the Legends' League and the priority always has been to win that.

'In 2016–17, I approached things the same way in that the aim was to try and win the Legends' League. However, I started off very well and established a healthy lead very quickly in the private league.

'I really did not pay too much attention to the overall leaderboard until I ended one particular Gameweek approximately forty-eighth in the world. That, obviously, did get my full attention.'

The pair then indulged in what could only be described as a period of semi-denial. Both knew they were doing well. Really well. But neither were quite ready to admit that, given the way things were going, they might be in with a chance of winning something rather bigger than a mini-league.

As Uwais put it: 'Even at that stage, I was quite focused in going through the same decision-making process. Fortunately, I am quite even-keeled like that.'

Ben, meanwhile, was rather more terse: 'I just ticked along.'

Only after Gameweek 27, with eleven more rounds of fixtures left, did Ben fully admit to himself that he was probably involved in an FPL title-winning race.

'From then on I kept tabs on the top three. Checking their transfers, their remaining players and seeing what unique players I had competing against theirs.

'My aims changed almost weekly, from I'd be happy with a top 100, to a top fifty, to a top ten, to top three ...'

Uwais, it transpired, couldn't have kept the realisation that he was in contention to himself even if he'd wanted to. The fact that he led the pack for most of the final nine Gameweeks of the season had turned him into something of a local celebrity.

'The greatest thing about being in the race for the FPL title was the fact that you get so many well wishes from friends and family. People you know well and many more that you do not know so well get in touch via text or phone call just to offer their well wishes.

'I remember once attending a wedding function with a few Gameweeks to go and so many people came up to me offering me all the best for the rest of the FPL campaign. For me, this was the best thing about it all, although it did feel a little surreal.

'I am a people person, and when you have so many random people coming up to you saying that they don't follow their own FPL progress and pay more attention to my own plight, that felt weird and exciting, really.'

PRE-MATCH

Uwais' and Ben's FPL stories for the 2016–17 season had been strikingly similar. But that had to change on Sunday, May 21. It just had to.

There was a crushing finality for both of them to contend with about the last day of the season – one of them was going to win the FPL title and the other was not.

With Gameweek 37 almost done, Ben had looked like he might actually be going into the final round of fixtures with a lead – for the first time all season – only for Uwais to come storming back and retain his place at the top of the table.

How they went about dealing with what was the biggest day of their lives, certainly in Fantasy terms and probably in reality as well, marked the point that their experiences of the season finally started to diverge.

Ben's morning did not start well.

'The day itself involved an unwanted, early start. I had a dream involving Christian Eriksen – a unique player for me against Uwais – and a PlayStation, one of the prizes. Clearly it was playing on my mind.

'I went to the gym, did a food shop, put up a mirror in the bathroom – I'd put that off for six weeks but that morning just seemed like a good time to do it, just as a distraction. I was just trying to keep my mind off Fantasy Football until closer to the teamsheets and kick-off.'

Uwais had other things going on to occupy his time. 'My final day on that Sunday began with a friendly match coaching our Under-8s. I volunteer as a coach for AHF FC and my son plays at the academy and club. So, having organised a friendly for that Sunday morning, this took my mind off things ever so slightly for a few hours.'

Uwais managed his time as well as he could. After his coaching stint, he gave a few interviews – he was Fantasy Famous, remember –

and then settled down to make the final changes to his team; decisions that he would have to live with for the rest of his life.

'The finality and seriousness of each decision meant I wanted to take as much time to reach the best possible solution for the issues I faced.'

Time, for Ben, seemed to be anything but the luxury item Uwais was savouring to its fullest. It was, at best, merely something to be endured.

'I tried to keep myself busy and try not to think about transfers. I hadn't made them yet. I had considered not making any changes, but really I just didn't want the whirlwind of options in my head any more.'

The 'whirlwind of options' – a perfect description for what both men were facing.

The final day of a Fantasy game's season is a fraught one for any manager still in with a chance of claiming something tangible from all those months of planning and plotting, be it victory in a mini-league, a good enough placing to earn some extra cash, or even just avoiding the ignominy of finishing last among family, friends or colleagues.

But to sit weighing up your options knowing that the choices you make will determine whether or not you will win the Fantasy Premier League title – a competition entered by millions around the world and played as equals by royalty, celebrities, professional sportspeople and all the rest of us – that is as close to the brutal finality experienced by the very few so very rarely.

We can all come back next year and have another go. The mini-leagues will still be there, as will the game itself. The only thing that will change is you yourself. You'll be a little greyer, or fatter, richer or poorer, wiser or even more reckless.

For Ben and Uwais, sat in their homes staring at the names of real players suffixed by wholly imaginary prices and points, they were at the tipping point; a one-shot deal that would bring them success or failure.

The stark reality that makes sport so cruelly compelling – someone will win, someone will lose – had arrived in their Fantasy lives.

They, too, could come back next year and have another go. But they would never be so close to the ultimate prize as they were right then and there, with time ticking down and decisions required.

As with any other Gameweek, those decisions would have to be made at least an hour before kick-off. Once that deadline had passed, there could be no more changes.

It's a tough rule, seeing as the team news for a Gameweek's fixtures generally comes after that deadline, but it's one area in which a skilled manager – one who studies team trends and understands the thought processes of a club's coach – can find an advantage. Conversely, selecting a player who then doesn't make the teamsheet can also be down to pure, dumb luck.

But the final Gameweek of the 2016–17 season had a strange twist to it; one very much in keeping with the world in which we all – pro footballers and us mug punters alike – now live. Huge numbers of football players have social media accounts these days. It can lead to some infamous mistakes, such as Sunderland striker Victor Anichebe's now legendary 'Can you tweet something like Unbelievable support yesterday and great effort by the lads! Hard result to take! But we go again!'.

For those with a slightly firmer grip on their accounts, or at least their account handlers, social media is a great way to interact directly with your fan base; a chance to counter the growing disconnect between the multi-millionaires who play the game and we wage slaves who fund them.

And on Sunday, May 21, shortly before the one-hour FPL transfer deadline at 2 p.m., Bournemouth's Josh King posted a picture on his Instagram account that made it abundantly clear he was injured and out of the final-day fixture at Leicester City.

This caused a frenzy among FPL managers. King had had a superb season, scoring freely after Christmas. He was playing up front for

Bournemouth, an out-of-position anomaly that meant he gained an extra point every time he scored because, although he was being used as a striker, he was classified in FPL as a midfielder, and with a budget price to go with it.

Suddenly, one post on social media had alerted hundreds of thousands of Fantasy managers to the fact that they were going to be without one of their key players for the final day of the season. Last-minute transfers took place across the globe, including one in Lancashire, England.

'Once King confirmed via Instagram that he was out and he was on my bench,' said Uwais, 'I made the decision to draft in Adam Lallana as a second transfer, the main reason being that he was going to start for Liverpool without a shadow of a doubt and he had a good fixture.

'I was always going to be bringing in [Lallana's team-mate] Philippe Coutinho for the final Gameweek, but the identity of the second transfer had not been as clear.'

His logic was sound for two reasons. As he mentioned, Liverpool had a great fixture – at home to a Middlesbrough side that had already been relegated, their players Championship-bound and halfway to the beach. And his opponent, Everton fan Ben, simply did not pick Liverpool players.

But the decision cost Uwais four points as it was his second transfer of the Gameweek. It meant he surrendered his two-point lead over Ben and went into the final ten matches of the season now two points behind.

Ben also had two transfers to make, but without penalty as he had saved his trade from the previous week to give him two free picks for Gameweek 38. How he reacted to the Josh King news – he also had the Bournemouth man in his team – could make or break his season.

'Finally 2 p.m. hit so I could see the team news as there was a lot of rotation possibilities. The big surprise for me, but no one else, was that

King wasn't playing. I'd had a quick check on injuries before I clicked my transfers but somehow managed to miss this.'

That mistake could prove fatal.

He'd decided to draft in (the then) Chelsea striker Diego Costa for the final day. To finance the move, he'd had to sacrifice an expensive midfielder – Costa's team-mate Eden Hazard – as he couldn't afford to simply swap in the Chelsea forward for his existing third striker, the aforementioned (and incredibly cheap) social media master Victor Anichebe.

That left Ben with one final decision to make – who to bring in as the midfield makeweight in the Costa deal.

He went for Junior Stanislas. The Junior Stanislas who plays, like the absent Josh King, for AFC Bournemouth. For a side enjoying the final-day comforts of mid-table obscurity, well away from either the big issues at the top of the league or the anguish below them, Bournemouth were going to have a major say in the outcome of the FPL title, whether they knew it or not.

And then it was done and Ben and Uwais could do no more. What control they'd had over their days was now beyond them. Their futures would make history, but they would have not the slightest influence over either.

KICK-OFF

Ben: 'I waited for the game to update so I could see Uwais' team. I felt quietly confident, but he had players capable of winning him the week single-handedly, so it was very much in the balance.'

Uwais: 'Ben had stuck with his principled stance of not drafting a Liverpool player. I was confident that if Liverpool drubbed Middlesbrough, that would probably be enough for me, all things considered.'

Ben: 'I live with my girlfriend, Pauline, but she could see I was tense, so she stayed with me until the games started and then went out into the garden. She could see how I was and just didn't want to sit with me. I was quite happy to be on my own, though. I had the BBC updates on my phone and I was pacing around the house.'

Uwais: 'We had decided to watch the Liverpool v Middlesbrough game at my brother's house. Whilst I was watching, my little brother Arkam was on Twitter. He is the social media specialist. He was going to keep us updated with regards to each and every development over the last day. The nerves were real, but I also felt quite calm and excited.'

3 p.m. Kick-off. All ten matches.

Ben: 'During the games I was quite restless. Normally I enjoy the games being on but I wanted it to be over.'

Uwais: 'Straight away, Junior Stanislas scored for Ben and, although that was a tad disappointing, I knew that the day was long so there would be plenty of twists and turns.'

Ben: ' I had a goal in the first minute and appeared to be ahead up until around seventy minutes.'

Uwais: 'Going into the second half, although I did not do the maths, in my head I knew I was maybe close to double digits behind. All of a sudden, Coutinho scores. And then Lallana scores to follow. There was pandemonium in the room.'

Ben: 'The last fifteen to twenty minutes, I was very anxious.'

Uwais: 'Fabregas [for Uwais] and Eriksen [for Ben] traded assists.'

Ben: 'The last few minutes in particular were painful as I didn't want any more goal updates and just wanted it to end.'

Uwais: 'It was only when Ben Davies scored in the eighty-third minute [for Ben] that I felt that it had definitely slipped away.'

Ben: 'Near the final whistle, Ben Davies got me a goal. That was the only time all day that I actually allowed myself to celebrate. I thought that it was the clincher, but when I refreshed Uwais' team he had a Fabregas assist appear. And then he got another. I reckoned if he got bonus points from those events, then the Davies goal would be wiped out and I'd be falling behind.'

Uwais: 'In the end, after all the bonuses were counted, to lose by five points and with Davies scoring to give Ben six points – there, in a nutshell, was the title.'

Ben: 'Second place would have been a great result, but given I was so close to first, the disappointment would have been huge.'

THE FINAL WHISTLE

Nobody knew for sure who had won the title until a couple of hours later. But once the final whistles had been blown, it was the eventual winner who was still contemplating how to deal with defeat, while the runner-up was already devising his coping mechanisms.

Uwais had spent that final day with his family close, and it was to them he immediately turned to soften the blow.

'It was special to go through those last ten Gameweeks with my own family. My son, who had turned eight in May, really followed my progress every single Gameweek. He would often come up to me when I would watch a game and ask "who do we have playing in this game, Dad?"

'On a number of occasions, we would watch games when we would have a few players playing and when those players got a goal or assist, he would celebrate and just to see the joy on his face was quite exciting. Good memories, for sure.'

Whereas Ben, presumably having fetched his girlfriend back in from the garden, was left in limbo by it all.

'In a lot of ways there was a bit of an anti-climax to it. Rather than the final whistle blowing and knowing there and then that I had won, I had a drawn-out two to three hours of it looking like I had won but it not being fully confirmed.

'Until the tables updated, I was still slightly concerned by a dubious assist or goal being re-credited to someone, which would change the outcome.'

But the outcome didn't change. Ben had won. By just five points.

'Once it was all done,' he went on, 'I was more relieved than anything else. I was glad it was over, happy that I had a number one rank locked in and started looking forward to the prizes.'

As everything started to sink in, it was Uwais, unsurprisingly, who had much to ponder.

'If I had not been in contention for the FPL title and ended up in the top ten at the end of the last day, it would have been fine. However, to be in the top two for the entirety of the final fourteen Gameweeks but to fall on the wrong side at the end was tough to take.

'You start to think about the possibility of winning the FPL title and, given that it was pretty much assured that I was either going to be the runner-up or winner going into the final Gameweek, you do realise that it is a fifty-fifty shot at achieving the nigh-on impossible.

'So, although it is a great achievement, I had got used to the idea of being in the top standings for the final ten Gameweeks and therefore you start to consider the "what if?" scenario of winning.

'It did not go my way and that is just something I have to come to terms with.'

For Ben, everything was that much simpler. 'I do still feel a sense of achievement regarding the win. It's still a topic of conversation and is something that I'm happy I can claim for ever.

'Winning FPL changed my life for about a week. I was a celebrity for a week, doing interviews, seeing various internet links about me, people getting in contact who I hadn't spoken to for a while and people telling their friends that they "know the guy who won it".

'After that, things have gone back to normal in the main.'

THE AFTERMATH

As to the future, the result has produced drastically different outlooks from the pair.

'To the victor go the spoils,' said Uwais, 'and Ben deserved to finish as top dog, but there is disappointment.

'However, you have to put it in its proper context. It is a game and, with real suffering out there in the world, this disappointment is trivial. You simply have to move on.

'I absolutely believe unequivocally that that season is the best it is ever going to be. There is simply no way you can achieve a similar result against such competition. That is disappointing, but you simply have to come to terms with it.'

Ben, however, disagrees. 'I don't rule out scaling those heights again. I feel each year I become more in tune with football and my opinions and thoughts become more in depth, seeing things more objectively; what really happened as opposed to the official story of the game.

'I feel I can still get a respectable position again. Maybe not first, but you never know.'

So what did they learn (and what can we steal) from their stellar seasons?

The obvious lesson is that even the most fundamental rules can be ignored. I'm not saying they should be, but they can be. If Ben Crabtree – FPL winner 2016–17 – can get away without picking players from a particular side for tribal, emotional reasons alone, then so can we.

It's just not the best lesson to be learnt from the pair. Instead, Uwais offered this:

'My own opinion is that selecting big hitters in away matches can often be a lot more rewarding than selecting them in plum home fixtures.

'This is not an exact rule, but I simply like the idea of certain big teams going away to grounds where the home team does need to open up.

'I captained Alexis Sanchez away to West Ham [in 2016–17] and he rewarded me with a hat-trick, an assist and three bonus.

'I had begun to buy into the idea of captaining offensive players from the big clubs away to mid-table clubs. I believe this is something I will be focusing on throughout the next few seasons in FPL.'

Ever the maverick, Ben went for a rather more standard suggestion than might be expected from a man happy to ignore Liverpool players, however in-form they might be: 'A piece of advice would be for players to leave their new transfers in the team long enough to play five to eight Gameweeks.

'Don't give up on players just to get flavour of the week as generally, in reality, that player was last week's outstanding performer.

'If you have a system that has some consistency to it, it's easier to analyse correct decisions and mistakes so you can tweak things in the right direction.

'I am also open to my way of playing not being the only way in which you can be successful. There are likely to be a quite a few differences between myself and the other nine players finishing in the top ten with regards to how we see the game, how much football we watch, how much we analyse stats, etc.'

The differences between Ben and Uwais, as it turned out, were marginal. But the gulf between them will forever remain huge.

Ben won, Uwais didn't. And the victor, rightly or wrongly, is the only one many people will ever remember. All because of a mere five points, provided by Tottenham's Ben Davies, six minutes from the end of what turned out to be a classic FPL season.

CHAPTER TWELVE

FANTASY TOWN

In the second-best film about baseball starring Kevin Costner – Field of Dreams – his character hears voices in his head. Fortunately for him, they don't tell him to avoid tap water, kill sex workers or shoot a head of state, insisting only that he constructs a baseball field in the middle of rural Iowa.

'If you build it, he will come,' they tell him.

It is built, he does come, the end.

In a similar fashion, although mostly without the aural hallucinations, an ancillary network has sprung up around Fantasy Football: websites, bloggers, self-styled gurus, podcasters, Twitter accounts, predictive software peddlers, feeble 'banter' pushers and trolls.

An entire Fantasy town has been constructed, and they have come.

As on any high street, the outlets range from the high-end to the pound shop, and all tastes are catered for, from the statistical to the amused. It is an unlicensed, Wild West kind of place in which, generally speaking, the strong and established hold sway, but anyone can turn up and have a go.

Before this entire frontier town analogy becomes as unworkable as the zip on Arsene Wenger's infinity coat, let's just say that the saloon is the place to be for Fantasy shits and giggles, and it is an establishment run by The Gaffer Tapes.

The Gaffer Tapes is a podcast that claims, with good reason, to be an award-winning affair – it took home the Judge's Award at the Football Blogging Awards for Best Football Podcast in 2016 and has been happy to repeatedly mention this fact ever since and for ever.

The trio behind the podcast are:

Name: Tom Holmes
Occupation: comedian, writer, published author
Real occupation: I work for an ad agency
Age: thirty-one
Interesting fact: I was one of Enid Blyton's Secret Seven

Name: Craig Hazell
Occupation: assistant TV producer
Age: thirty-three
Interesting fact: I once trended on Twitter. True story

Name: Ash Kernsworth
Occupation: app developer
Age: thirty-four
Interesting fact: I am a top 100 FPL player and European petanque champion

Humour, as much as Fantasy information, is at the heart of The Gaffer Tapes. And it has one thing in spades that many other podcasts would dearly love but can't simply create out of thin air – a genuine chemistry between its protagonists.

The three Gaffers didn't meet over a mutual love of Fantasy Football and decide to start a podcast as a result. Instead, the trio's mutual love for each other went in search of a subject and stumbled upon Fantasy Football.

'Tom and Craig met on the stand-up comedy circuit and instantly fell in love.

'Tom and Ash met through their respective wives and swiftly bonded over their love the Ultimate Fighting Championship and drinking alcoholic beverages in public houses until you can't remember what your name is.

'Tom introduced Craig and Ash and an inseparable triangular bond was created: like Vic and Bob ... and another one.

'We toyed with various ideas for a podcast, but Ash's revelation that he once finished eighty-first in the world at Fantasy Premier League sealed the deal and the next thing we knew we were sat in a pub in Windsor drinking lager (Tom), cider (Craig) and Tia Maria and orange juice (Ash ... no, seriously) and coming up with features for the newly named The Gaffer Tapes podcast.'

Groups of men around the world often think that the drink-fuelled stuff they come out with on a night down the pub is pure comedy gold. It is, of course, nothing of the sort, just a steady stream of poor in-jokes and increasing jibber-jabber. Alcohol merely filters out the inhibitions and, in time, the quality control setting that would otherwise tell you in no uncertain terms that the idea of Glenn Himmler Und His Orchestra playing Torchlight Serenade is kind of funny, but only then and there and after eight pints.

The Gaffer Tapes is cut from much of the same cloth (without the Nazis), but manages to be both funny and mostly coherent nearly all the time. And without the need for alcohol, except for one infamous case during the final podcast of the 2016–17 season.

'We started recording podcasts on an iPhone in June 2014 to about a dozen people, and can now boast (and we *do*) 20,000 listeners a week from about fifty countries.

'Finding out that actor Dominic Monaghan, from Lord of the Rings, Lost, and that Eminem music video where he gets off with Megan Fox, was a listener was *madness*, but to have him on as a guest twice has been incredible ... going for a beer with him was pretty cool too.

'Every time we get a voice-clip or message from someone – particularly if that person is from another country – is so flattering;

we still can't quite believe when people take the time and effort to get in touch.

'A listener in America once informed us that he left the room whilst his girlfriend was in the late stages of labour to set his line-up before the deadline. Quite incredible.

'Another time, a lovely lady from Canada sent us an email which we read out on the pod to surprise her boyfriend, who is apparently our biggest fan, for his birthday. Stuff like that is *so* cool.'

*

The people behind the Always Cheating podcast are rather more sanguine about receiving messages from North America. It's where they live, after all.

They are:

Brandon Kelley: thirty-eight, marketing at a large trade book publisher, NYC/Brooklyn, married, no kids, Fulham supporter.

Josh Landon: thirty-five, marketing director at a non-profit, NYC (work)/Brooklyn (apartment), married, one baby girl, long-suffering Arsenal supporter.

It turns out that Always Cheating came about in similar fashion to The Gaffer Tapes, as Josh explained.

'I think we started it primarily because we needed a way to justify – to ourselves and our significant others – just how obsessed we (and many of our friends in our insanely competitive mini-league) were about the game. For years before we had done a different podcast back when the "two guys talking about nothing" style of podcast was still in vogue (but was it ever, truly, in vogue?).

'The podcast itself is probably a little more personal and less hardcore than your typical Fantasy podcast – it's very much grounded in how the two of us are approaching the game, i.e., two serious, passionate fans but two people who admittedly aren't quants. People seem to like it for just that reason – it's not trying as hard to sell you on a point of view as some of the others.

'Topics include strategy, statistics, predictions, rants, and a fair amount of perspective on the oddity of being a massive FPL fan in a country where mostly people couldn't name a single team in the Premier League.'

Brandon's reasons for following football were fairly standard. 'I've always been a soccer fan. The PL stuck out as an English-speaking league (easier to follow obsessively abroad) with a ton of captivating storylines to follow.'

Josh, however, cites one of the game's more infamous events as the moment he gave himself up to the sport. 'It was really the 2006 World Cup – and Zidane's shocking headbutt – that started me on the path to soccer fandom.'

Fun fact: the exact words that Italian defender Marco Materazzi said to Zidane to provoke the headbutt were 'I prefer the whore that is your sister'. Materazzi's insistence that he would never have insulted Zidane's mother because 'my mother died when I was fifteen' could be seen as an example of moral relativism, whereas on Twitter it would be described as 'banter', or even 'free speech'.

Brandon believes that increasing numbers of Americans 'get' football every time a World Cup comes around. 'Hands down the biggest "Eureka moment" nationally was our nation hosting the World Cup in 1994, which immediately led to the birth of Major League Soccer.

'The Premier League seems to be growing exponentially now, though, especially since NBC (one of our largest TV broadcasters) acquired the Premier League rights in the US and makes every single game available to anyone with even the most basic TV subscription package.'

The time difference is not a major issue for the football (and Fantasy Football) fan in the States. Not on the east coast, anyway. 'Premier League games air very early in the US, which means there's little to no competition on the airwaves during the 7:30–12:30 kick-offs through Saturday morning.'

But there is a genuinely sinister threat awaiting those Americans who give themselves up to football, according to Brandon. 'The only real challenge to fans in America is not getting lumped into another hipster trend piece in The New York Times.

'Otherwise, it's nothing but a pleasure to follow the league Stateside. As for the FPL, there's no doubt it'll grow here as the league itself grows. Through MLB and NFL, Americans are already fantasy sports obsessed.'

*

While Always Cheating has its American roots to help it stand out from the crowd, the relatively new British podcast Who Got The Assist had no such easy selling point when it jumped into what was already an overcrowded pool.

The duo behind the pod are:

Tom Cantle: twenty-eight, lives in London, works for a behavioural science agency but with a background in market research.

Nick Harris: twenty-eight, working in financial services as a client relationship manager for a company in London.

'I've known Tom since the age of twelve as we went to the same secondary school,' said Nick, 'but I only really started speaking to him at the age of fifteen and we initially bonded over the topics of history and politics and, er ... girls and booze.'

Fantasy Football came later, and when they decided to create their podcast, they elected to use their professional expertise to inform their personal obsessions, as Tom explains.

'We want to "hero" the economy in how we approach things, as this has become such a massive part of the game. Nick works in finance, so he applies some of his professional knowledge to give our assertions some more gravitas. But we'll be really thinking about this in how we approach Who Got The Assist as it's the thing we tend to think about most of the time – "xx rising/xx falling" is something we tend to talk about a fair bit.

'Given my job in behavioural science, we mention to some extent the psychology that impacts the FPL manager, perhaps talking about one or two biases per week on our pod.

'Another thought we've had is identifying and calling out the prevailing narratives in the FPL community – we're borrowing the term "meta" from gaming here. By looking at this, naming it (possibly using attempts at humour) and talking about what people are doing – and why they should or maybe shouldn't be listening to the "dominant narrative" – we think is also really interesting for readers/listeners.'

The one key factor linking all these podcasts is that they're hosted by men. But there are alternatives to the 'sausage fest' that is Fantasy Football in general, and podcasting in particular.

FPL Nymfria, a 'thirty-something' graphics professional in the UK, hosts a YouTube channel that details her Fantasy life, providing a running commentary of her season and offering hints and tips to those seeking guidance.

It's not her real name, but the perils of being a woman on social media often demand a level of separation between the online and the real. And, alas, football and sexism continue to go together like Fifa and 'loyalty payments'.

'I started my YouTube channel because I'm passionate about football, especially the Fantasy Football side of things. I wanted to share my experience with others and I noticed there weren't any female YouTubers doing that yet, so I thought I'd see if people were interested in what I had to say about Fantasy Football and, thankfully, the feedback has been pretty good so far.'

The feedback hasn't always been of the positive kind, however. 'I was once asked "how can a woman even play FPL?!" Now, given the gentleman's previous messages, I knew he didn't mean it in a practical manner, like he wanted to know the methods I used to play the game. It was definitely meant in a "you probably shouldn't be playing this" kind of way.

'I've also had other female FPLers share their bad experiences with me, and it's hard to hear/read.'

When she mentioned her experience on Twitter, it ended up trending. 'I had an awful lot of male and female support alike; at the time it even sparked a trending hashtag: #PointyBits.

'It made me realise that the gentleman mentioned above, at least vocally, seemed to be in a minority. I've had a lot of encouragement from all kinds of FPLers whatever their age, sex, religion, etc. In the main, it's a great community to be a part of.'

Nymfria believes that whatever differences there are between men and women count for little when it comes to playing Fantasy Football. 'There's no doubt male and female brains collate and use information differently. That's science.

'But I don't think I play FPL any differently. I don't play FPL "as a woman", I play FPL as "an FPL player". I do all the things anyone else would do to play the best game I possibly can. I check injuries, team news, transfers, etc ... just as anyone else serious about the game would.'

The same can't be said about how she's judged as an FPL player. 'If anything, I have found, purely on personal experience, that I have been judged more harshly on my ability to play the game because I haven't grown up learning about football in the "conventional" way.

'I would say it's mostly true, unfortunately, that the world of Fantasy Football is still a traditionally male world. And not just in Fantasy Football but in football in general. There has been massive headway made in introducing female presenters etc to the game, but as to whether they are there to be taken seriously, or just because of diversity, is a question only the TV broadcasters can answer.

'But the coverage of the brilliant female football teams we have now definitely helps.'

One blogger who has turned the odd football stereotype on its head is FPL Holly, a twenty-seven-year-old teacher from Hull.

Holly – another one happy to keep her full name out of proceedings – is for the most part a classic Fantasy obsessive. 'I spend at least ten hours a week on FPL. I'm constantly refreshing Twitter for any news and losing sleep over captaincy choices. But my husband doesn't like football and can get a bit prickly if I'm spending an excessive amount of time on it.'

Holly produces a weekly blog for the Fplbet website. It's well-written fare, for the most part involving captaincy tips. But there is a twist – she also includes recommendations from her 'Clueless Husband'.

I can already hear the anguished cries of 'sexism!' from a few men out there and, I guess, they have a point to a degree. Flip it and have a male pundit detailing the choices of his 'Useless Wife' and there would be, let's just say, some debate.

But that's probably missing Holly's obvious subversion of the nonsense that women have suffered at the hands of 'normal' football fans since the dawn of footballing time. And, as Nymfria can concur, sexism is still alive and well today.

So I'd like to think that most of us men can just enjoy the irony and revel in the wilfully random choices of a Fantasy manager who once picked Wayne Rooney as his captain because he'd seen the striker in the showbiz section of the Daily Mail that week.

Or, to put it another way: get over it, snowflake. I have, although the fact that Holly's Clueless Husband is currently ahead of me in the overall rankings is proving rather harder to take.

There are myriad excellent FPL pundits out there – Jay Egersdorff, Triggerlips, FPL General and Fantasy YIRMA immediately spring to mind – but there are many more offering sage advice with patience, generosity and sincerity to the fore. In fact, Nymfria's negative experience seems to be a rarity among Fantasy fans on Twitter which, given the inglorious history of that particular platform, is something of a surprise.

There is a genuine sense of an FPL community online, with like-minded individuals providing hints, tips and help to anyone in need free of charge and, to all intents and purposes, on demand.

That, in itself, is pleasing enough. But when you consider that all of us Fantasy managers are essentially in direct competition with each other, that level of sharing, kindness and support is something rather special.

And when real life sticks its cruel little head in, the community can be seen at its finest.

The untimely death, in October 2017, of Twitter stalwart Phil Goldring (aka @FPL_Loon) prompted a stream of heartfelt messages from people who knew the Canada-based Spurs fan only through a mutual love of Fantasy Football.

In one of his last tweets, Phil himself had declared: 'Props to the #FPL community for the sense of belonging to something that an unemployed single guy (no kids) who's not on a team is missing'.

That belonging, ultimately, could not win out over the real-world pressures that engulfed him, but you suspect that a man noted for his warmth and gently mischievous sense of humour would have appreciated the community's move to honour his death by captaining Harry Kane in the Gameweek that followed. Kane racked up sixteen points.

An equally bittersweet tale involved popular FPL manager Simon Humber. A short post on the Transfer Hub blog, run by Triggerlips, appeared at the end of April 2015. 'Simon Humber, one of the original members of Transfer Hub, passed away today. He had been suffering from ocular melanoma, which came as a great surprise to many, as he was always cheerful and never lost his great sense of humour. Taken far too soon, he leaves behind a young son.

'Many of us on Transfer Hub will remember him for his rotation spreadsheet, which he was keen to pass on to the group. He was also a regular poster on Fantasy Football Scout, where he posted under the name Absinthe.

'Around a month ago he posted in the Transfer Hub group, asking which players would be good to buy until the end of the season. Many didn't realise the significance, but he knew he wouldn't be around to manage his team, but still wanted a good finish.

'Dedicated until the end.'

The awful news produced a wave of reaction – fond memories of a well-liked player, requests for information on where to send charitable donations and even, from Triggerlips himself, the news that 'next season our league will be named the Simon Humber Cup, there will also be a trophy in his honour'.

His final post on Fantasy Football Scout was a simple 'cheers all', a thank you that was to be reciprocated in a truly beautiful way by his employers. Simon worked as the creative director on EA Sports' FIFA series of football games, which prompted a tribute from EA's VP and GM for the game, David Rutter.

'When you make video games, you spend a great deal of time with people, and shipping an annual title makes a team very close. I worked with Simon daily for seven years and feel like I – and the team – lost a family member. In terms of his legacy within FIFA, he was the daddy of Ultimate Team, and played a big role in career mode – many of the features coming this year were ones he was leading development on.'

Simon was a huge Portsmouth fan and the company decided to honour their man by including Fratton Park in FIFA 16. That, in itself, was a lovely touch, but if you have a copy of the game, take a look behind the goal and you'll find a small wreath of flowers laid to honour Simon's life and loves. An FPL mini-league called The Simon Humber Trophy continues to thrive, with more than 330 teams taking part during the 2017–18 season, and Fantasy Football Scout (FFS) members My Pretty Pony and TopMarx organised a charity football tournament in his honour in 2018.

As mentioned, Simon was an active member of the FFS website. It is a site that dominates the Fantasy landscape for any number of reasons, most of them revolving around its founder, Mark Sutherns.

At this point that I am duty bound to declare a major conflict of interest here. I have been writing, in various guises, for FFS for a number of years. I'm a freelancer, but Mark is the nearest thing I have to a boss these days. You'll just have to trust me when I say that what follows is as unbiased and accurate an account as I can possibly muster.

His story is a tale of the rise and rise of someone who is the closest thing Fantasy Football has to an ultimate pundit.

To even get the commission to write for FFS, I had to beat hundreds of other applicants, apparently. That didn't alert me as to the seriousness of the website. I was just happy to have landed a regular role that paid well – two more clues that I wasn't dealing with some fly-by-night operation.

When I was informed that I would be helping out on articles for the FPL website, written under the pseudonym The Scout, it finally started to dawn on me that Mark had his fingers in some serious Fantasy pies.

After a season's worth of articles, I knew Mark to be fairly demanding/a perfectionist, but an otherwise patient person who wouldn't let copy go out in The Scout's name without it being just so. Considering he ended up rewriting much of what I produced, I wasn't confident that I'd be getting any repeat business. I was wrong, fortunately.

The next season he upped the work, this time for The Sun Dream Team site and ESPN's Fantasy game. I also got to write about the official Uefa game for the 2016 European Championship, as well as a new 'Daily Fantasy Sports' offering from American company DraftKings.

FFS, I began to realise, was a bit of a go-to brand when it came to providing expert tips and coverage of nearly all the big official Fantasy games. All these major players, from FPL to governing bodies to global media companies, were coming to this obscure English website for partnership deals.

Except it wasn't that obscure. Not in the Fantasy Football world.

FPL winners used its extensive, members-only statistics area and cited its Rate My Team software as a major help in them securing their title. High quality, in-depth articles were published daily and, as I had seen first-hand, tie-in deals were in place with companies both nationally and across the world.

FFS, as neither William nor Craig Shakespeare has ever put it, was some serious shit.

It is one of the more curious aspects of life as an online writer that you often end up developing a good working relationship with someone you've never physically met. I finally got to shake Mark Sutherns by the hand and look him in the eye – he's a fairly gangly man so I had to look up – some three years after he first started paying me. I knew what he looked like by then because FFS had signed a major deal with the Premier League to massively expand the coverage The Scout would produce on a now daily basis for the FPL site.

That deal allowed Mark to dedicate himself full-time to being a Fantasy Football pundit, writing daily articles and appearing on social media and as the resident expert on the weekly TV show on the FPL website. It was a meteoric rise that had turned a do-it-yourself-when-you-get-back-home-from-work venture into, arguably, the world's biggest independent website dedicated solely to Fantasy Football. And, as it turned out, it was all down to Mark's childhood incompetence.

'When I was a kid, my dad managed a football team. But I was rubbish at football, so bad that I wasn't even good enough to get into a team run by my own dad.

'So I started learning as much as I could about football. I was buying Rothmans Football Yearbooks and reading them, literally reading them from cover to cover. I built an encyclopedic knowledge of football from the age of eight onwards as a way to get my dad to notice me.'

The Sutherns' household was already a bit of a knowledge palace. Mark's father was a semi-professional quizzer who had appeared on television, his pub team winning ITV's World of Sport quiz title. Reference books were everywhere, the thirst for knowledge a given, football at its core.

And, to an impressionable eight-year-old, seeing his father on the telly cemented the notion that knowing stuff could take you places.

The foundations were in place and were then built upon by another classic British, do-it-from-your-shed enterprise – the Championship Manager computer game. 'The Collyer brothers [the game's creators] were heroes of my childhood. They created the game in their bedroom and Fantasy Football just took that further.

'It was a way of pitting myself against my friends – that's the essence of it, trying to beat your mates at something that quantifies your knowledge of football.

'When Fantasy Football came along, I thought this was something I could play and use my knowledge, turn my knowledge into something useful. I was quite a social person with it. I liked the typical things you talk to blokes about. I had a lot of close friends and we used to feed off each other.

'When Fantasy Football arrived, we were going to join a league and do it religiously. I'd stay behind and photocopy all the stats, set up a database, etc. I was well into the data behind it from the start.

'And there was an element of loving numbers – I knew appearances and goals for players, all that stuff. So I looked at numbers as a way of getting better at the game. But it was mainly another way of proving I knew about football.'

Grown-up Mark had moved to Bath and was working as a computer games writer before taking a marketing job in London for a games company. Fantasy Football was a major part of his personal, but not professional, life by then.

'I was doing some forum work and there was this guy on one of them, about Fantasy Football, called Granville, and I remember saying "who is this guy? He thinks he knows it all".

'And the bloke standing behind me just said "that's me".'

Granville, aka Lee Cowen (or in Mark's words 'an opinionated Mancunian'), introduced him to FPL. A friendly rivalry sprang up – one that endures to this day and can be heard on the FFS ScoutCast – and the idea to create a Fantasy Football website grew from that. 'Had I not met Granville, I probably wouldn't have bothered setting up the site.

'I remember coming home from work and seeing a hundred people had been on the site. I was delighted. I loved it. Bit by bit it grew and

I realised there were other people out there who were interested and it snowballed.'

The site was still just a hobby at that stage, costing Mark £20 a month in hosting fees and the time he could spare after work to keep it updated and running as smoothly as possible. Except it wasn't running smoothly at all.

'Every Saturday morning, when people were picking their teams, the website used to go down. It couldn't take the traffic. I'd have to ring the host to try and get the site back up. It was horrible. And then the host rang me at work one day to say we're taking you off our server because you're crashing all the other websites as well.

'I had no revenue at that point and it was suddenly going to cost me £250 a month for a new host. I had to figure out a way to make money or just close it down.'

Bookmaker Paddy Power was invited to advertise on the site. They came along, saw the traffic and agreed. And they weren't the only ones to see the commercial potential of a site pulling in ever increasing numbers of visitors.

'I got an email from a couple of Americans who offered me fifty grand for 50 per cent of the business and another fifty grand as a salary. I didn't know what to do. It was tempting, but I didn't really trust them.'

Mark turned to an old colleague from his Bath days, Chris James, who had since branched out into mobile gaming. 'We talked about the idea of monetising the site. I looked at the US Fantasy sites and saw what they were doing. I took the model they used – members' areas and the like – and it all fitted into place.

'I loved the stats and the data. It was feeding my own obsession and I thought that if I can use this stuff, people might pay money to access them. I didn't have money for the Opta licence, so Chris put in the money for a stake in the business.'

FFS became the first site to offer paying members use of football statistics to help inform their Fantasy Football decisions.

Mark built it – and they came.

'I got two and a bit thousand members in the first year and made a profit. I didn't really have any ambitions to take it beyond that. If I made a couple of grand a year, I was happy.

'But I was spending three or four hours after work on it every day. I couldn't let it go then. The members made me think there was something in this, as did the Americans' interest.

'The other turning point came when we were asked to pay a licence fee for the fixtures.'

That was a watershed moment for many small, independent websites and football fanzines. A company called Football DataCo appeared and began demanding money from anyone who published football fixtures. Their argument was that the fixtures were an intellectual property owned by the footballing authorities.

As a result, the company began charging a standard fee for the reproduction of fixture lists, which currently stands at £266 plus VAT to print the fixtures of one English club. Newspapers printing the fixtures of all clubs are charged around £3,931 plus VAT by DataCo for a date-ordered listing.

For Mark, it required him to make a major decision. 'It was a lot of money. The site had to become more professional to make money, to turn it from a hobby into a business. It went from a labour of love to a full-time job.

'I never wanted that, I just wanted it to be a bit of fun. But I'm very grateful for where I am, for all the support from the members and the people who have helped out. Chris effectively transformed my hobby into a business and has masterminded its growth ever since. Indeed, I've been very fortunate to get the right help at the right time. For example, I met Ed (Eliot) – our Technical Director – just when we needed to develop the site. I was at my fiancé's best friend's wedding and it just so happened that I was sat next to a lady who was married to an elite web developer with time on his hands. You can't buy or learn that kind of luck.'

Although Mark is coy about detailing just how many members the site now has, it's definitely more than the original 'two and a bit thousand'. Throw in partnership deals with the Premier League, Uefa, Sky, Yahoo and various others and you've got compelling evidence of the real money that can be made from a prime spot in Fantasy Town.

Running a website about a game is one thing. Becoming a world-renowned (in the rarefied world of Fantasy Football, that is) expert in your field is quite another. It takes knowledge, experience and a proven track record.

Mark has all three.

His Sutherns Comfort team finished its first FPL season, in 2006–07, in 2,217th place. A similar result followed the next year, and then he jumped to 268th in 2008–09. He's been outside the top 30,000 just the once, and has added finishes of 382nd, 115th and a career-best forty-second (in 2014–15) to his CV.

It's therefore no surprise that he consistently features in the higher reaches of the Hall of Fame all-time best managers table published by FFS.

A natural worrier who often agonises over whether to bring in new content or commercial partners for his website, it's entirely predictable that the same nervous energy infuses his choices as a Fantasy manager. 'There are decisions that haunt you. A Sanchez/Hazard decision from the 2016–17 season, I made the transfer at 1 a.m. and I was up all night. The mood swings you get, I don't want it to, but they are pretty ridiculous.'

Throw in the added ingredient of being a fully paid up pundit, and it's a wonder he sleeps at all.

'Every transfer you make matters. It affects you. Where I am now, I have to go in front of a camera and talk about it. I can justify my obsession because of that. I'm lucky. But I want my team to do well, and also the players that I pick for others to do well.

'I care so much about my professionalism and what I do now. I want to give sound advice, to prove that there's an element of skill in the game.

'It's harder because there's a bit of pressure on it. You're aware that you've built yourself up, and others have too. It becomes a bit more of a burden.'

When a new FPL season comes around, I just hope that I'll do roughly as well as the last one. Mark, however, is in it to win it. But the fact that he's playing the game in full view of millions of managers worldwide adds an extra level of pressure to the whole business.

'I look at a season with excitement as well as trepidation. The more you chase it, the harder it gets. But if you're going to be at the top, you're going to have to expect that. We've created a world where FPL matters a lot to a lot of people. There is pressure once you get near to the top, but I enjoy putting that pressure on others as well.

'We want to sell this game to people, tell them that this is a good thing. So when people win it, we want to go "you're not going to be forgotten".'

So how does he go about being one of the best Fantasy Football managers out there? 'I never make a decision without backing it up. You can make a mistake, but if I make one and look back and see why, that makes me feel secure in making those decisions.

'If I make a gut-feeling decision it's not enough for me. I never do it. I build a case for and against and weigh it all up. Nothing is done quickly. I do the research. If I did something purely on gut instinct, I would beat myself up for weeks about it.

'This is the level I do it at. I have to justify it as I write and broadcast about it.'

Seeing as he created a website based on his love of data, that too comes into the equation. But one of the sources of that information is not of the standard, stats-in-a-table, kind.

'It can come down to a comment a manager has made the day before in a press conference that triggers something and makes me think he's going to do that, or play that guy. It can be such a minute detail that can swing things your way. No algorithm in the world can examine Jose Mourinho's stance, tone of voice or body language to interpret what that means to his selections the next day better than you or I can. It's not gut instinct, it's your impression.

'Every Premier League manager, I build up a relationship with. I know, almost, that I can read Wenger or Mourinho to an extent. You watch an interview and make a comment on it. You can see what they say, and what they don't say. This is all data.'

And although Mark does use the range of predictive and team-rating software that is out there and available for all Fantasy managers, he's in no way wedded to the idea that technology is all you need to succeed.

'I don't buy the idea of people who've never played Fantasy Football being able to use a bit of software which will make them win it. I just don't buy that. I hope not, as well.

'Part of it is the emotion of it, the investment you put into it based on your decision-making process. It's not me doing it if it's based on a cold piece of software. You're abandoning all responsibility for your decisions. Yes, the algorithms will feed into my decision. I'm not saying they don't work, but I don't believe they will enable a new breed of dominant Fantasy Football manager. There's so many elements to breed success that I don't think there's any danger of it becoming a cold, calculated pursuit.

'I think there's a breed of player out there with strategy and experience who are getting better and better, honing their skills season by season and they're going to win it. The top 500 is populated by managers who've been there and done it.'

Mark is one of them.

And for the rest of us to ever dream of getting anywhere close to these people, we're going to need his eye for detail – the eye that, for instance, views a press conference as a means of gaining a tiny, but possibly, vital piece of data that means he ends up buying a player who is actually going to make a difference.

It seems almost laughably obvious, but every Fantasy manager will have seen a player, been sold on that player and then brought him in, only for this bright new hope to end up on the subs' bench or, worse still, not even in the squad at all.

Avoiding such schoolboy errors takes more than schoolboy knowledge. It requires commitment, dedication and, above all else, time.

These attributes have served Mark Sutherns very well, both as a Fantasy Football manager and as the creator of a global Fantasy brand. If we can bottle them, they might do the same for us. Without the global brand bit.

And I did play football as a kid, and beyond. I wasn't brilliant but was once tapped up to play for a rival Thursday night six-a-side league team, so that's at least one thing I will always be better at than Mark 'The Scout' Sutherns.

CHAPTER THIRTEEN

THE FUTURE

Over the past three decades, I've been able to track the increasing popularity of Fantasy Football by the reactions of people to its very mention.

So, in the 1990s it would elicit a raised eyebrow and a shrug that said 'I have no idea what you're talking about and wish this to remain the case as I don't like football and am unsure as to your motives regarding the word fantasy'.

By the 2000s, this had been replaced by a frown of dim recollection, as if the person had either dreamt about something similar, or perhaps once heard about it on the news. A similar reaction could be also obtained by asking people to name the capital of Djibouti.

Since the turn of the present decade, the default response has become an understated, but generally confident, nod of recognition, usually followed by an admission that someone they know plays the game.

Fantasy Football might not be mainstream just yet, but it's really only a matter of time.

The main game, FPL, grows bigger, and at a greater rate, year by year. Draft games either pick up new fans or retain ever-loyal armies of old ones. Even within the newspaper industry – a sector that has been beaten close to death by the internet – a title's Fantasy Football game tends to remain alive, kicking and probably one of the main reasons why some people still feel any loyalty to that particular brand.

Fantasy Football even has its own magazine these days. Its founder, Jamie Reeves, has a long, and mostly successful, Fantasy history.

'The first league I ever played in was calculated by the league admin, who would total up scores manually and you'd have to write to him to make changes. After every match week he'd post you a letter with each team's total score and an updated version of the league table.

'In my young age, I always wondered why he chose to print these off in faded pink, but looking back that's probably due to the fact his ink cartridges were always running low due to printing hundreds of pages each week.'

Having lived through the formative years of Fantasy Football, he was well placed to see the marked effect it was having on some like-minded souls.

'I once met a guy with Demba Ba tattooed on his backside thanks to FPL.

'I met the arse-tattoo guy in Turkey. If I remember correctly, he was a Man United fan and he got the Demba Ba tattoo to pay homage to his FPL performance during that famous season at Newcastle [Ba scored sixteen goals, at a dirt cheap price, in 2011–12]. At my time of meeting him, Ba had just joined Chelsea, so he wasn't feeling quite so great about his decision.'

Jamie decided – as far as anyone knows, that is – not to decorate his own backside with his own favourite player, instead turning to writing about Fantasy Football online. He soon realised that he was operating in an increasingly crowded market, which got him thinking.

'The Fantasy Football industry has displayed year-on-year growth for as long as I can remember, and subsequently I felt that the tipster market had started to become somewhat saturated and formulaic.

'I wanted to create a place to showcase the best and most useful articles, to promote my favourite writers and their most forward-thinking topics, and most importantly, to ensure the occasional diamonds in the rough are not missed.'

That showcase turned out to be a magazine about Fantasy Football which, after presumably seconds of brainstorming and focus group goalthink granularity going forward, was called Fantasy Football Magazine.

'I only ever intended this to be released digitally, but after an avalanche of messages asking for a printed version, I figured out the logistics and launched a crowdfunding campaign to cover the start-up costs involved with launching a print publication.'

Jamie was taken aback by the success of that funding campaign. So quick did he raise the cash that he even lived to regret a Twitter-based call to arms that promised he'd captain Sunderland's Victor Anichebe – a Fantasy Football legend for all the wrong reasons – during a Double Gameweek towards the end of the 2016–17 season if his funding target was met ahead of schedule.

Sure enough, the target was reached and Anichebe took the armband, lasting a full thirty minutes of the first match before getting injured and bringing Jamie a massive one-point – doubled, of course – haul.

Not that he cared in the long run. By the time the crowdfunding campaign was done, his initial target of £7,500 had become an £11,595 final figure – a 155 per cent return.

'I can only talk from the experience of somebody who grew up in the 90s, when Fantasy Football was still print-based, but I honestly feel that it's now ingrained within our culture here.'

Ingrained it may be, but that wasn't enough to keep Fantasy Football Magazine afloat. Despite – or actually because of – the magazine being a highly professional and beautifully designed product, only a handful of issues were produced before Jamie and his team had to mothball the entire project.

They cited a number of reasons, but the bottom line was that the magazine was simply too expensive to create and distribute. Costs were being covered and commissions honoured, which meant that everyone but the team behind the enterprise was getting paid.

As an email sent to subscribers declared: 'Unfortunately, the fees involved with producing a quality magazine (image licences, print & distribution, design, etc) proved harder and harder to cover when operating independently. Despite overwhelming support from our readers, it is no longer viable to continue publishing.'

But as Jamie told me: 'It just needs a big re-evaluation and a new strategy.' So we might not have seen the last of Fantasy Football Magazine.

Jamie and his team weren't the only ones to see the commercial potential in Fantasy Football's growth and a major threat to the UK Fantasy status quo appeared in 2016.

Daily Fantasy Sports (DFS) revolutionised sports betting in America. It did so mostly by not being betting at all.

The concept was simple – deposit money into a website account, pay a stake to enter a particular game and win money if your entry beat other people's. The games were based on tried and trusted American Fantasy sports – baseball, basketball and American football – but with a twist. Instead of investing huge amounts of time and effort creating a Fantasy team to do battle with opponents over an entire season, DFS enabled you to pick players involved in fixtures on one particular day.

Typically, you would build a mini-team of, say, eight players who were playing for maybe six teams across three fixtures. You would then enter your selection in a contest involving a set limit of other Fantasy managers for a guaranteed prize pot.

The winner would take home the main cash prize, but payouts would usually extend to around half of all the players involved, enabling many to at least recoup their stake. There were no rollovers or void results and it was not a case of the house winning and you losing – there had to be winners. The money was there to be won, with the games' organisers taking their cut from those managers whose teams performed the worst.

DFS proved to be an instant hit in America because online sports gambling was illegal. Two main companies emerged as the new market's big hitters – FanDuel and DraftKings – and once they settled the question that DFS was truly a game of skill, not luck, and therefore not actually betting at all, they grew very large very quickly.

As FanDuel's co-founder and CEO Nigel Eccles told Scottish newspaper the Daily Record in a 2016 interview: 'Fantasy sports has been played in the US for fifty years. It's played by over fifty million people and there really hasn't been any question until recently about its legality. There's clear federal laws, there's clear case laws about Fantasy sports.

'I think what we have really seen in the last six months is that the explosion in the daily Fantasy market has brought the attention to the fore. I think the question has more been about how do we regulate this industry?

'This has become a multi-billion-dollar industry – there needs to be appropriate consumer protection and regulation in place. That's where the bulk of the discussion has been and that's where our focus is.'

The new industry was not without controversy, as Mr Eccles alluded to in his mention of 'appropriate consumer protection and regulation'.

Allegations of 'insider dealing' between employees of FanDuel and DraftKings emerged, with DraftKings workers supposedly making $6 million on their rival's website. Both companies denied the claims, but subsequently banned their employees from playing for money on rival websites.

The hard-won notion – proved by a number of studies commissioned by DFS companies – that this new strand of sports betting was not betting at all also created another negative issue. Because skilled players consistently won, thereby demonstrating that luck did not play the key part in their success, the casual DFS player was little more than a minnow to be devoured by the sharks, at least according to an article in the Sports Business Journal.

'Investors are overlooking a fundamental operating challenge: the risk that the skill element of daily fantasy is so high that DFS pros will wipe out recreational players in short order. For a real-money contest to achieve sustained popularity, it needs the right balance of skill versus luck. Chess is popular but almost no one plays it for money because it's far too skill-based; the better player wins almost every time.

'Poker thrives because an amateur can beat the best players in the world. Indeed, on June 13 at the World Series of Poker, a fifty-one-year-old football coach defeated seven pros in the final table of a $5,000 tournament to win $567,000.

'DFS affords a huge advantage to skilled players. In the first half of the 2015 MLB [Major League Baseball] season, 91 per cent of DFS player profits were won by just 1.3 per cent of players.'

Online poker had been a huge business precisely because mug punters could mix it with the big boys (and girls) and they could get lucky. It was great news for the little man, so it ended up getting banned in the US.

The research proved that this was not the case with DFS. As a game of skill, it became legal and hugely popular. But as a game of too much skill, the threat was that its popularity would soon wane.

That didn't stop both FanDuel and DraftKings enthusiastically leaping into the UK and European market, with the huge popularity of Fantasy Football in general, and the Fantasy Premier League in particular, key reasons for their move.

In a world of attention deficit disorder, snap actions and instant rewards, DFS was the zeitgeist-tapping solution to a problem we didn't even realise we had, what with it being too long and involved to consider in the first place. FanDuel and DraftKings dreamt of a product that would 'bring the excitement of an entire season down to one day'.

'I would say the UK market is a bit like the US market when we launched in 2009,' Eccles said in the Daily Record interview. 'I think that our product is a step change better. It's a completely mobile experience.

'Not only does it collapse that season down into one day, the drafting experience is faster and slicker, the player information is great, the live scoring experience is just really fast and exciting.

'In essence, we think this is the future of Fantasy Football in the UK.'

Anyone wondering why Eccles would be so thoroughly quoted in a Scottish newspaper is to be applauded for their perception. The reason was simple and a nice twist to the story in itself: FanDuel had conquered America, but it was a Scottish start-up.

It started out as Hubdub, an Edinbugh-based web platform that enabled users to bet virtual money on predicting real-world events such as presidential elections.

As Eccles told the Venturebeat website: '2008 was an election year, and we thought it would be cool to build a prediction market where you could predict the outcome of running news stories. And the election was one of the biggest ones.

'Users loved it; we had a ton of engagement. But the fatal flaw was that there wasn't really a business model. So even though we were getting the scale in users, we just couldn't figure out how we would turn it into an interesting business.'

At that point, Hubdub employed seven people and had raised venture capital investment for what threatened to be a classic internet business – great idea, really popular, but nobody wanted to pay for it.

The team headed to an industry event, South by Southwest (SXSW) in Austin, Texas, to try to figure out what to do. 'We said we seem to know how to build games that people like to engage with, but we really want something with more of a robust business model,' explained Eccles. 'And we also wanted something that people were willing to pay for.'

From a series of brainstorming sessions, DFS was born. Eight years on, FanDuel were employing 360 people in New York, Orlando, Los Angeles and, true to its Scottish roots, Glasgow.

Prior to the big European push, the firm had raised $275 million, with investors such as Google Capital and Time Warner eager to get their slice of a DFS pie that was about to conquer the world just as it had the States.

News that FanDuel and DraftKings were planning to merge and create an uber-DFS conglomerate merely strengthened the certainty that the UK and Europe, with its quaint attachment to season-long Fantasy Football played for little or no financial reward, was about to get a very nasty shock to its system indeed.

The year following Nigel Eccles' interview with the Daily Record was an eventful one. And mostly disastrous.

I never played FanDuel myself, although the reports I heard from those that had were mixed, but mostly positive. I did try the DraftKings version, during Euro 2016, and was monumentally shit at it.

That was not a criticism of the game itself. It was entirely down to me. I did enjoy, to a degree, the immediacy of it all. You could watch a match in which your players were featuring and see, in real time, the consequences their on-pitch actions were having to your overall score.

And those actions were diverse. The scoring system could not be accused of a lack of depth. Yes, goals and assists were vital, but players also picked up points for making crosses or tackles, for instance. And they lost points for being tackled or committing a foul.

It was, in short, an exhausting affair as I saw relatively minor occurrences on the pitch having major impacts on my overall score. The rush of seeing your man score a goal was, in many ways, far more intense than that experienced in good old FPL or a season-long draft game. It was all the other rushes and downs, large and small, that were the issue.

DFS, to me anyway, was overstimulating, adding so many extra layers of involvement in a match as to render it overwhelming. I struggled to enjoy a match in which a poorly timed tackle from an Austrian centre back left me cursing my selectorial stupidity. Then again, I struggled to enjoy watching Austria at all during Euro 2016.

I was one of those DFS minnows being swallowed whole by the sharks and it was not a particularly pleasant experience. And I was getting paid for it.

But that was just me, and the generally negative experience of one especially hapless user was the least of FanDuel's or DraftKings' worries.

For starters, the US regulators had not taken kindly to their planned merger, with the Federal Trade Commission announcing plans to seek a preliminary injunction to block the move. They claimed it would have given the wannabe behemoth more than 90 per cent of the DFS market, aka a monopoly.

The other problem was the loyalty many Fantasy Football players outside the States clearly felt towards the likes of FPL.

As I wrote a good deal earlier in this book, there is a strange dichotomy at the heart of Fantasy Premier League. On the one hand, you have a major global player with brand awareness and a rampant money-making machine at its core. On the other, the game it has begotten is a mainly-for-fun, purists' delight that wins you a nice holiday and a selection of sponsored baubles.

Money might have been a huge Premier League driver for some, but it was well down the FPL pecking order for most, confined to wholly unofficial mini-leagues in which players could win a few quid here or there. The vast majority don't play FPL for the money, they do it for the love.

The major reason for that was – and still is – the fact that online sports gambling in the UK is not illegal. Nor is it seen as some kind of shady, Mafia-driven hotbed of crime and grime, as anyone who has had to sit through the interminable in-play sports betting adverts on television will confirm. I mean, I love a bit of Ray Winstone, but I want him hitting a fellow Borstal boy with a sock full of snooker balls, or wearing a way too tight pair of nasty yellow trunks. I do not want him to tell me, for the thousandth fucking time, that the only way is to in-play with Ray.

There is a clear demarcation over here that those DFS giants over there failed to grasp, or at least thought they could break down: we like to play Fantasy Football and we like to bet on sports. What we can't seem to be arsed to do is combine the two.

In 2017, a year after launching big in the UK, FanDuel announced it was pulling out.

It was an appropriately skewed end to what had been a topsy-turvy beginning. The Brits, after all, were meant to break America only after conquering their own damp little patch. FanDuel had gone about it the wrong way round.

The stories of UK pop bands, actors, TV presenters and countless other talented and popular people, and Piers Morgan, trying and failing to make it big in America were legion. They would then return to Blighty, their hubristic tails between their legs, to pursue careers involving varying levels of what-might-have-been bitterness.

FanDuel flipped all that on its head, failing to break their home turf and slinking back to America to the comfort of their billion-dollar enterprise.

Not that DFS has entirely given up. As Jamie Reeves points out, there are other players in the reckoning.

'FanDuel and DraftKings withdrawing from the UK market was a huge blow for daily Fantasy over here. We needed those guys to invest massively, offering big enough pools (they have milli-makers in the US, where average Joes like us win a million on Fantasy) to tilt the FPL paradigm and attract those stubborn season-long purists.

'The main player now is Yahoo, but Premier Punt and FanTeam are two that survived the DFS exodus and now operate in their second or third years.

'As for the new boys, Dribble (affiliated with Sky) is an interesting product, meanwhile Fantasfida opened up last year and have a very sleek product. But I think we're starting to accept that DFS will never compete with FPL in the UK. It's almost a cultural loyalty that we play FPL season-long and bet on sports books weekly.'

One of the DFS new boys seeking to fill the vacuum created by the travails of FanDuel and DraftKings is Sportito, UK-based but with its trademark owned by an Italian firm called ASAP Italia. The brand is already 'the Official Fantasy Sports partner of QPR and Burnley

FC' – further proof of the ongoing assimilation of Fantasy Football into the sporting mainstream – and one of its cheerleaders is the well-respected pundit FPL General, who also goes by the name of Mark McGettigan.

Mark writes a column for the Sportito website, but is under no illusions as to the challenges all DFS operators face.

'Most people don't know what daily Fantasy Football is. I was surprised by how many folk I interact with on Twitter, who have been playing FPL for years, who are unfamiliar with DFS. One guy wrote to me asking "what is daily Fantasy Football?" And he was from the UK.'

Mark also believes some may be put off by worries over online identity theft and fraud – to play DFS, after all, requires people to hand over bank and credit card details. But the major obstacle remains the trip that Fantasy Premier League has on the majority.

'The number one challenge is getting Fantasy Football enthusiasts to part with their hard-earned cash when the best platform (FPL) is free. For most fantasy managers, FPL is enough for them, they are not interested in playing daily Fantasy Football.

'Serious FPL managers will have invested cash in mini-leagues at the start of the season, therefore may be unwilling to put cash into daily Fantasy sites.'

Both the initial failure of DFS to wow abroad like it did at home in the USA and the struggle for recognition the new outfits are experiencing point to the enduring strength of the established Fantasy Football models in the UK country and beyond.

One of the reasons behind that strength, according to another popular pundit, the Christmas Island cheerleader Chief, @FPLHints, revolves around something that money simply can't buy.

'We sometimes take FPL too seriously for our own good and I have no doubt more casual managers have become addicts, which makes it harder to get a higher rank in FPL. But as a result of this influx, the FPL community has grown and is growing. Fantasy Football has gone mainstream.

'One of the reasons why I continue to play FPL is due to the friendships and rapport that I have built over the years. Because of that, I still like giving advice on an ad hoc basis.

'At the end of the day, it's a game that lets us forget about the mundane reality of life, even if it's for a couple of hours on a Saturday.'

As for the numerous draft games out there, the future seems to be equally bright.

Simon Wardle was the Draft Fantasy Football champion in 2016–17, an achievement that has led to a number of writing jobs within the draft game industry, although his win had particular resonance for him rather closer to home.

'Best of all, I got to tell my daughter that I was the best in the world at something, and she was impressed. My wife? Not so much.'

Simon is convinced that the attempts of FPL to get in on the draft act with the launch of their own draft game in 2017–18 will actually strengthen the hand of the more established operators in the field.

'I firmly believe that it will only be a positive thing as it spreads the draft word to a much larger base. And once players see that there is a superior product already out there that is a couple of years ahead in development already, then they will jump ship.

'The big selling point of having both your salary cap and draft on one site is not enough of a deal-breaker for me as it really is not that hard to balance multiple games, especially with apps nowadays.

'Personally, I will be sticking with the tried and true, glitch-free option.'

Simon is equally bullish about the strength of Fantasy Football – be it draft or salary cap – when pitted against Daily Fantasy Sports. In fact, he believes they can complement each other.

'The emergence of daily Fantasy games is also going to keep the Fantasy growth going as this is a great method for the casuals to get involved without having to be committed to a whole season of monitoring their teams.

'I know this sounds crazy to us hardcore players, but not all out there are as obsessed as we are.'

So FPL is booming, draft games flourishing and even DFS, despite the setbacks, might well find its niche in Europe. Is there anything that can go wrong? The worry, for some, is that we are on the verge of 'Peak Fantasy'.

Poker player and FPL blogger Martin Coleman is one of those worriers. Actually, ex-player is more apt – he drifted away from online poker when it was banned in the US. As a high-rolling shark, the ban deprived him of a regular supply of online lunch, making steady earning that much harder to rely on.

'Notwithstanding the fact that women were becoming increasingly successful, "Man wins poker tournament" was the sarcastic headline that best captured the moment the poker community reached peak poker.

'My induction into the world of tournament poker coincided with the boom I described the genesis of in a blog. It also coincided with the launch of poker magazines on newsagents' shelves.

'I recorded the growing numbers of popular poker shows on TV. I craved more in-depth study of my new subject though, so I ventured online and found poker chat rooms, forums and strategy websites springing up everywhere.

'I bought and read the books that these sites signposted me to. Social media entered the fray, and I found myself increasingly plugged in to the travelling circuses that were the likes of the European Poker Tour (EPT) and World Series of Poker (WSOP), and the first podcasts I ever listened to were poker-specific.

'And then "Man wins poker tournament", and I realised I was bored of it all. I'd read the poker equivalent of the Kama Sutra, but there's only so many ways you can play a hand. I became unfaithful.

'Truth be told, I had already been having a bit on the side. I'm not ashamed to admit there was overlap between my old relationship and my new one. Yes, you guessed it, I'd found Fantasy Football.'

Dirty, cheating Fantasy slut he might be, but Martin was still clean enough of mind to notice the trends he'd seen developing in the poker world were also being played out in Fantasy land – but in reverse.

'Because of technological advances perhaps, my Fantasy Football journey began with social media, on to websites, then podcasts, YouTube videos, and I've not long since passed a magazine launch, with the next stop a dedicated book due out next year.'

Never mind Peak Fantasy, Martin just managed 'Peak Meta': referencing a book in the book to which the reference refers.

'Maybe it's a case of once bitten, twice shy, but I feel like peak Fantasy Football is on the horizon. There are already countless Twitter accounts, innumerable websites and enough podcasts to fill an entire week's listening schedule. There's only so many ways you can choose a captain. When faced with too much choice, we can feel overwhelmed and not choose at all.'

Jamie Reeves disagrees. 'The future is looking good. It's a concept that really satisfies a diverse demographic. We are nowhere near peak fantasy.'

Fantasy Football Scout's Mark Sutherns backs that point up. 'I can't see saturation point yet. The Premier League is a huge and popular spectacle. I don't see that diminishing. It's football. That's going to be around for ever and the PL will be at or near the pinnacle of it.'

So what is still to come if we're not at the peak just yet?

'I think Fantasy Football is getting more into the mainstream,' Mark adds. 'I think the time will come when we see matches analysed on TV. We will see pundits analysing the game in Fantasy terms. It's a way of talking about player and team form. The audience is clearly there. It would be silly if that wasn't recognised.

'The broadcasters will figure out that the audience is out there for the game to be spoken about through the lens of Fantasy Football. You can talk generally about Fantasy Football. FPL is the dominant game, but looking at football from a more general Fantasy perspective is possible. The rules overlap.'

The 2016–17 FPL winner, Ben Crabtree, also cites television as the next step. 'Commentators and pundits now throw in occasional comments about someone ruining a Fantasy week or being a great pick, so there is a lot more awareness about it.

'I think it could eventually mirror American sports. People love the Premier League and the audience is global compared with American sports, for instance. I'm in a league with my Australian friends from when I lived there. They were already huge fans of the game and got me on to a TV programme called The League, which is actually about an NFL fantasy league.

'An FPL version of this programme with a subtle Office-style humour, not necessarily documentary style, would be brilliant.'

I'm not so sure about that, but if there are any Hollywood executives out there willing to pay for a movie treatment, there's got to be room in the script for an incredibly warm and wise writerly figure, voiced by Morgan Freeman, or perhaps played by George Clooney.

Jamie Reeves is another expert expecting a small-screen boom. 'Univision, the largest Spanish-speaking channel operating in the US, have their own Fantasy game for Liga MX and their broadcasters highlight players and their Fantasy prices whilst the actual game is taking place.

'Whether or not FPL will reach that level of integration is hard to say, and it does depend somewhat on the commercialisation of the game. But we've seen this begin to happen in the UK with Sky Sports advertising their SkyBet Fantasy Six-A-Side product ahead of live broadcasted matches.'

And he's willing to see things go a lot further than that. 'Wait until we're all plugged into our VR headsets with an FPL overlay on live matches and leagues popping up at half-time.'

If I thought watching Austria while playing DraftKings was overwhelming, I clearly ain't seen nothing yet.

CHAPTER FOURTEEN

IMPROVEMENT

I have played Fantasy Football since the mid-1990s and Fantasy Premier League from its first full season onwards. I have been an enthusiastic, dedicated and loyal Fantasy fan; never giving up, always striving.

Unfortunately, what I've also never been is any good.

Before the 2016–17 FPL season, my best-ever finish was 35,961st in 2006–07, with an honourable mention for 2008–09's 55,055th. And in the interests of balance and full disclosure, it would be remiss of me not to cite 2012–13's worst-ever 894,555th or the equally shambolic 771,871st two years earlier than that.

My biggest problem was a stubborn refusal to be in any way disciplined or logical in the way I played the game. I loved taking wild punts on unproven players based on nothing more logical or scientific than 'fuck it, you never know'. As a result, some of the world's biggest Fantasy turkeys have stuffed up my teams, from the Carlos Kickaballs of the 1990s – Nottingham Forest's Andrea Silenzi and West Ham anti-legend Florin Raducioiu immediately stumble through my mind – to the more recent phenomenon of previously class-leading models Andriy Shevchenko and Fernando Torres becoming Chelsea tractors as soon as they took the Abramovich rouble.

Even when these disaster-magnets had been utterly proven unfit for purpose, I grimly stuck with them in case they turned it all around and I could have the last laugh. Instead, it always ended in tears.

My insistence on taking things personally didn't help either. I refused to have one Premier League goal-scoring machine in my team because his drug-dealer brother once threatened to kill a photographer I worked with; I couldn't bring myself to tap into the emerging talent that was the 2004 Arsenal wunderkind Cesc Fabregas until he finally ditched his truly ghastly highlighted mullet; while John Terry rarely graced my teams because . . . John Terry.

In short, I was a Fantasy veteran with the mind of a casual.

All that changed when I started working for Fantasy Football Scout and then began writing this book. The idea of discovering and then acting upon the tips and tricks of great managers was not some idle academic exercise inapplicable to the real business of Fantasy improvement. As soon as I talked to these Fantasy legends, I started applying their wisdom to my team.

And boy did it work.

By the end of the 2016–17 season, I finished 8,458th out of more than four and a half million FPL managers. I was easily inside the top 1 per cent and not so far away from the top 0.1 per cent.

I would like to say that this improvement has been sustainable, so I will. I would also like to stress that this is a lie because as I write this, two-thirds of the way through the 2017–18 campaign, my season is going down the toilet.

There's one major reason for this sorry state of affairs: me.

But there's a serious point to be made here: you can have too much advice at your disposal, too many conflicting viewpoints that end up producing little more than paralysis through analysis.

So whatever you do as a Fantasy Football manager, do it on your terms. There's a ton of advice out there, so take what you want and what you need, but never lose sight of yourself in the process. You are the boss, both literally and in Fantasy terms. Never forget that.

Having said all that, here are a range of specific Fantasy issues and how regulars on the popular Fantasy Football Scout podcast, the ScoutCast, approach them. Those regulars are: Lee Cowen, aka Granville; Joe Lepper, aka Jonty; Chaz Phillips, aka Az; and Andy Mears, who just sticks to Andy and should be applauded for it.

I've also canvassed the views of Fantasy Football Scout's rather publicity-shy senior editor, Paul McKinnon, and arguably the finest Fantasy Football manager of them all, Jay Egersdorff, because they know, technically speaking, some serious shit.

The issues they tackle are: transfers, team value, team formation, how best to approach new players to the game, points hits and fixtures.

But be warned, like the meaning of life, peace in the Middle East and how Michael Owen ever got a job as a TV pundit, there are no easy answers. These experts are undeniably skilled at providing different solutions to the same problems.

Transfers – is there a best time to do them and how to use them to increase team value?

Granville: 'I have shifted on this fairly recently. I used to leave transfers until the last minute in case of an injury or some other mishap. My favourite example of this was one Friday afternoon I transferred in Luca Modric and by the evening he'd been rushed into hospital with appendicitis.

'It's a fairly rare occurrence that a player will lose his availability during the week and, with this in mind, I have been known to go early with my transfer, particularly when a price rise/drop is imminent.'

Az: 'At this moment in my FPL career, I have to say I am a keen "waiter". If there are midweek cup or Champions League games, the reward of a 0.1 rise is surely outweighed by the risk of losing the player you've just transferred out and having to transfer another one in for a points hit.

'Furthermore, it's important to remember that the 0.1 rise is nothing unless it is coupled with another 0.1 rise, as you need the 0.2 rise to make any "profit".'

Andy: 'Knowledge is power. I tend to side with waiting until as late as possible, so I have the most amount of information and can base my decisions around this instead of whether a player is going up or down in price.

'I do think, though, that as with a lot of FPL decisions, you shouldn't rigidly think that there's a one-size-fits-all approach. While I like waiting until the last minute for transfers, I won't always do this, especially at the start of the season when prices tend to be more volatile, there's more active managers than at any other point in the season and knee-jerk transfers are made.

'There's always a player we hadn't considered that does well or someone we thought was a bench warmer who turns out for the starting XI. Those players you might want to quickly get in before their price rises.'

Jay: 'I always make transfers as late as possible. This is because I like to gather and utilise as much information (team news, press conferences, news releases) as possible before making my transfer decision.'

Jonty: 'Being tardy with moves means you have more information at hand, especially from press conferences.

'In the 2017–18 season a good example was when Chelsea boss Antonio Conte revealed that striker Alvaro Morata was injured the day before a Gameweek deadline. Those that waited were able to simply transfer him out, in my case for Liverpool's Roberto Firmino, who went on a scoring run by happy coincidence.

'Those Morata owners that made a move earlier in the week elsewhere in the squad then had to either spend points or another free transfer to remove the Blues striker or push him to the bench.'

Building team value – why and how?

Jonty: 'Many see the market as a game in itself. The pursuit of money, coupled with the risk of transferring in a player who may end up injured before deadline, is an added thrill to the game.

'These thrill seekers can also benefit from far greater team value, which can help later in the season when player prices can rise so high that they become unattainable.'

Paul: 'If building team value is a priority, then early-Gameweek trades will yield the best results. Typically, a player will rise in price by a maximum of £0.3m over any given Gameweek, so the earlier you make them, the better chance you have of profiting.'

Az: 'A lot of managers obsess over team value. While I know the pains of being 0.1 short of that perfect transfer, really your team value should naturally increase over the season as you bring in players who are performing well and drop those who are not.

'If you really want to increase your team value, targeting well-known players in the media (such as Harry Kane) and players from the most popular team in the Prem (Man United) is a good strategy as a lot of "casuals" bring in these players and they are the most likely to see large price hikes.

'Another key thing to keep in mind is a player's price paid, selling value and current price. If you buy Mohamed Salah for 9.0 and he rises to 9.3, you can take a price fall back down to 9.2 as you will still be able to sell him for 9.1. A lot of managers don't realise this and make early, panicked transfers because they think price falls will affect them.

'Always make sure you understand the rules of the game and the quite complicated selling system.'

Andy: 'I think team value is thought of too highly by FPL managers and a high team value at the end of the season doesn't always reward you how you think it will.

'The difference between a squad with high team or selling value versus one that is lower is often down to just one player. It's your Alonso v Mawson, or Sanchez v Eriksen.

'It's not the be-all and end-all of your season. In fact, quite often with a lower team value, you'll be forced to look for those bargains or diamonds in the rough.

'Those with high team value will likely not be looking at them because they can afford the higher priced safe option. Instead of making the safe expensive plays, those low-owned diamonds can be the rank booster your team needs at the end of the season.'

Formation – is there a default set-up that brings the best results?

Jay: 'I prefer to use as few defenders as possible because they can lose points for conceding goals.'

Granville: 'I still go with three defenders by default and always try and have a minimum-price defender who's "nailed-on" in his team.

'With the introduction of the wing back into many Premier League sides, there has been a points shift from centre backs to full backs and now we have a number of defenders approaching 7.0 in price (or more).

'I see them as a cheap way to pack more attack-minded players into my squad, quite often at prices below an equivalent midfielder.

'As for 3–5–2 v 3–4–3, I'm flexible depending on the situation.'

Az: 'My take on formations is that you have to roll with what's happening in the game.

'Adopting a flexible approach to your formation is something I am experimenting with after being an avid 3–4–3 player for all this time. But now, with wing backs and less striking options in teams, it's an exciting time to be an FPL manager as you explore setting up your teams in different ways to gain an advantage over others.'

Paul: 'A Fantasy manager should always be looking to get as many attacking players on the pitch as possible.

'Maybe that's just from a romantic point of view but I'd rather be cheering on the chances of goals and assists than crossing my fingers for clean sheets. That means rolling out a three-man defence, either in a 3–4–3 or 3–5–2, with seven offensive options in the starting XI.

'In terms of attacking potential, "wing backs" is too broad a term when pinpointing the best options. Defenders with dead-ball duties and/or those with a penalty box goal threat who are likely to earn bonus points when their team returns a clean sheet should be the main targets.'

Jonty: 'Traditionally, a 3–4–3 formation has been favoured by many FPL veterans because it fits nicely with the variety of different types of players. But it is important to be flexible.

'The increasing use of wing backs means a 4–4–2 formation can also be successfully deployed. The likes of Marcos Alonso at Chelsea are really a midfield winger in all but name, which adds to the appeal of a four, or even five-man backline.'

New players – do we risk summer signings in our initial squads?

Jonty: 'Buyer beware! Sometimes a successful player at Championship level or abroad can fail in the Premier League. Sometimes they can be a roaring success.

'Key successes have included Swansea's Michu, who scored an impressive eighteen goals in his debut 2012–13 season after arriving from Spanish side Rayo Vallecano.

'It is always worth taking a risk on one, or even two, of these new recruits. But making sure you have an exit plan is key, as history shows many will fail. Gameweek 1 sides that are loaded up on such players are set for disappointment.'

Paul: 'There are numerous factors to consider, so it's imperative to do as much homework as possible. First and foremost, the new player must be a regular starter for his side.

'Keeping an eye on pre-season matches is also essential. These fixtures not only give an indication of an individual's form ahead of the campaign kick-off, they also highlight where he will fit into his new team's formation.

'Delve into the data from their previous clubs and ask yourself if the player's new team is as attack-minded and dominant as his previous one.

'A new arrival may have scored twenty-something goals and fired shots aplenty for his last team but if he moves to a Premier League side that is battling to beat the drop, both the quantity and quality of opportunities could be restricted.'

Granville: 'I always like to have a new player to the league in my Gameweek 1 team. Feels fresh.'

Point hits – to take, or not to take?

Az: 'I think a points hit is best utilised when it is in conjunction with two free transfers – an almost "mini-Wildcard" for four points.

'This allows you to change formation, if necessary, bring in a heavy-hitting player and remove as much "deadwood" as possible.

'I also think a points hit is acceptable when you would be otherwise priced out of a move if you didn't make it that week. Sometimes, spending four points for a player who you really want is a lot more satisfying than being stuck with someone who you don't really care for.

'Lastly, I have learnt from previous seasons that the old adage "never take a hit for a defender" just isn't true any more.'

Andy: 'Points hits are consistently discussed within the FPL community. A lot of the time I think too much is made of them and people use "recency bias" to decide whether they're a good idea or not.

'Those that have a good season and don't take hits tend to decide that hits are a bad idea. The opposite can be said for someone who has a good season taking multiple.

'I've just come off the back of a season (16–17) where I had my best finish (4,935th overall), yet took ninety-six points worth of hits, a number that a lot of top FPL managers would be shocked at. For me they're a tool, and one that FPL managers should look to use where needed, thinking long term.

'Psychology plays such a big role in an FPL manager's thinking and decisions often affect their mood. I think hits are one way managers like to deal with this.

'A good points hit can let you move around multiple players to get the team you really want for the next Gameweek. You'll feel happy and good about your team coming up to the deadline and running up until the first game kicks off. After, that it's up to the players on the pitch.

'If the hit doesn't work out then it's likely a bad mood incoming, as well as time to start looking at the next hit you'll need to take to rectify last week's mistake.

'It can be a never-ending cycle for FPL managers and hits are often used like a drug to chase the next high.'

Granville: 'I like them. Firstly, it accelerates your squad into the team you want without waiting an extra week.

'Look at how often your plans change from week to week. It always feels like a big deal to start a week at -4 or -8, but look at it as a percentage of your total score rather than your weekly score. It's really insignificant.'

Paul: 'A Fantasy squad should be assembled in a manner that allows you to dip into the market and react to player form without the need for major surgery.

'Points hits can pay off handsomely around Double Gameweeks, though – if the player you are transferring in is set to play twice in a round of fixtures, then you are limiting the risk attached to his acquisition.'

Jonty: 'Most seasons, I take between five to ten points hits.

'Instead of leaping on every bandwagon that comes along, I prefer to plan my moves in advance and am happy to wait a week or two. This tactic has been instrumental in my six top 10,000 overall ranking finishes.

'The one season where I abandoned this strategy, in 2016–17, ended up being my worst and I finished it lucky to scrape into the top 100,000.

'That year, I took around twenty hits, often two each week. They become moreish after a while as the thrill of chasing the hottest emerging talent took hold. But FPL is a thirty-eight-round competition and a long game approach is needed.'

Fixtures – is there really any such thing as a 'good fixture' and does home trump away?

Jay: 'I believe reviewing fixtures is key and, when making a decision between two players over who to start, will always favour the home team.'

Granville: 'I'm feeling less inclined to follow them nowadays. Many top four matches end up high-scoring and it's the fixtures versus the minnows that sometimes catch you out as packed defences are never easy to open up.

'Some players are simply better, or as good, away from home.'

Az: 'The fixture ticker is such an important tool in an FPL manager's arsenal – sometimes sides will get a run which may include three fixtures at home out of four or five matches.

'These are the players I target and, if coupled with some FPL form, then returns are highly likely. However, when a team is at home they are under more pressure to attack – so clever, counter-attacking teams can actually benefit from being away.'

Paul: 'Fixtures should never be a factor when bringing in the likes of premium-priced, proven Premier League performers such as Harry Kane or Sergio Aguero. Essentially, a player's FPL cost should correlate with his ability to provide points.

'The real value of home and away comes to the fore when you are alternating cut-price defenders in accordance with their respective fixtures.

'Look for those budget-friendly backlines who are far more resilient in front of their own fans –typically, teams will concede fewer goals at home.'

Jonty: 'I'm a big fan of following fixtures and getting in players with a strong run ahead of them.

'Fixture spotting is more about identifying form teams encountering weaker teams. Look ahead to the next four to six Gameweeks. The FPL website has a colour-coded fixture difficulty system in place. If there is more red than green, then avoid.'

Tips galore and now with added confusion, as even these experts can't agree on everything. That underlines my earlier point – take what you will from tips, tricks and advice, but always own what you end up doing. You make the decisions, ultimately.

There is one more thing that has barely been mentioned in this book. In fact, when I received replies to a questionnaire which asked, among other things, why people played Fantasy Football, one answer was conspicuous by its almost total absence.

Fantasy Football is meant to be fun. Yes, it enrages and baffles, frustrates and dismays. But it's still meant to be fun. Embrace it, live it, allow it to distract your mind from the myriad horrors of everyday existence. But always, always, enjoy it.

Remember the chastening experience of Matthew Martyniak. Don't let Fantasy Football consume you. Be its master, not its slave. Keep it all in perspective.

While writing this book, my mind has frequently returned to the George Bernard Shaw comment I quoted earlier in these pages: 'We don't stop playing because we grow old; we grow old because we stop playing.'

We Fantasy Football managers all play a game about a game. That makes us some curious brand of uber-player; never old, forever young. Immortal, almost.

I'd like to think we can all live with that.

CHAPTER FIFTEEN

HOW TO PLAY AND ASSORTED RARITIES AND B SIDES

If you've come this far, you almost certainly know how to play Fantasy Football already. But for the sake of inclusivity, below you'll find a rough guide to what Fantasy Football is and how to play it.

If you do not wish to be informed about what you already know, skip a bit and you'll find a host of other odds and sods to keep you busy for a wee while yet.

What is Fantasy Football?

For 'The Novice': The easiest way to describe Fantasy Football to the uninitiated is to start with the game's two component words:

Football.

Yes, it's a game all about football. And that, by the way, refers to real football, not the American or Australian versions. Or any of the rugby variants that appropriated the word 'football' despite the sport mostly involving players running around with a ball in their hands.

Fantasy.

Here perhaps best described as 'pretend'. Confusion could arise because the word 'Fantasy' does have other connotations.

For clarity, therefore, Fantasy Football does not involve picking a bunch of hobbits to play up front for your team, although that tactic seems to have served Pep Guardiola well over the years. Nor does it involve threesomes, a bathtub full of Swarfega or selecting a half-naked fireman to play 'in the hole'.

In essence, then, it's a game of pretend football, but involving real players whose real actions have real impacts on your entirely made-up team.

For 'The Casual': Fantasy Football is a pleasant distraction from the horrors of life, be they the humdrum (partner's nail clippings/psychotic child/that 'workplace incident' that just won't go away) or the important (climate change/global terrorism/that 'workplace incident' that just won't go away).

The game allows you to turn your knowledge of football into something quantifiable while enjoying light-hearted rivalries with friends, family and colleagues (although that 'workplace incident' did rather sour one particular mini-league).

A few minutes here and there every week and hey presto! Team sorted, captain selected, let the fun begin.

For 'The Hardcore':

Spreadsheets are power
Fun is weakness
Death to Pleasant Distractions

The budget

Like many of the best games, Fantasy Football involves spending pretend money. The amount tends to be 100 million because it sounds a lot and it's easy to contextualise. So, for instance, if you blow forty-five million on a star striker, you know immediately that he's just taken up 45 per cent of your budget.

There are two main types of Fantasy Football – fixed budget and draft (or auction).

Fixed budget games, like Fantasy Premier League, provide you with a list of players who come with predetermined prices. Managers compile a team within budget and then compete against other managers who have picked their team from the same pool of players at the same prices.

This means that you could conceivably end up with a team that has exactly the same players as that of a rival manager. But over the course of the season, you are allowed to transfer players in and out of your team, so the chances of two teams having the exact same players across a whole campaign are ridiculously slim.

The skill comes in recognising players that are in form, or about to be in form, and buying them in while staying within your budget. And on the flip side, you need to recognise when it is time to let a player go.

In draft games, a group of managers – usually small, no more than twenty, often a lot less – meet up either physically or virtually and have an auction.

Again, they have a budget, but this time no player is given a set value. Instead, managers must decide how much they want to spend to get certain players into their team.

Once a player is bought, he remains in that manager's team, and that manager's team alone. At no point in a draft game of Fantasy Football can two managers own the same player.

The auction continues until everyone has compiled their squad of players. The money tends to be spent on big-name players and then managers make up the rest of their squad by taking it in turn to pick players for free.

The skill here involves managing your money to maximise what you can buy. There will come a time in the auction when only one manager has any money left to spend, meaning they can bring in a number of players at knock-down prices because nobody else can bid against them.

Any number of mind games are also played to, for instance, trick rival managers into spending too much on a big-name player.

The actual auction is, to many, the highlight of a Fantasy Football season. It's fun, sociable, frantic, exciting and then, when you finally look at the team you've ended up with, only then do you understand what an enormous cart of horse shit you've purchased and realise that you've got not a single chance of winning your league that year.

The scoring system

There are any number of different Fantasy Football games out there, but all generally follow the same basic principles. I've used the Fantasy Premier League's scoring system and features here as it is, by a matter of millions, the most popular game in the world.

You are provided with a set amount of pretend money to build a pretend squad of real Premier League players.

Every week, you then select what you consider to be your best XI and their subsequent performances give you a score for that 'Gameweek'.

At the end of the season (involving thirty-eight Gameweeks), the manager with the highest score wins.

Most games allow you to make transfers so you can buy a particularly successful player while ditching those who are, to use a technical term, shite.

Different types of players score in different ways.

Attendance

Every player in your team gets a point just for turning up, much like at the sort of school sports day that has Daily Mail leader writers foaming at their bile-twisted facial gashes. If your player sets foot on the grass for even one minute of a match, there's points to be had.

Players that manage sixty minutes or more receive an extra point for all that hard work.

Goals

Anyone who scores a goal receives points. But defenders and midfielders are awarded more points than strikers, as scoring goals is what strikers are paid to do. Unless they're playing for Tony Pulis.

Assists

Anyone who sets up a goal for someone else – known as an assist – receives points, typically slightly less than those awarded for a goal.

Assists can come from a glorious cross, a beautiful through-ball, a simple pass, a shot that rebounds to the eventual goalscorer or a completely unintentional ricochet off the arse of a player who was too busy pulling the shirt off an opponent's back to even be looking at the ball.

Defending

Seeing as defenders and goalkeepers don't get to do so much of the two key points-scoring areas mentioned above, they are rewarded for keeping a clean sheet, i.e., not conceding any goals.

But should they concede a ton of goals, then points are deducted.

In Fantasy Premier League (FPL), midfielders also get a single point for a clean sheet and goalkeepers are given extra points for making a load of saves.

Goalkeepers also receive points for saving penalties.

Discipline/incompetence

Should a player receive a caution, they will be docked points.

Should a player get sent off, they are docked even more points.

Players who score own goals are duly punished, as are hapless spot-kick takers who miss penalties.

*

FPL then tweaks the scoring system further in a bid to spread the points available across the whole team, rather than just seeing them tumble into the entitled laps of the prolific striker or midfield creative genius.

Captaincy

A Fantasy manager must pick one player to captain their side every week. This can change from match to match.

The designated captain receives double points. Should your captain not play at all, a vice-captain is also on hand to pick up the slack.

Your captaincy decision can make or break your managerial week and is, arguably, the major cause of hardcore agonising.

Bonus points

FPL also awards bonus points in each match played.

The best performer receives the maximum three points, with co-stars given two points and a one-point pat on the head awarded to diligent others.

The system by which bonus points are awarded is, to many, fiendishly complex and often controversial.

A raft of stats are used to decide which player performed the best, including (but most definitely not limited to):

- Scoring the winning goal
- Scoring a shedload of goals
- Creating a lot of chances
- Remembering to defend (and in particular hoofing the ball away a lot and getting in the way). These actions are known collectively as CBI – clearances, blocks and interceptions

Seasoned FPL managers are often convinced that bonus points are awarded, or more pertinently not awarded, for the following reasons:

- My captain scored. I really needed those bonus points (x2), so they were denied me out of spite
- I was refused a single bonus point for my player's barnstorming performance because the people running the game didn't have that player in their Fantasy teams
- Illuminati chemtrails

Formations

Just like the real thing, FPL enables a manager to use different formations to get the very best out of their players.

Nearly every formation imaginable is covered here, although the FPL rule that you must field at least three defenders does mean Guardiola's frequent use of the 0–1–10 formation (with the one being the goalkeeper employed as a box-to-box midfielder) is not available.

But 3–5–2 to 5–4–1 and everything in between is allowed, with a manager able to change formation every single Gameweek should they so desire.

There is no ideal formation – the top two players in the 2016–17 season, for instance, used either 3–5–2 or 3–4–3 the most, but never exclusively, during their bids for FPL immortality.

Transfers

FPL allows a manager one free transfer every Gameweek so you can ditch your injured, your incompetent and your slacker without being penalised.

If, however, you wish to change more than one member of your squad in a Gameweek, it will cost you. For every transfer over and above your one free one, you will be docked four points. These are known as 'hits' and are the subject of much debate among seasoned managers.

Team value

Every player in FPL starts the season with a value. The best players cost you more money to bring into your team with, typically, star strikers costing the most.

But every player's value will fluctuate during the season – the better and more popular the player, the more they will end up costing. Canny trading, where you buy players before their value shoots up or sell them at their peak price, has an effect on the overall value of your team.

This is particularly important when you play your Wildcard.

The Wildcard

FPL has, over the years, tweaked the game to provide extra layers of playability. These are known as 'chips'.

The Wildcard is the ultimate example.

FPL managers are currently handed two Wildcards per season – one to play between the start of the season and the transfer window opening on January 1 every year, and the second between January 1 and the end of the season.

The Wildcard allows a manager to completely change the make-up of their squad without taking a points hit.

It is, among other things, a canny way to keep the game relevant and interesting for those who have made such a hash of the first few weeks of the season that they are considering just giving up. The Wildcard enables them to turn the base lead of their side into sweet and shiny gold – a very thin and feeble mixed metaphor of a Fantasy caterpillar goes in, a beautiful butterfly emerges.

The second Wildcard can be used exactly as the first – to paper over the cracks of your incompetence once again.

But the best managers know better.

As the season progresses, teams get involved in cups, matches are postponed and fixture pile-ups kick in. As a result, towards the end of a league campaign, some teams end up playing twice in a single Gameweek. This is known, in a deeply unimaginative move, as a Double Gameweek.

The Double Gameweek is Fantasy catnip. Or crack. It can make or break a manager's whole campaign. If they can skilfully manage their team to ensure that the eleven players who start a Gameweek will all be playing twice, then they can score a lot of points.

That's when they use their second Wildcard, discarding all but the very best players with just the one fixture and bringing in a fresh wave of assets with the potential to score two sets of points.

As Double Gameweeks tend to occur towards the end of the season, a well-played second Wildcard can win the canny manager their mini-leagues and shoot their teams way up the overall rankings.

The other chips

Four other chips have been introduced in recent years and, much like the Kardashians, the odd one or two actually have some inherent worth.

The Triple Captain chip is pretty obvious – for one Gameweek only, your captain scores you three times the points, rather than the usual two. But it's not a guaranteed winner, as one manager, civil engineer David from Scotland, was happy to confirm.

'A guy at my work played his Triple Captain on Philippe Coutinho ... in that game he was just returning from injury, but was red-carded. So my colleague got -6 as a result.

'This year he played his Triple Captain on Salomon Rondon, who did nothing but score two points, so my colleague got six.

'The Triple Captain had only been around for two years, so my colleague played two Triple Captain chips and scored a grand total of zero.'

Much like the second Wildcard, the Bench Boost chip has the potential to massively improve a manager's score, if played during a Double Gameweek.

You are not allowed, however, to play more than one chip in a Gameweek, so planning is required. The received wisdom is to play your second Wildcard the week before a Double Gameweek and then your Bench Boost during it.

If it works, you'll end up with a potential FIFTEEN players scoring you double points, because the Bench Boost chip enables your entire squad – two goalkeepers, five defenders, a further five midfielders and all three of your strikers – to score points during the Gameweek in which you play it.

It doesn't always work out that way, however.

Last, and least, used to be the All Out Attack (AOA) chip, which allowed you to field all of your midfielders and strikers for one Gameweek, with only two defenders (rather than the minimum three) required on your teamsheet.

It sounded good on paper but, as often as not, the extra attacker you brought in scored fewer points than the defender you sacrificed.

AOA was the Scrappy Doo of Fantasy chips – unnecessary, unwanted and unloved. It was the most gimmicky and least used of all the chips. If it were a horse, it would have been taken out and shot. Or sold to a leading supermarket retailer. As a result, the powers-that-be scrapped the chip for the start of the 2017–18 season, replacing it with a new one called the 'Free Hit'.

Just like the Wildcard, the new chip on the block enables managers to change their entire team, if they so desire, without being docked points for making so many transfers.

The only difference is that the Free Hit is a one-week only deal – your team can be completely changed, but only for the Gameweek in which you play it. Once the fixtures are done, your team reverts to the players you owned the week before.

Draft games

The Fantasy Premier League game is not the only one in town, just the biggest. And for the 2017–18 season, FPL introduced another game to run in parallel with their main event.

It was a draft game – one in which managers meet, either physically or virtually, to undertake an auction where they buy players for their squads.

As mentioned above, the key difference with a draft game is that once a player is acquired, no other manager then owns that player. So every point scored by a Harry Kane or a Paul Pogba goes to one manager, and one manager alone.

FPL's foray into the draft game potentially threatens the market share of other, well-established operators out there – in particular the UK's original Fantasy provider, Fantasy League, and their Fantasy League Auction product – as well as more recent offerings such as Togga.

Fantasy League's response to the development has been, perhaps surprisingly, bullish, with founder Andrew Wainstein declaring: 'Yes, FPL Draft should affect things – perhaps positively more than negatively. Whilst its free, it's a much less flexible and engaging format than ours and could open up the market to our style of games.'

How FPL's draft offering fares remains to be seen, although what is not in doubt is the supremacy of its main game, which attracts hundreds of thousands of new managers every year.

Fantasy League insist their version of the draft game 'creates a more realistic and engaging way of playing Fantasy Football and it's demonstrated by high retention of users, most leagues running for ten or more years'.

That last point, regarding the loyalty of its users, is key to the survival of the game when pitted against the FPL behemoth.

Daily Fantasy Sports

A new type of Fantasy Football has arrived in Europe over the last couple of years – Daily Fantasy Sports, or DFS as they like to be known.

A number of UK users will immediately think of sofas sold with the lure of interest free credit when DFS is mentioned, but its backers – two companies called DraftKings and FanDuel – have brought their product across the Atlantic on the back of its huge success in America. Other big names, such as Yahoo, have also joined the fray.

DFS offer customers the chance to dip in and out of the Fantasy Football waters without having to commit to a season-long slog of team management.

Instead, games revolve around specific matches, or small groups of them. Managers pick a team of players, typically eight-strong, and points are accumulated from their performance in one match.

DFS generally cost money to enter. Each contest has a fixed amount of entries allowed, with cash paid out to the highest-scoring teams. It's the closest thing to gambling that Fantasy Football has thus far become, although both companies have produced a number of studies to show that their games are ones of skill, not luck.

Why? Because online sports gambling is illegal in America and DFS have emerged to fill a clearly very large appetite for such things Stateside.

The introduction of DFS to Europe has not been without issues, which have been examined in this book.

The only thing I'd like to add is that I tried out DraftKings during the 2016 European Championship and I sucked. That is more a comment on my skills than any criticism of what DraftKings had to offer. I just felt the need to share.

The FPL Name Game

The Puntastic (Players)

Wanyamas In Pajamas
Wijnaldum and Dumber
Giggs Boson
Gylfi Pleasure
Moratatouille
Men Behaving Chadli
1FlewOverLukakusNest
Lingardium Leviosa
Victor Moses Lawn
Boxing Can Girouds
Technical Knockaert
Thierry Ennui
TheHuthIsOutThere
De Jong Trousers

The Puntastic (Club Remix)

Bayern Bru
Bayern Sell
Inter Bred
Borussia Teeth
Kenfica
Bayer Neverlusen
Fritzl Palace
Criminal Mainz
Grand Theft Porto
Fiorentina Turner
Colonel Getafe

The New Rock 'n' Roll

Batshuayi I Like It
Dzeko & The Bunnymen
Kings of Leon Osman
RockULikeAHarryKane
Comfortably Nyom
Pjanic at the Isco
Tinchy Sneijder
I wanna be Altidored
Nahh then Vardy bum
Smack Matic Up

Ayew The Only One To Have That Idea?

Ayew Serious
Ayew Fer King Gueye
Ayew Luk King @ Mee
AyewBlindFerFuchsAke
JesusRoseFerMeeAyew
Lookman, Ayew Ake?

The Fabregas Fan Club

Let's Talk About Cesc
The Cesc Pistols
Absolutely Fabregas
Cesc And The City
Fabreghastly
Cesc&Drogs&AshleyCole
Cesc On Fire
Unprotected Cesc

The Shoehorn In As Many Players As Possible

Dier Gunn Alli
Dunk Mee Jesus
HartVormIngsToure
JesusRoseOnomahNDiay
Michu at De Gea Ba
Hit DefoeKingTargett

The Innuendo Bingo

Smash Your Back 4 In
Your Mum's Athletic
Mee Long Slimani
Net 6 and Chill
Dunk Mee Willian
Pulis Enlargement
Exeter Gently

The Self Aggrandizer

Ooh Ah Andy Carr
The Winning Team
The Special One
#1

The Nominatively Determined

Norfolk 'n' Chance
Suffolk 'n' Bad
Mediocre At Best
I Know Nothing
Clueless
Average Joes

Artfulpointsdodger

Panicked Wildcard

The Underachievers

I Suck at FPL

Who cares

Control-ALT-Defeat

Expecting Toulouse

The Haven't Got Time For This

aaa

Team Name

Enter team name

Team Name Pending

Placeholder

Update this later

Tbd

My Team

Football Team

QWERTY UIOP FC

The Got Too Much Time For This

uʍopǝpᴉsdn sᴉ ǝnƃɐǝl

The Why Would You Even Do That?

Kiddyfiddler FC

The Uncategorisable

Catsdon'tbendthatway

Spleeb Splorb

What is Correlation?

The Best Mini-League Name I Could Find

The Kolo Toure Is Afraid Of His Own Dog Appreciation League

The FPL Dream Teams Per Season

As collated by, and with huge thanks to, FPL Discovery (all-time best
   figures in bold):

2002–03 (3–4–3)
GK: **Friedel (187 points)**
DEF: Hyypia (151), Silvestre (141), Gallas (138)
MID: Scholes (186), Kewell (182), Giggs (172), Lampard (167)
FOR: Henry (271), Beattie (192), van Nistelrooy (188)
TOTAL POINTS: 1,975.

2003–04 (3–4–3)
GK: **Van der Saar (187)**
DEF: Hyypia (168), Terry (155), Bridge (153)
MID: Pires (216), Lampard (216), Malbranque (194), Giggs (163)
FOR: Henry (242), Shearer (185), Saha (167)
TOTAL POINTS: 2,030.

2004–05 (3–5–2)
GK: Cech (178)
DEF: **Terry (196)**, Riise (160), Gallas (150)
MID: Lampard (269), Pires (174), Scholes (159), Duff (159), Downing (159)
FOR: Henry (231), A Johnson (183)
TOTAL POINTS: 2,018.

2005–06 (4–3–3)
GK: Van der Sar (168)
DEF: Terry (184), Gallas (175), Finnan (170), Ferdinand (165)
MID: Lampard (222), Gerrard (176), Gamst Pedersen (168)
FOR: Henry (239), van Nistelrooy (198), D Bent (184)
TOTAL POINTS: 2,049.

2006–07 (3–5–2)
GK: James (173)
DEF: Taylor (164), Lescott (164), Carragher (163)
MID: Ronaldo (244), Lampard (202), Fabregas (182), Gerrard (180),
   Arteta (178)
FOR: Rooney (184), Drogba (170)
TOTAL POINTS: 2,004.

2007–08 (3–4–3)
GK: James (167)
DEF: **Lescott (196)**, Ferdinand (171), Laursen (163)
MID: Ronaldo (283), Fabregas (205), Gerrard (200), Barry (178)
FOR: Adebayor (200), Torres (193), Santa Cruz (182)
TOTAL POINTS: 2,138.

2008–09 (4–5–1)
GK: Schwarzer (175)
DEF: Vidic (187), Lescott (172), Carragher (161), Bosingwa (156)
MID: Lampard (226), Gerrard (216), Ronaldo (206), Kuyt (193), Barry (162)
FOR: Anelka (179)
TOTAL POINTS: 2,033.

2009–10 (3–4–3)
GK: Reina (164)
DEF: Evra (168), Dunne (158), Terry (150)
MID: **Lampard (284)**, Fabregas (214), Milner (184), Malouda (169)
FOR: Drogba (242), Rooney (224), Tevez (210)
TOTAL POINTS: 2,167.

2010–11 (3–4–3)
GK: Hart (175)
DEF: Baines (178), Hangeland (154), A. Cole (150)
MID: Nani (198), Adam (192), Malouda (186), Kuyt (177)
FOR: Tevez (185), Berbatov (176), Drogba (176)
TOTAL POINTS: 1,947.

2011–12 (3–4–3)
GK: Hart (166)
DEF: Evra (159), Kompany (145), Walker (140)
MID: Dempsey (209), Bale (195), Silva (184), Walcott (169)
FOR: Van Persie (269), Rooney (230), Aguero (211)
TOTAL POINTS: 2,077.

2012–13 (3–5–2)
GK: Hart (158)
DEF: Baines (177), Evra (152), Ivanovic (143)
MID: Bale (249), Mata (212), Cazorla (205), Walcott (194),
   Michu (190)
FOR: Van Persie (262), Suarez (212)
TOTAL POINTS: 2,154.

2013–14 (3–4–3)
GK: Howard (160)
DEF: Coleman (180), Terry (172), Baines (169)
MID: Y Toure (241), Gerrard (205), Hazard (202), Lallana (178)
FOR: **Suarez (295)**, Sturridge (197), Rooney (190)
TOTAL POINTS: 2,189.

2014–15 (3–4–3)
GK: Fabianski (151)
DEF: Ivanovic (179), Terry (177), Jagielka (142)
MID: Hazard (233), Sanchez (207), Silva (191), Cazorla (168)
FOR: Aguero 216, Kane (191), Austin (176)
TOTAL POINTS: 2,031

2015–16 (3–4–3)
GK: Cech (159)
DEF: Bellerin (172), Alderweireld (166), Koscielny (153)
MID: Mahrez (240), Ozil (200), Eriksen (178), A Ayew (171)
FOR: Vardy (211), Kane (211), Lukaku (185)
TOTAL POINTS: 2,046

2016–17 (3–5–2)
GK: Heaton (149)
DEF: Cahill (178), Alonso (177), Azpilicueta (170)
MID: Sanchez (264), Alli (225), Hazard (224), Eriksen (218), De
   Bruyne (199)
FOR: Kane (224), Lukaku (221)
TOTAL POINTS: **2,249**

The Best Film About Baseball Starring Kevin Costner

Bull Durham

The Capital Of Djibouti Is . . .

Djibouti

More On Those Interesting 'Gaffer Tapes' Back Stories

Name: Tom Holmes
   Interesting fact: I was one of Enid Blyton's Secret Seven.
   The details: 'Tom was a child actor and featured in about a dozen audiobooks, as George in the Secret Seven, various characters in the Famous Five, and a boy called Daniel who steals a hamster in the Animal Ark series.'

   Name: Craig Hazell
   Interesting fact: I once trended on Twitter. True story.
   The details: 'Craig actually trended on Twitter when the final episode of Coach Trip Series 10 was shown on TV. Him and his mate Will had

been in it from the very start and were incredibly popular. Everyone was tweeting to say they should have won the show … although all they would have won was another trip on a coach, so they were more than happy to let another couple win (disclaimer: Will and Craig are not a "couple").'

Name: Ash Kernsworth

Interesting fact: I am a top 100 FPL player and European petanque champion.

The details: 'Ash genuinely is "European junior triples petanque champion". I know, right?! First time we'd heard about it too.'

Author's epilogue: Despite repeated/maybe actually only one request(s), Ash declined to explain to me the difference between petanque and boules.

The Worst Fantasy Football Campaigns On Kickstarter

Name: Chris Radford

Date: 2013

Idea: 'The Sports Planet – Fantasy Football App' – a brand new multi-layered Fantasy Football application built into a modern sports forum

Description (in campaigner's own words): 'My Football (Soccer) based Fantasy Football idea is different to many of those in the world as we speak. Most worldwide football fans have heard of 'The Premier League' and as we speak there are numerous competitors who have already picked up on the band wagon and created a basic premier league fantasy football app.

'… any lay football fan could sign up to our site and then open an application that allows them to build a fantasy team and build it up to the required level that they wish.

'The key however, is the "Super League Combination" something that there is currently no similar application around on the web as we speak. The super league logic would in principle be the idea that somebody can pick a team that has players from all 4 divisions in their team and thus they don't have to stick to players from 1 league.'

Problem: Why would anyone, as we speak, want to pick a team of players from all four divisions when there's no Fantasy Football game that involves such a thing?

Funding goal: £15,000

Funds pledged: £1

Result: 'This project's funding goal was not reached'

Name: Jack Goodwin

Date: 2015

Idea: Total Fantasy Football League

We all love the Premier League Fantasy Football – but sometimes we want to be part of an exclusive league, run FOR and BY the fans!

Description (in campaigner's own words): 'Do you love Fantasy Football? Do you enjoy being a part of a league? Do you want MORE? You wan' some?! ... We'll giv' it yer!

'For the last two years I have run an internal company Fantasy Football League which has grown from 30, to 50+ managers. Each year it's bigger, better, and more interactive.

'Many of the managers in the league have approached me asking if I was planning to branch out to the wider audience so that EVERYONE can become a part of this league!

'Why us? To be honest, you could all easily create your teams FREE on the Fantasy Premier League (FPL) website and run with it, why not? But really ... is that ALL you want from your team?'

Problem: You could all easily create your teams FREE on the Fantasy Premier League and run with it ... so that's exactly what you did.

Funding goal: £2,000

Funds pledged: £230

Result: 'This project's funding goal was not reached'

Name: Victor Onwudiwe

Date: 2013

Idea: ShoootOut Football – ShoootOut Soccer

ShoootOut/Football – Soccer – A 'Games Triangle' that takes gaming out of the realm of fantasy, and back into the world of reality.

Description (in campaigner's own words): 'Except you think virtual, or have in effect assumed a virtual identity, it's almost impossible for any player to relate to any of today's games. ShoootOut Football/Soccer is about to change all that. ShoootOut Football/Soccer will take gaming out of the realm of fantasy, and back into the world of reality.

'We seem to have lost our heads in the "cloud". Except you relocate to some other planet, most games will seem more like an "out of body" experience. We all daydream and occassionally want to delve into some other universe. There's nothing wrong with fantasy, it's the complete dominance of that genre that's the problem.

'The term "reality" is not for the exclusive use of the Kim Kardashians of this world, or the other more intrepid subjects of similarly formatted television frivolities. Reality is just as relevant to games as it is to other forms of entertainment. While our natural curiousity might lead to the odd excursion into some other universe, we must never lose sight of the need for us to get back to reality, ASAP.

'Games began life as real physical activity, before migrating to tables, world of videos, online, apps and virual reality. Not necessarily in that order.

'ShoootOut Football/Soccer "Games Triangle" is a project designed to reinject reality into gaming, ie, contemporaneous, whilst re-connecting gaming with it's roots.

'The "Games Triangle" is the creation of three versions of the same game, designed for three different platforms; 1. Video Game 2. Table-Top Game 3. Real-Life, Surface-based Version of the same game.'

Problem: Our return from some other universe seemed to involve flicking a ball into one of five holes in a plastic tabletop football thingy.

Funding goal: £35,000. Yes! Thirty-five big ones!

Funds pledged: £500 (from one backer)

Result: 'This project's funding goal was not reached'

Name: Sam Cottle

Date: 2015

Idea: Politics Live

Think Fantasy Football for politics. A virtual parliament where you can choose anyone from the population to represent you.

Description (in campaigner's own words): 'Welcome to the People's Parliament!

'The idea is to initially create a virtual version of the House of Commons where users can select the candidates they want to be Prime Minister, the 21 cabinet ministers and an MP for their local area from a pool of candidates.

'The candidates could be anyone, so long as they meet the legal requirements for holding elected office in the UK and have a verifiable social media account (e.g. Facebook or Google); and to be added to the pool they need five separate nominations from users.

'The results of user selections will be aggregated on a rolling basis with the most popular candidates for each position appearing in the virtual parliament.

'The candidate pool will be pre-filled with all of the representatives from all the UK political parties who are running for office in the May general elections, as well as a selection of celebrities/public figures who we think might be fun to throw into the mix.'

Problem: Sam himself nailed it by admitting 'the main risk to the site is the potential for lack of popularity'.

Funding goal: £25,000

Funds pledged: £0

Result: 'This project's funding goal was not reached'

And one Fantasy sports effort from the USA ...

Name: Greg Reifsteck

Date: 2014

Idea: 'Big Balls Fantasy Football Videocast and Podcast: Season 3'

Description (in campaigner's own words): 'Real Sexy Superfans give you fantasy football picks. No washed-up NFL players in suits giving you picks read off of a teleprompter.

'Since most fantasy football shows are sausage fests we have added ladies that know their football and fantasy strategies. We feel this makes our show unique and more exciting for the now 10 million women that play the game.'

Problem: Most of those ten million women weren't that interested in receiving their NFL picks from busty 'ladies' in bikinis.

Funding goal: $3,000

Funds pledged: $200

Result: 'This project's funding goal was not reached'

Nicest Celebrity Brush-Off

Hello David,

No Fantasy Football for me. I support Schalke. We stopped living the
dream in 1958.

Enjoy writing the book though!!

Henning

Henning Wehn

German Comedy Ambassador

London Town

Graham's law of diffusion

'Gases diffuse at the rate which is inversely proportional to the square root of their densities.'

No, me neither. But pass it on.

Websites

This is by no means a definitive list, more a thank you to the people
 mentioned in this book.

The Gaffer Tapes: http://www.thegaffertapes.com/

FPL Observatory: http://barcoleyna.blogspot.co.uk/

Mathematically Safe: https://mathematicallysafe.wordpress.com/

The Psychology of Fantasy Football: http://www.fantasyfootballs
 cout.co.uk/2016/05/26/the-psychology-of-fantasy-football/

FPL Hints: https://fantasypremierleaguehints.blogspot.co.uk/

Who Got The Assist: http://whogottheassist.com/

Always Cheating: http://www.alwayscheating.com/

FPL Nymfria: https://www.youtube.com/c/FPLNymfria

FPL Holly (inc Useless Husband): http://fplbet.com/

Christmas Island Tourism: https://www.christmas.net.au/